Our Whole Lives

Sexuality Education
for Grades 10–12

Our Whole Lives

Sexuality Education
for Grades 10–12

Eva S. Goldfarb, Ph.D. & Elizabeth M. Casparian, Ph.D.

Judith A. Frediani
Developmental Editor

Unitarian Universalist Association

United Church of Christ

BOSTON

The Sexuality Education Task Force Core Committee (1994–2000) is responsible for the development of the *Our Whole Lives* curricula and companion resources. Members have included:

Reverend Makanah Elizabeth Morriss (UUA), co-chair
Reverend Gordon J. Svoboda II (UCC), co-chair
Reverend Lena Breen (UUA), co-chair
Reverend Jory Agate (UUA)
Kathleen Carlin (UCC)
Dr. Duane Dowell (UUA)
Judith A. Frediani (UUA)
Reverend Sarah Gibb Millspaugh (UUA/UCC)
Jennifer Devine (UUA)
Reverend Patricia Hoertdoerfer (UUA)
Faith Adams Johnson (UCC)

ISBN 978-1-55896-396-2

Printed in the United States of America.

10 9 8 7 6 5
20 19 18

Curriculum Development Assistant *Dorothy M. Ellis*
Text Designer *Sandra Rigney*
Cover Designer *Isaac Stone*

Acknowledgments

We gratefully acknowledge the work of the original Sexuality Education Task Force (1991–1993), whose members assessed the need for sexuality education materials in the two denominations, researched the possibilities, articulated the philosophy and goals, and proposed a budget for this ambitious project. Those members included:

Reverend Roberta M. Nelson (UUA), Chair; Reverend Jory Agate (UUA); Debra Anderson (UUA); Kathleen Carlin (UCC); Dr. Duane Dowell (UUA); Faith Adams Johnson (UCC); Vaughn Keller (UUA); Reverend Makanah Elizabeth Morriss (UUA); Dr. William Stackhouse (UCC); Reverend Gordon J. Svoboda II (UCC); and Cynthia W. Young (UCC).

We gratefully acknowledge the North Shore Unitarian Universalist Veach Program, whose funding made their work possible.

The *Our Whole Lives* leaders who patiently field-tested the draft curriculum provided critical feedback to make this curriculum more leader-friendly and more appealing to participants.

The most important feedback came from the senior-high youth who participated in the program. They helped in the revision of the program through their written evaluations as well as verbal and nonverbal reactions to information and activities.

Special thanks to the field-test leaders, parents, and youth from the following congregations and secular sites for their valuable contributions to this curriculum:

Unitarian Universalist Fellowship of Fayetteville, Arkansas; Neighborhood Church, Unitarian Universalist, Pasadena, California; Unitarian Church of Evanston, Illinois; Congregational Unitarian Church, Woodstock, Illinois; Unitarian Universalist Church, Bloomington, Indiana; Sanford Unitarian Universalist Church, Sanford, Maine; Unitarian Universalist Church of Silver Spring, Maryland; The Learning Center for Deaf Children, Framingham, Massachusetts; Foster Memorial Church, United Church of Christ, Springfield, Massachusetts; Edgewood United Church of Christ, East Lansing, Michigan; Family Planning Program, Plymouth, New Hampshire; Garden City Community Church, United Church of Christ, Garden City, New York; Unitarian Universalist Church of Asheville, North Carolina; United Church of Chapel Hill, United Church of Christ, Chapel Hill, North Carolina; All Souls Unitarian Church, Tulsa, Oklahoma; Hope Unitarian Church, Tulsa, Oklahoma; Fellowship Congregational Church, United Church of Christ, Tulsa, Oklahoma; Porter Leath Children's Center, Memphis, Tennessee; Planned Parenthood Education and Training Department, Olympia, Washington; and Olympia Unitarian Universalist Congregation, Olympia, Washington.

We gratefully acknowledge use of the following material:

"Group Facilitation Techniques," by Pamela M. Wilson, from the introduction to *Our Whole Lives: Sexuality Education for Grades 7–9.*

"On Not Having Kids" by John Huber. Copyright © 1982 San Jose Mercury News. All rights reserved. Reproduced with permission. Use of this material does not imply endorsement of the San Jose Mercury News.

X by Lois Gould. Copyright © 1978 Lois Gould. Published by The Stonesong Press. Reprinted by permission of the Charlotte Sheedy Literary Agency, Inc. on behalf of the author.

"Sexual Being" adapted with permission from "Circles of Sexuality," *Life Planning Education*, Washington, D.C.: Advocates for Youth, 1995.

"Kyle Dale Bynion" and "Rachel Corbett" from *Two Teenagers in Twenty: Writings by Gay and Lesbian Youth*. Edited by Ann Heron. Published by Alyson Publications, Inc., 1983; 1998. Reprinted by permission of the publisher.

Excerpt from *Contraceptive Technology*, 16th revised ed., Hatcher et al. New York: Irvington Publishers, 1994. Reprinted with permission.

"I Am Woman," by Helen Reddy and Ray Burton © 1971 (Renewed) Irving Music, Inc. and Buggerlugs Music Co. All rights reserved. Used by permission. Warner Bros. Publications U.S. Inc., Miami, FL 33014.

"Beating the Stats" by Brad Bailey. Reprinted with permission from SEX, ETC., a National Newsletter by Teens, for Teens, a publication of the Network for Family Life Education, Rutgers, the State University of New Jersey.

The order in which the names of the authors appear was selected at random. This was a joint effort of equal contribution by both authors.

Contents

Introduction   ix

Leader Resource List   xxi

Handout List   xxii

Required Materials and Resources   xxiii

Parent Orientation Sessions   1

Opening Session   21

SESSION ONE   Sexual Health **Learning About Our Bodies**   25
Workshop 1   **Language**   25
Workshop 2   **Body Image and Feelings**   29
Workshop 3   **Anatomy and Physiology**   34

SESSION TWO   Sexual Health **Taking Care of Our Sexual Selves**   41
Workshop 4   **Sexual Response Cycle and Sexual Functioning**   41
Workshop 5   **Reproductive and Sexual Health Care**   48
Workshop 6   **AIDS and Other STDs**   55

SESSION THREE   Sexual Health **Making Safer Choices**   71
Workshop 7   **Contraception**   71
Workshop 8   **Condoms and Negotiating for Safer Sex**   84
Workshop 9   **Sexy Safe Fantasy**   90
Workshop 10   Sexual Health **Closure**   92

SESSION FOUR   Lifespan Sexuality **Exploring Our Sexual Development**   95
Workshop 11   **Gender Roles**   95
Workshop 12   **Identity, Roles, and Orientation**   99
Workshop 13   **Sexual Orientation**   109

SESSION FIVE   Lifespan Sexuality **Becoming a Parent**   119
Workshop 14   **Conception, Pregnancy, and Birth**   119
Workshop 15   **Parenting License**   127
Workshop 16   **Parenting Alternatives**   130

SESSION SIX   Lifespan Sexuality **Expressions of Sexuality**   135
Workshop 17   **Sexuality Time Line** 135
Workshop 18   **Sexuality and People with Disabilities** 143
Workshop 19   **Sexual Expressions and Relationships** 146
Workshop 20   Lifespan Sexuality **Closure** 153

SESSION SEVEN   Building Healthy Sexual Relationships **Communication**   157
Workshop 21   **Verbal and Nonverbal Communication** 157
Workshop 22   **What Makes a Good Relationship?** 163
Workshop 23   **Questions of the Other Gender** 166

SESSION EIGHT   Building Healthy Sexual Relationships
                   Intimacy, Masturbation, and Lovemaking   169
Workshop 24   **Defining Intimacy** 169
Workshop 25   **Masturbation Myths and Facts** 173
Workshop 26   **Sexual Behavior** 178
Workshop 27   **Images of Love and Sex in Music and Video** 182

SESSION NINE   Building Healthy Sexual Relationships
                   Recognizing Unhealthy Relationships   185
Workshop 28   **Power and Responsibility** 185
Workshop 29   **Power in Relationships** 188
Workshop 30   **Breaking Up and Moving On** 191
Workshop 31   Building Healthy Sexual Relationships **Closure** 196

SESSION TEN   Sexuality and Social Issues **Reproductive Rights**   199
Workshop 32   **Abortion** 199
Workshop 33   **New Reproductive Choices** 206

SESSION ELEVEN   Sexuality and Social Issues **Power and Control**   215
Workshop 34   **Sexual Exploitation, Sexual Harrassment, and Erotica** 215
Workshop 35   **Date Rape** 218
Workshop 36   **Between Consenting Adults** 224

SESSION TWELVE   Sexuality and Social Issues **Equality**   231
Workshop 37   **Gay Pride Parade** 231
Workshop 38   **Gender Equality** 235
Workshop 39   Sexuality and Social Issues **Closure** 239

Closing Session   241

Resources   249

Introduction

Parents, educators, and communities all face the challenge of creating environments that support and nurture sexual health. Young people need sexuality education programs that model and teach caring, compassion, respect, and justice. Such programs should be holistic, moving beyond the intellect to address attitudes, values, and feelings that youth have about themselves and the world.

Our Whole Lives: Sexuality Education for Grades 10–12 is one component of the *Our Whole Lives* lifespan series, which includes

Our Whole Lives: Sexuality Education for Grades K–1

Our Whole Lives: Sexuality Education for Grades 4–6

Our Whole Lives: Sexuality Education for Grades 7–9

Our Whole Lives: Sexuality Education for Young Adults, Ages 18–35

Our Whole Lives: Sexuality Education for Adults

Unlike many other sexuality curricula currently available, this program is comprehensive and progressive. In an inclusive and developmentally appropriate manner, it addresses sensitive topics that other programs usually exclude. Although the curriculum was developed by the Unitarian Universalist Association and the United Church Board for Homeland Ministry, United Church of Christ, this text is completely secular and free of specific religious doctrine or reference. The underlying values of the program, however, reflect the justice-oriented traditions of both denominations.

This curriculum is designed for groups ranging from ten to fifteen participants, but it has been implemented successfully with groups as small as eight or as large as twenty-five. It has also been used successfully in a variety of community settings, including schools, youth-serving agencies, and religious communities.

GOALS OF THE CURRICULUM

The overall goal of the *Our Whole Lives* program is to create a positive and comprehensive lifespan educational program that helps participants gain the knowledge, values, and skills they need to lead sexually healthy, responsible lives. This curriculum is designed to help adolescents

- affirm and respect themselves as sexual persons (including their bodies, sexual orientations, feelings, etc.) and respect the sexuality of others.
- become more comfortable and skilled in discussing and negotiating sexuality issues with peers, romantic partners, and people of other generations.
- explore, develop, and articulate values, attitudes, and feelings about their own sexuality and the sexuality of others.
- identify, and live according to, their values.
- increase motivation and skills for developing a just sexual morality that rejects double standards, stereotypes, biases, exploitation, dishonesty, and abuse.

- acquire the knowledge and skills needed for developing and maintaining romantic or sexual relationships that are consensual, mutually pleasurable, nonexploitative, safe, and based on respect, mutual expectations, and caring.
- acquire the knowledge and skills needed to avoid unintended pregnancy and sexually transmitted diseases.
- express and enjoy sexuality in healthy and responsible ways at each stage of their development.
- assess the impact of messages from family, culture, religion, media, and society on sexual thoughts, feelings, values, and behaviors.

PROGRAM ASSUMPTIONS

Our Whole Lives is based on a set of assumptions about the rights of young people. Specifically, we believe that teenagers have the right to

- ask any questions they have about sexuality.
- receive complete and accurate information about sexuality.
- explore any issues of sexuality that interest them.
- have support in making their own decisions about sexual matters.
- express their sexuality in ways that are healthy and life-affirming.
- be treated with respect by leaders and participants in this group.

The curriculum is based on the following assumptions about human sexuality:

- All persons are sexual.
- Sexuality is a good part of the human experience.
- Sexuality includes much more than sexual behavior.
- Human beings are sexual from the time they are born until they die.
- It is natural to express sexual feelings in a variety of ways.
- People engage in healthy sexual behavior for a variety of reasons, including to express caring and love, to experience intimacy and connection with another, to share pleasure, to bring new life into the world, and to experience fun and relaxation.
- Sexuality in our society is damaged by violence, exploitation, alienation, dishonesty, abuse of power, and the treatment of persons as objects.

PROGRAM VALUES

Although *Our Whole Lives* is designed to be relevant to youth from a wide range of family backgrounds and religious traditions, it is not without values. The program gives clear messages about key sexuality issues. These issues fall into one or more of four broad areas—self-worth; sexual health; responsibility; and justice and inclusivity.

Self-Worth
- Every person is entitled to dignity and self-worth and to his/her own attitudes and beliefs about sexuality.

Sexual Health
- Knowledge about human sexuality is helpful, not harmful. Every individual has the right to accurate information about sexuality and to have her/his questions answered.

- Healthy sexual relationships are
  - consensual (both people consent)
  - nonexploitative (equal in terms of power, neither person pressures or forces the other into activities/behaviors)
  - mutually pleasurable (both receive pleasure)
  - safe (no or low risk of unintended pregnancy, sexually transmitted diseases, and emotional pain)
  - developmentally appropriate (appropriate to the age and maturity of persons involved)
  - based on mutual expectations and caring
  - respectful (including the values of honesty and keeping commitments made to others).
- Sexual intercourse is only one of the many valid ways of expressing sexual feelings with a partner. It is healthier for young adolescents to postpone sexual intercourse.

Responsibility
- We are called to enrich our lives by expressing sexuality in ways that enhance human wholeness and fulfillment and that express love, commitment, delight, and pleasure.
- All persons have the right and obligation to make responsible sexual choices.

Justice and Inclusivity
- We need to avoid double standards. People of all ages, races, genders, backgrounds, income levels, physical and mental abilities, and sexual orientations must have equal value and rights.
- Sexual relationships should never be coercive or exploitative.
- Being romantically and sexually attracted to two genders (bisexual), the same gender (homosexual), or another gender (heterosexual) are all natural in the range of human sexual experience.

UNDERSTANDING MIDDLE ADOLESCENCE

Major physical changes (puberty) and cognitive and social developments mark adolescence, the stage of development between childhood and adulthood. Although adolescence extends from about the age of ten to the age of twenty-two, this curriculum is aimed at the middle adolescent, the youth between the ages of fifteen and seventeen. For most adolescents, these are the high school years.

Physical Development

Because boys enter puberty on average two years later than girls, middle adolescents (somewhat like the early adolescents of junior high school) are not all at the same stage of development. Girls are likely to have almost reached their adult height while boys are less likely to have done so. While both sexes are likely to have achieved sexual maturation of the primary sex characteristics (that is, become capable of reproduction), boys are more likely to continue experiencing noticeable growth and change in the size of the genitals, the development of body hair, the tone of the voice, and the development of muscles. In other words, middle adolescents are not out of the woods yet when it comes to dealing with changes in their bodies and questions about their ultimate stature, physical attributes, or general appearance.

Given the dramatic changes of puberty, it is not surprising that adolescents may be preoccupied and dissatisfied with how they look. An adolescent's body image will be influenced by society's concept of attractiveness, communicated through a variety of mass media and by messages from peers and parents.

Health

The health status of adolescents is somewhat of a paradox. In some ways, teenagers are the healthiest age group as they tend to have fewer colds and ear infections than children and suffer fewer of the illnesses and physical damage that adults experience as they age. Yet, adolescents experience greater health *risks* than either children or adults, largely because of risky lifestyles (more true of males than females), dangerous environments, and the adolescent myth of invulnerability. Adolescents are much more likely than any other age group to be injured in motor vehicle accidents, misuse alcohol and drugs, experience unwanted pregnancies, and have inadequate diets. More than 50 percent of the twenty million annually reported cases of STDs occur in teenagers and young adults under the age of twenty-five. Teenagers use alcohol and tobacco more than any other age group. Adolescents have the least satisfactory nutritional status of any age group. Although teenagers tend to consume adequate or excessive calories, they tend to skip meals and eat too much refined sugar, starch, and fat. Iron-deficiency anemia is one of the most common nutritional disorders of this age. At least 15 percent of all teens are significantly overweight, yet extreme thinness and the eating disorders anorexia nervosa and bulimia are not uncommon.

Cognitive Development

Adolescence is a period of significant development in cognitive abilities, including the acquisition of formal operational thought. Unlike the concrete operational thought of childhood, formal operational thought involves the ability to reason about abstract ideas and possibilities, not just realities; to apply scientific reasoning to problem solving; and to combine ideas logically. These abilities help teenagers argue more effectively with their parents, and help them cultivate friendships, find solutions to their life problems, and study abstract concepts in school.

The high-school years also see an improved capacity to process information and to develop areas of expertise. Middle adolescents can respond well to educational opportunities that nurture critical thinking, reflection on complex issues, and the process of decision making.

Moral Development

Middle adolescents are in the process of developing a personal morality, that is, an understanding of what is right and wrong. Moral thinking develops in two forms: as increasingly logical and abstract principles of justice and fairness, and as increasingly sophisticated ways of caring about the welfare of friends, family, self, and others. Laurence Kohlberg originated a major theoretical model for the development of justice and Carol Gilligan originated the major theoretical model for the development of caring. Other researchers have further developed their work.

In her book, *In a Different Voice*, Carol Gilligan suggests that boys and girls tend to view moral dilemmas differently. Boys tend to think in terms of abstract moral principles that are applied to specific situations and to emphasize independence, autonomy, and the rights of others. Girls tend to develop an ethic of caring that integrates abstract moral principles with the context to which they may be applied and that responds more to *needs* than to *rights*. If a friend is sick, a male, applying the principle that you respect another's autonomy and right to get some rest, may decide to leave his friend alone until he gets better rather than check on how he is doing. A female, on the other hand, may see the sick friend as someone who needs care. For the female, not contacting the friend may seem like neglect, not respect.

These differences are only tendencies, not absolutes drawn on gender lines, but the debate over how boys and girls view moral dilemmas has drawn attention to the nature of moral development and the need to include the experiences and perspectives of girls and women in research and theory.

In Summary

With their ability to think critically, logically, and abstractly, middle adolescents are capable of processing increasingly complex information, forming opinions based on their own reasoning, and offering solutions to perceived problems and conflicts. They can be active and creative participants in discussions, debates, and role plays. Like adults, they do not always apply logic and reason to every situation.

The moral development of the middle adolescent includes elements of both a sense of abstract justice and a sensitivity to particular situations and the needs of the people involved. A middle adolescent can be very idealistic with a strong sense of right and wrong. Violations of this sense of justice can lead to cynicism or skepticism.

Middle adolescents need experiences with adults and peers that increase their self-esteem; encourage independence and effective decision-making; support them in developing and living their values; provide a supportive peer community and an opportunity for increasingly stable, intimate, and mutual friendships; and offer learning opportunities that engage their interest and develop their competencies. *Our Whole Lives* is designed to address each of these needs.

STRUCTURE OF THE CURRICULUM

This program is designed in a modular way to maximize its usefulness with senior-high youth in a variety of settings. It comprises forty-one workshops, most of which take from 25 to 60 minutes. They are organized into twelve 2- to 2 1/4-hour sessions and 1-hour opening and closing sessions. The viability of each workshop makes it possible to conduct this program in meeting times as short as 45 minutes. The thematic coherence of each session makes a 2-hour meeting productive for groups that can meet for that period of time. Because of its flexibility, *Our Whole Lives for Grades 10–12* may be offered

- as weekly 2-hour sessions
- as biweekly or monthly 2-hour sessions
- as regularly scheduled 45- or 60-minute workshops
- as a week-long program at a conference
- as a combination of weekend retreats and regular meetings.

In addition to the twelve program sessions, *Our Whole Lives for Grades 10–12* includes a 1-hour opening session and a 1-hour closing session. Four 10-minute program session closures help participants periodically reflect on and integrate what they have learned.

The program uses four themes to address major topics in sexuality of interest to teens:

1. *Sexual Health:* Sessions 1–3 begin building group trust and cohesion; address sexual language and its impact; look at how people perceive and feel about their bodies; and review what we know—and explore what we do not know—about sexual and reproductive anatomy and physiology.

2. *Lifespan Sexuality:* Sessions 4–6 explore important dimensions of sexual development, including gender identity, gender roles, and sexual orientation; look at the processes of conception, pregnancy, and birth and at parenting responsibilities and alternatives; and consider healthy expressions of sexuality throughout the life cycle.

3. *Building Healthy Sexual Relationship:* Sessions 7–9 explore communication issues and skills; look at the nature and role of intimacy in sexual behavior, including masturbation; consider the meaning and impact of images of love and sex in popular music and video; and identify the elements of unhealthy relationships through a consideration of power and responsibility within each relationship.

4. *Sexuality and Social Issues:* Sessions 10–12 include discussions of reproductive rights, abortion, and ethics in reproductive issues; address sexual exploitation, harassment, and abuse, including acquaintance rape; and provide participants with an opportunity to express their values in the context of equity and justice issues relating to sexuality, including gender equality and gay pride.

Organization

Each workshop includes the following elements:
- *Rationale:* a short narrative addressed to the facilitators to help set the context for the workshop.
- *Time Required:* the amount of time required to complete the workshop. Workshop times vary from 25 to 60 minutes and are usually either 30 or 45 minutes.
- *Goals:* clearly articulated purposes for the activities in each workshop.
- *Objectives:* one or more observable learning objectives.
- *Materials:* a listing of all materials necessary for the activities.
- *Preparation:* a detailed guide to any preparation needed for activities.
- *Activities:* one or more scripted and timed activities.

Every third session ends with a 10-minute reflection exercise to integrate previous learning.

IMPLEMENTING THE CURRICULUM
Introducing Our Whole Lives *in Your Organization*

Before conducting this program, secure the endorsement and support of your organizational leadership and the parents of the participants. While procedures will vary from one organization to another, the following may be helpful in enlisting such support.
- Communicate clearly the philosophy and goals of the *Our Whole Lives* program, especially to the parents, educators, and decision makers in your organization. Hold an informational meeting and/or meet with specific groups as appropriate.
- Make the materials and resources available for all interested parties to see.

- Describe your plans for providing qualified, trained leadership. If you already have qualified teachers, introduce them to parents and others in your organization.
- Be available to answer questions from any interested people.

The Role of Parents

One goal of *Our Whole Lives* is to nurture communication between parent and child and to support parents in their role as the primary sexuality educators of their children. For simplicity, this program refers to all loving adult caregivers, such as grandparents, aunts, and foster parents, as *parents*.

The following are crucial for obtaining parental approval and support and establishing a trusting relationship between the educating institution and the home:

- *Parent Orientation Session*: Hold an orientation session in which parents have the opportunity to gain an overview of the program, view the curricular materials, ask any questions they may have, and express their hopes and concerns for their children's education. Require all parents who wish to enroll their teens in *Our Whole Lives for Grades 10–12* to participate in the session.
- *Parent Permission Form*: Obtain the written permission of parent(s) or guardian(s) before enrolling youth in *Our Whole Lives*. The process for securing this permission will vary somewhat from one organization to another.

The script of the orientation session and the parent permission form follow this introduction.

Leadership

The leaders or facilitators who implement the curriculum are important determinants of the program's success. Thus, it is very important for leaders to be highly skilled in communication and facilitation, in managing the learning process so that activities accomplish objectives, and in using a variety of teaching techniques, including role play. Leaders must have the ability to create an atmosphere that engages adolescents and to use language and communication styles that are relevant to the specific youth in the program. Group leaders must have the patience and creativity to respond to the various personalities and maturity levels represented in the group. Finally, leaders of middle adolescent groups must be willing to empower group members to grow in their own leadership ability. Facilitators can share leadership with youth in such areas as choosing the topics to be covered or the order in which topics are covered, designing group opening or closing rituals, coleading some of the exercises, and determining group behavior covenants and the consequences for violating them.

Our Whole Lives is intended to be facilitated by a male/female cofacilitation team. This is an ideal that provides the group with two adult voices, male and female perspectives, and an opportunity to see two people share leadership with mutual respect. Cofacilitation also gives each leader an additional pair of eyes and ears and a helping hand with preparation, problem solving, and the ongoing challenges and joys associated with program implementation. Unfortunately, not every organization will have the capacity to dedicate two facilitators to this program. In that case, one caring and creative facilitator can lead the program effectively. However, if at all possible enlist a compatible male/female team to lead your group.

Training

This program requires trained leaders. Unless the proposed facilitators are experienced sexuality educators, it is essential that they attend a workshop to prepare for this experience. Training is critical for the following reasons:

- It offers the opportunity to see many of the activities modeled by trainers as they were intended to be conducted.
- It gives facilitators a supportive environment to practice skills and get constructive feedback from trainers and other curriculum implementers.
- It allows facilitators to network with others in the same position and to share ideas about what will and won't work with their groups.
- It provides an opportunity for facilitators to get in touch with their own feelings, opinions, and experiences regarding sexuality.

New facilitators often flounder when they are given a curriculum to implement without training. After training, most facilitators are genuinely excited about the materials. As a result of their own training experiences, they typically feel more equipped to deliver the curriculum as intended. At the same time, they recognize the need to adapt the materials constantly to make them as relevant as possible to a particular group.

For information about teacher training opportunities, contact the Our Whole Lives Consultant at the Unitarian Universalist Association (UUA), 25 Beacon St., Boston, Massachusetts 02108, 617/948-6423, owl@uua.org, or the United Church of Christ national offices. These offices have information about training for teachers in both secular and religious communities.

Experiential Learning

People of all ages learn best when they are in a comfortable environment, treated with respect, actively involved in their learning, provided with opportunities to share their experiences and knowledge, and given adequate time to discuss and integrate what they have learned into their lives outside the program. Educational programs that actively involve participants in the learning experience are referred to as *experiential*.

Activities in *Our Whole Lives for Grades 10–12* have been designed to recognize the knowledge and experience that participants bring to the program. Rather than lecturing or telling participants how to live their lives, the *Our Whole Lives* curriculum is an experiential curriculum that engages participants in experiences that enable them to draw their own conclusions, examine their own attitudes and values, get excited about new ideas, try out new skills, and practice new ways of relating to others.

GROUP FACILITATION TECHNIQUES

Group facilitation refers to the ability to manage the group and interact with participants in a manner that furthers their ability to achieve the objectives of the group. The following guidelines will help you manage the group process more effectively:

- *Be prepared.* Receive the training you need to facilitate this program and then read the curriculum thoroughly. Prepare for each session by obtaining materials and organizing your notes in advance. Arrive at your room early, preferably 30 minutes before the session begins.
- *Know the youth in your group.* Use participants' names when you address them and acknowledge the contributions that they make. Help all members feel that they are an important part of the group.

- *Encourage group discussion.* Ask open-ended and/or provocative questions, ones that cannot be answered with "yes" or "no" but instead lead to energized discussion. Most facilitators know this principle in their heads but do not always translate it into action. Sometimes the problem is in the questions rather than the content. Participants are less likely to respond to poorly worded or complicated questions. Encourage all group members to participate in their own ways. Listen and respond to both content and feelings.

- *Help participants understand what occurs within the group.* Point out similarities and differences in members' contributions. Call the group's attention to comments that have been overlooked. Encourage participant/participant discussion rather than participant/leader discussion. Help members label and evaluate their own reasoning. Elicit or contribute summarizing comments that capture the important concepts addressed during an activity or session.

- *Attend to the group.* Maintain eye contact with *all* group members. Be aware of their body language, facial expressions, involvement in the program, etc.

- *Pace the program appropriately.* Move things along quickly enough to keep participants from being bored but slowly enough to make sure they absorb what is being discussed. When the pace is too slow or directions are unclear, participants are likely to get distracted, begin side conversations, and tune out.

- *Use effective language.* Speak in a clear voice, using interesting inflections and avoiding monotones. Use language the youth can understand and relate to. Avoid distracting gestures. Do not hold the curriculum in your hand or rely on it as a prop when you conduct activities.

- *Be approachable and unshakable.* Often, in the earliest sessions, youth will hold back or test you. They are "checking you out" to see how you will react to attitudes or opinions that most adults object to. Let it be known that when you ask a question you want their real answer and not their perception of the right answer. Typically youth are very wise. They can figure out what adults want to hear and feed them the "right" answers. Unfortunately, this dynamic does not further honest dialogue about critical issues.

- *Use humor.* A sense of humor can go a long way in maintaining youth's interest in the group. It is great to laugh at yourself or at situations or just to have some fun in whatever way is natural for you, but don't force humor, and *never* make a joke at a group member's expense.

- *Be yourself.* Allow your own personality to emerge as you lead the group. The more you come across as an authentic human being with real emotions, a sense of humor, and strengths and weaknesses, the more participants will relate to you.

- *Know your own limitations.* Be aware of knowledge gaps and know when to refer participants to other resources. If you are not *completely* sure of an answer to a question, say "I want to check that information. I'll tell you at the next session."

- *Be patient and flexible.* Working with middle adolescents requires a lot of energy because the needs within any one group may vary greatly. Be prepared for youth to throw a monkey wrench into your well-organized plans from time to time. Sometimes you will need to stay with a topic longer than planned or abandon an activity that you thought would be extremely relevant.

- *Respond to problem behaviors.* Most groups experience potentially problematic behaviors such as monopolizers, quiet members, clowns/jokers, and disrupters. The following section presents general guidelines for avoiding problem behaviors and provides some suggestions for handling problems that do occur.

Handling Common Group Dynamics

Most groups display the same types of role-playing among members. There is always a clown, for instance, or someone who always starts the conversation or someone who makes trouble. Some roles (task roles) can help or hinder the group in accomplishing its goal; other roles (social roles) can help or hinder the group in its work as a unit. These roles can be either positive or negative. No matter whether the roles are task roles or social roles, certain kinds of problems almost always emerge in a group. What follows lists several of the most common types of problems.

The Monopolizer. The monopolizer talks too much. Sometimes he/she is knowledgeable, and it is tempting to let him/her take over. It is never a good idea. He/she is likely to say inappropriate things to other group members and to take the group away from its task. He/she also can cause resentment among other members. A facilitator should feel authorized to interrupt a monopolizer, talk to him/her privately away from the group, or, as leader, ask the group to help address the problem. Sometimes it helps to avoid making eye contact with the monopolizer. If he/she is well-intentioned, acknowledge the monopolizer's contribution but remind him/her that others need to contribute as well. The facilitator is the group leader and should not let someone else take this role away from him/her.

Silent Members. The silent member may be shy, afraid of being "wrong" in front of the group, or may simply be a quiet learner. If the silent member is not making eye contact, it is difficult to know whether she/he is paying attention. Sometimes members are quiet because of their cultural backgrounds. Strategies for involving silent members include calling on them by name but allowing them to pass if they seem uncomfortable, chatting with them informally after the group or during breaks to see how things are going, checking with other staff about the behavior of silent members in other activities, or pairing them with more talkative people during an activity. Reinforce any responses (verbal or otherwise) that silent members make and try to notice any nonverbal cues indicating that they would like to comment.

Side Conversations. Side conversations are very frustrating for facilitators. They occur because close friends sit together, something interesting not related to the program has happened, group members are not interested in the topic, or the topic is so interesting that group members cannot wait their turn to speak. Strategies for handling side conversations include

- making a statement such as, "I'm hearing a lot of different conversations going on at one time. That makes it hard for us to communicate. Please talk to the whole group when you have something to say."
- pausing during the side conversation, thus allowing other group members to hear the conversation.
- drawing members into your discussion by asking their opinions or giving them other tasks to perform.

- giving group members a short break, openly acknowledging their need to complete their business.
- talking to group members during a break to find out why they are carrying on side conversations and to seek their future cooperation.
- changing the activity or group format to make the session more engaging of participants' attention and energy.

Participants Who Entertain. Some group members always have to be on stage; they are the class clowns. They can disrupt the work of the group. Here are some suggestions:

- Stand or sit close to the entertainer (class clown).
- Give the class clown some extra responsibility so that his/her energy can be used in a positive rather than negative way.
- If the clowning is not disruptive, it can serve a useful function for the group. Humor can be a healthy release of pent-up energy or anxiety.

Development of Subgroups. Subgroups of two or more individuals often develop within a group. Subgroups tend to form around common roles, beliefs, attitudes, emotional responses, or likes and dislikes; they also tend to form on the basis of race, ethnicity, gender, age, and so on. Subgroups can provide support and protection for individuals within the larger group. This is particularly true for group members who hold less prominent positions in the group. Members often communicate differently within the various subgroups, whether they are discussing a specific topic or information about other group members. For example, young people in subgroups may be more honest with one another, expressing opinions or feelings that they do not feel comfortable stating in the larger group.

It is important for facilitators to reach out to subgroups and try to get to know each member. It is unrealistic to discourage such a natural grouping; however, it is possible to help subgroup members participate in the larger group.

Polarization. Polarization is the pulling away of individuals or subgroups from one another and from the group's shared purpose. Sometimes people pull away when they perceive that what they believe has been discounted or denounced. Other times, two or more individuals or subgroups actively disagree, become angry with each other, and fail to resolve their conflict. In most cases, it is easy to notice polarization dynamics—members may move away from the group, may sit outside of the group arrangement, or may not participate constructively in the work of the group. If polarization occurs, you can

- do nothing, except observe and personally acknowledge that polarization is taking place. This action is especially appropriate if you are dealing with a person who is trying to get attention. Alternatively, you may try to find a different, more positive way to give him/her attention.
- handle put-downs and disagreements appropriately when they occur to help prevent polarization.
- encourage polarized members to rejoin the group.
- stop the work of the group and provide an opportunity for group members to talk about how they are feeling.

- speak individually with members who may be feeling polarized, before or after the group meeting.

Verbal Abuse.   Treat verbal abuse as a form of violence. Stop it immediately and apply the consequences for breaking this rule. No group leader or participant ever has to accept verbal abuse directed toward him or her. A cooling down period during which both the facilitator and the group member can relax a little before trying to work things out can be helpful. If things are very tense, a mediator can help.

RESOURCES

This curriculum includes many leader resources for use with specific sessions. These resources provide leaders with background information and materials for use in conducting various program activities. In addition, informative supplemental materials, including recommended books, videos, Web sites, and organizations, are listed in the Resources section of this Leaders' Guide. These resources address many aspects of adolescence and sexuality and may be helpful to parents and youth as well as facilitators.

List of Leader Resources

Parent Orientation	Leader Resource 1	Time Line Activity Card List
Session 1	Leader Resource 2	Body Parts Smarts
	Leader Resource 3	Female Sexual System
	Leader Resource 4	Male Sexual System
Session 2	Leader Resource 5	HIV/AIDS Quiz
	Leader Resource 6	HIV/AIDS Facts
Session 3	Leader Resource 7	Contraception Scenarios
	Leader Resource 8	Contraception Scenarios Hints and "Answers"
	Leader Resource 9	Reasons for Not Wanting to Use a Condom
Session 4	Leader Resource 10	X
	Leader Resource 11	Stories of Gay, Lesbian, and Bisexual Adolescents
	Leader Resource 12	Statements for Forced Choice Exercise
Session 5	Leader Resource 13	Events of Conception
	Leader Resource 14	Pregnancy and Fetal Development
Session 6	Leader Resource 15	Sexual Being
	Leader Resource 16	Sexual Relationship Definitions
Session 7	Leader Resource 17	Communication Cards
	Leader Resource 18	Communication Scenarios
Session 8	Leader Resource 19	Myths and Facts About Sex and Masturbation
	Leader Resource 20	Sexual Behaviors Definitions
Session 9	Leader Resource 21	Breaking Up: Role Plays
Session 10	Leader Resource 22	Abortion Debate Role Play
	Leader Resource 23	Abortion Mini-Lecture
	Leader Resource 24	Reproductive Technologies Case Studies
Session 11	Leader Resource 25	Consenting Situations
	Leader Resource 26	"What If?" Cards
Session 12	Leader Resource 27	Gay Pride Parade

List of Handouts

Parent Orientation   Handout 1   Program Outline

Handout 2   Our Whole Lives Program Goals and Assumptions

Handout 3   Our Whole Lives Program Values

Session 1   Handout 4   Language of Sexuality

Handout 5   Parts of the Body (Female)

Handout 6   Parts of the Body (Male)

Session 2   Handout 7   The Story of Jake and Nora

Handout 8   Toll-free Hotlines and Local Resources

Session 3   Handout 9   Contraceptive Facts

Session 5   Handout 10   Parenting Criteria

Session 6   Handout 11   How I Feel

Handout 12   Sentence Completions

Session 8   Handout 13   With Whom Would You Do It?

Handout 14   Sexual Behaviors Continuum

Session 9   Handout 15   Personal Ad

Session 10   Handout 16   Sexual Exploitation and Sexual Harassment

Session 11   Handout 17   Diane's Story

Handout 18   Mark's Story

Session 12   Handout 19   I Am Woman

Handout 20   Leader Evaluation

Handout 21   Participant Feedback Form

Required Materials and Resources

Most Sessions

Newsprint, markers, and tape
Pens or pencils
Writing paper
3" × 5" and 5" × 8" index cards
Handouts and Leader Resources (provided)

Parent Orientation

Material to make one poster
Optional: grab bag of materials to use in "Safe Sexy Fantasy"

Session One

Drawing utensils such as markers or crayons

Session Two

American Cancer Society breast self-exam and testicular self-exam brochures, videos, and/or models (see Resources for ordering information)

Session Three

Male condoms
One female condom
Dental dam. (If a dental dam is not available, have scissors and either plastic wrap or an extra condom from which to make one.)
At least two demonstration penis models or substitutes, such as cucumbers, bananas, or large test tubes
Optional: prize for contest winner
Grab bag of materials to use in "Safe Sexy Fantasy"

Session Four

An invited panel of bisexual, gay, and lesbian speakers (see Session Four, Workshop 13 Preparation for details)
Optional: Two Teenagers in Twenty, edited by Ann Heron (Boston: Alyson Press, 1995)

Session Five

Optional: prizes for winning team

Session Seven

Workshop 21:   Blue and yellow index cards

Session Eight

Workshop 25:   One box of graham crackers or Kellogg's Corn Flakes™ wrapped in foil or wrapping paper.

Workshop 27:   Player for CDs and DVDs
DVD player and television
Examples of popular songs and/or music videos about love, sex, and/or relationships

Session Nine

Workshop 28:   Pink and blue index cards
Optional: stickers—one different kind for each pair
Blindfolds (bandanas or scarves) for each pair

Session Ten

Workshop 32:   *Optional*: props for the dinner table role play, such as a large table, plates, glasses, hats, etc.

Session Eleven

Workshop 34:   Examples of sexual exploitation and sexual harassment for group discussion
Age-appropriate examples of nonexploitative erotica from art or literature

Workshop 36:   Red and green index cards

Session Twelve

Workshop 37:   Poster board
Poster paints

Closing Session

Large box with a lid
Low table or small mat
Small object(s) to share—for yourself or the whole group (see Preparation for details)
Special refreshments as desired

Our Whole Lives

Sexuality Education
for Grades 10–12

Parent Orientation Sessions

A WORD TO THE LEADERS

The goals of this orientation session are

- to inform parents about the curriculum,
- to offer a rationale for this comprehensive approach to sexuality education,
- to gain input from parents, and
- to gain parental support for the program, which is most important.

Parental responses to the curriculum will vary, depending on the organization and community. If you are offering this program in a religious setting and have the support of the leadership, parents usually are supportive. If you plan to offer the program at a secular site where controversies have raged, you can expect another one now.

Our Whole Lives is a progressive approach to sexuality education that addresses the totality of human sexuality in an age-appropriate manner. It is based firmly on the values of self-worth, sexual health, responsibility, justice, and inclusivity. As a result, the program affirms equity between the genders and the inclusion of bisexual, gay, lesbian, and transgender people, two issues that are often excluded from traditional curricula. Criteria for sexually healthy relationships are explicitly identified as a yardstick for making decisions. Thus, *Our Whole Lives* helps young people adopt these very humane values and provides them with information and skills they need for life.

Most parents care deeply about their teenagers and want to do the best they can to influence them in positive ways. Parents may or may not have the skills or resources to do the best job possible. When dealing with parents, maintain an attitude of respect and understanding. You are their ally; you share with them the goal of helping their teens become healthy and responsible sexual beings.

Many parents today are genuinely scared for their teenagers. They worry about all of the negative things that could happen to them—sexual abuse, harassment, rape, pregnancy, premature parenthood, sexually transmitted disease. The biggest fear for most parents seems to be that their child will develop AIDS. They are also often afraid of doing the wrong thing: starting sexuality education too early or too late, giving misinformation, or robbing their sons/daughters of their childhood innocence.

In addition to these fears, some well-intentioned parents continue to believe the following myths:

- Information about sexuality is harmful to children and youth.
- Sexuality information leads to experimentation.
- Giving adolescents information about contraception and condoms in addition to information about abstinence sends a double message that encourages teenagers to have sexual intercourse.

1

- Bisexual, gay, and lesbian children only grow up in other people's families. Parents control the sexual orientation of their children.

Because they believe these myths, many parents and educators focus their energies on helping children and youth avoid negative consequences related to sexuality. Of course, no loving parent wants a son or daughter to be sexually abused, emotionally harmed, or infected with HIV or another sexually transmitted disease. However, when adults focus on the prevention of problems as their primary goal, they may inadvertently communicate such harmful or inaccurate messages as: 1) sexuality is more negative than positive; 2) sexual behavior is dangerous because it can kill people; 3) sexual feelings, especially for females, are unnatural and must be controlled; 4) females must control males in sexual encounters; 5) all romantic encounters are heterosexual.

These messages may be offered with good intentions and by caring people, but they can have a chilling impact on a young person's ability to become a healthy sexual adult. Many children and youth are unable to shed these lessons once they enter adulthood. Most parents say they want their children to grow up to be loving, responsible, and responsive sexual partners in "appropriate" adult relationships, but how does a parent raise such a child? What facts, attitudes, and skills do children and youth need to develop into adults who are sexually healthy and responsible?

One of the best answers to these questions is for parents to encourage their children's participation in this comprehensive program. It is normal for parents to worry about their teenagers. Your role as facilitator is to listen, to be completely open, and to provide any information that parents request. When parents see that you know what you are talking about, that you care about their children, and that you are a well-trained, ethical person, their comfort will increase dramatically.

Many parents did not grow up in homes in which sexuality was discussed openly. As a result, they may carry old scars and lack models for creating an environment that is affirming of their children's sexuality. Once they begin to review their own sexuality education during this session, they may begin to assess and heal their own wounds. Many parents acknowledge that they do not want their adolescents to grow up with the ignorance, secrecy, and shame that they experienced around the topic of sexuality.

It is critical that you communicate with parents before you begin to work with teenagers. Send home letters and make public announcements about plans for the upcoming program. Invite parents to one or more orientation sessions. Depending on the organization, you may need to obtain written permission for youth to participate. In other organizations, it may be sufficient to inform parents in writing and have them sign a form if they do not want their children to participate.

DESIGNING YOUR PARENT ORIENTATION

This parent orientation is designed in two parts. Session A requires 2 hours, and provides a broad overview of the program content, philosophy, and goals. Session B requires 75 minutes and offers hands-on experience with representative activities from the curriculum.

You may choose to present both parts in one half-day session, perhaps with a shared meal. You may choose to schedule Session A and Session B as separate meetings. Finally, you may find that Session A provides an adequate orientation for your group and that you do not need Session B.

GOALS FOR WORKSHOP PARTICIPANTS

To help participants
- gain an overview of the program and its underlying values.
- identify a broad definition of human sexuality.
- identify ways in which parents can support their teenagers' participation in the program.
- receive support in their role as the primary sexuality educators of their children.

WORKSHOP SUMMARY

Parent Orientation, Session A

Welcome and Introductions	15 minutes
How Many of You?	10 minutes
Time Line	45 minutes
Sexual Being	20 minutes
Overview of the Program	20 minutes
Closure	10 minutes

Parent Orientation, Session B

Experiencing the Program Activities:

Language	20 minutes
Sexy Safe Fantasy	30 minutes
Gay Rights Posters	15 minutes
Guided Fantasy	10 minutes

PARENT ORIENTATION, SESSION A

Introducing the Program

MATERIALS

☐ Newsprint, markers, and tape
☐ Leader Resource 1, Time Line Activity Card List
☐ Leader Resource 18, Sexual Being
☐ Handout 1, Program Outline
☐ Handout 2, Our Whole Lives Program Goals and Program Assumptions
☐ Handout 3, Our Whole Lives Program Values
☐ 3.5 × 5" and 5 × 8" index cards

PREPARATION

- Read this session and decide together how to share leadership responsibilities.
- Arrange for an appropriate meeting room where the group will not be interrupted.
- If parental attendance at this orientation is required for youth to participate in the program, follow up with any parents/guardians who have not made a commitment to come.
- Photocopy the handouts listed in the Materials Checklist.

- Because people like to know what they will be doing at a meeting like this, prepare an agenda on newsprint. Simply listing the activities from the Workshop Summary section will suffice.
- For the overview of the program, list the program assumptions and goals on newsprint.
- List the following suggested group ground rules on newsprint to post at the appropriate time.
  - Listen with an open mind.
  - Be nonjudgmental.
  - Ask any questions. No question is dumb.
  - Participate as much as possible but share the time.
  - Keep what is said in the group confidential. Respect others' right to privacy.
  - Use "I" language.
  - Pass if you wish.
  - Avoid making assumptions about other people. If anything, assume diversity.
  - Have fun.
- For the Time Line activity, create index cards for each of the ages and events in Leader Resource 1, Time Line activity Card List. We recommend 5 × 8" cards for the events and 3.5 × 5" cards for the ages. Laminating the cards is useful but not necessary. Because some events may be considered controversial, you may add or remove cards, depending on the group you are facilitating.
- For the Sexual Being activity, create a colorful poster of the circles diagram in Leader Resource 18, Sexual Being. Review Components of Human Sexuality, a part of Leader Resource 18, Sexual Being, to help explain the concepts of the diagram.

Activities

WELCOME AND INTRODUCTIONS   15 minutes

1. Welcome parents to this orientation session. Introduce yourself and describe a little about your background and training. Ask each parent to share the following information:
- Name.
- Names and ages of children.
- Expectations for this orientation session.

2. Write the expectations on newsprint as they are named. At the end of the sharing, summarize the expectations and explain how they will be addressed during the session. Post the agenda that you have prepared on newsprint and give a quick overview of today's session.

3. Bring up the issue of group ground rules. Explain that many people are nervous about attending a program dealing with sexuality because they fear that they will be embarrassed, sound stupid, or be judged or gossiped about. Suggest that the following ground rules may help participants feel comfortable during the session. Post the rules and invite discussion.
- Listen with an open mind.
- Be nonjudgmental.

- Ask any questions. No question is dumb.
- Participate as much as possible but share the time.
- Keep what is said in the group confidential. Respect others' right to privacy.
- Use "I" language.
- Pass if you wish.
- Avoid making assumptions about other people. If anything, assume diversity.
- Have fun.

4. Ask for reactions to the idea of ground rules for conversations about sexuality. Then ask if there is anything parents would add to the list. Explain that it is important to establish a safe and comfortable environment and that you will follow a similar process with the youth.

WARM-UP: HOW MANY OF YOU?   10 minutes

1. This activity is a warm-up that helps participants get to know each other and relaxes the atmosphere a bit. Explain that you will read some descriptions and if the description fits a participant, he/she should stand and look around to see who is standing with him/her. After a few seconds you will ask them to sit down and listen to the next description. Read the following descriptions:

How many of you
- grew up in this area?
- have grandchildren?
- use the Internet?
- had an argument with your child(ren) this week?
- are the oldest child in your family?
- are the youngest child in your family?
- are the only child in your family?
- are a middle child in your family?
- have a parent living with you?
- are a single parent?
- have a good friend of a different race or ethnic background?
- have a good friend who is bisexual, gay, lesbian, and/or transgender?
- got a good sexuality education at home?
- got a good sexuality education from school?
- can talk openly with your teenager about sexuality?

TIME LINE   45 minutes

1. This is a great activity for pointing out how important it is for parents to be the primary sexuality educators of their children. Because there are a wide array of opinions on most of the topics, parents choose the time when they feel an event is best for their children and then express that value to their children later.

2. Lay out the age cards you have prepared from Leader Resource 1, Timeline Activity Card List, in chronological order on the floor at the front of the room. Place the Always and Never cards near the age cards.

3. Deal the event cards from Leader Resource 1 face down to participants. Explain that these cards represent events that are likely to happen to their children at some time in their lives. They will be asked to place their event card(s) under the age at which they would most prefer for their children to experience that event. If they do not want their children to experience that event ever, they can place the event card under Never; if they want their children to experience the event throughout their lives, they can place the card under Always. Have all participants place their cards on the line at the same time.

4. After the cards are placed, ask the group to gather around the time line to discuss the results.

Read each card aloud in chronological order. Then read the Always and the Never cards. Discuss the chronological placement of each card, beginning with birth. (Many parents may be hesitant to admit which cards they placed, especially if a number of people vocally disagree. Do not force parents to reveal which cards they placed, but you may point out that their reluctance is a good example of the peer pressure we typically expect our children to resist.) Point out how few (or how many) parents felt they received a good sexuality education at home. Make the point that many parents did not have role models for how to talk to their children about sexuality.

5. With the group seated in a circle, help participants process the activity with the following questions. Be sure to write the responses on newsprint.

- How do you want your children's experience to be similar to or different from your own?
- How can you, as your child's primary sexuality educator, help make this happen?
- How can parents and community organizations, for example schools, clinics, religious groups, etc., work together to achieve these goals?

SEXUAL BEING   20 minutes

(Leader Resource 18 is adapted from "The Circles of Human Sexuality," *Life Planning Education*, rev., [Washington, D.C.: Advocates for Youth, 1995].)

1. Display the Sexual Being poster you have prepared. Explain that you will give a brief presentation on human sexuality to show how much is included in that concept. Taking one circle at a time and using information from Leader Resource 18, Sexual Being, explain what each term includes. Point out that all five circles of sexuality are part of what makes us sexual human beings. Emphasize that having sexual intercourse is only *one* behavior in *one* of the five circles. Reinforce the value of sexual intimacy without sexual intercourse and the importance of sharing love and caring in a relationship. Point out how many of the events in the Time Line Activity were not related to sexual intercourse but were related to sexuality.

2. Distribute Handout 1, Program Outline, and discuss how each unit relates to one or more of the circles of sexuality. Invite parents to react to the proposed content. Ask if there is anything missing that they would like included. Then ask if there is anything included that they would like omitted. Seek differing opinions from parents and discuss why some are uncomfortable with a topic and why it is included.

OVERVIEW OF THE PROGRAM   20 minutes

Review the following information informally, referring to the list of program goals and assumptions you have prepared on newsprint. Look for parents' nonverbal responses. Encourage them to ask questions and make comments.

1. Unique Opportunity

Let parents know that the *purpose of this program is to help their youth gain the knowledge, life principles, and skills they need to express their sexuality in life-enhancing ways.* Explain that this is a unique opportunity for their teenagers to get honest, helpful information about sexuality from adults and each other. Youth will be free to bring up any sincere questions, concerns, or opinions in the group and their issues will always be respected and addressed in age-appropriate ways.

2. Program Goals

Distribute Handout 2, Our Whole Lives Program Goals and Assumptions. Ask parents to read the goals for the program. Then ask:

- Are these the goals you hoped the program would have?
- Are there other goals that are important to you? [Some may mention specific topic areas. If these are covered in the program, turn their attention to the program outline which was handed out earlier and show them in which session the topic will be addressed.]

3. Program Assumptions

Explain that this program is based on some assumptions about the rights of young people. Say that we believe teenagers have the right to

- ask any sincere questions they have about sexuality.
- receive full and accurate information about sexuality.
- learn about any sexuality issues that interest them.
- have support in making their own decisions about sexual matters.
- express their sexuality in ways that are healthy and life-affirming.
- be treated with respect by leaders and participants in this program.

4. Program Values

Tell participants that the program also supports some basic values related to human sexuality. Distribute Handout 3, Our Whole Lives Program Values, and review it with the group. Ask:

- What are some of the main messages included in these program assumptions, goals, and values?
- What is your reaction to these statements?

5. Communication with Parents

Explain that from time to time the youth will be encouraged to discuss something or do an activity with their parents. Acknowledge that some youth will want to do this, while others may not. The activities will never be mandatory, but it is wonderful when youth give their parents the opportunity to engage in conversation about these issues. A benefit of this program for some families will be increased communication about sexuality.

CLOSURE 10 minutes

1. Take some time to answer any remaining questions from parents.
2. Thank everyone for coming and wish them luck in their roles as sexuality educators.

Experiencing the Program

This part of the orientation gives parents an opportunity to experience several activities from the program to gain a fuller sense of how material is presented and how the program's values and assumptions come alive. Depending on your time frame, you may want to choose only two of these activities.

MATERIALS CHECKLIST

For Language

☐ Newsprint
☐ Markers for each participant
☐ Masking tape

For Sexy Safe Fantasy

☐ Paper
☐ Pens/pencils
☐ A grab bag of items to be used in the fantasies.

For Gay Rights Posters

☐ Newsprint
☐ Markers
☐ Masking tape

PREPARATION

- For the Language activity, write the following questions on newsprint:
  - Which words do you feel comfortable using?
  - Which words make you uncomfortable? What is it about these words that makes you uncomfortable? What other feelings do these words bring up for you?
  - Which words would you use with your teenager? A doctor? A close friend? A sexual partner? Your parents?

Write each of the following words on the top of a newsprint sheet, one word per sheet: Penis, Vulva, Sexual Intercourse, Breasts, Oral Sex, Masturbation. Post the sheets on the walls around the room.

- For the Sexy Safe Fantasy activity, gather a variety of items to be used in creating a sexual fantasy and place them in a large grab bag. Be sure that there are at least as many items as there are participants. Just about anything will do. Items might include: telephone, feather boa, candles, music tapes, radio, massage oil, nightgown, scarf, honey, flowers, teddy bear, silk underwear, book of erotica, book of poetry, and chocolate syrup.

Activities

LANGUAGE   20 minutes

(Adapted from Workshop 1)

1. Give each participant a marker. Then, divide the group so that there are an equal number of people standing in front of each posted word. Tell participants they will have 1 minute to write as many terms as they can think of for the word printed on the newsprint. Each participant in a group may write the words he/she thinks of or the group may choose one member as the "scribe" (2 minutes). Encourage participants to think about all types of terms, including slang, common words, family words, etc., not only "proper" terms.

2. After 2 minutes, have participants move in a clockwise direction to the next newsprint sheet and give them about 1 minute to add to the list started by the group that was there before them. Continue this process. Keep moving the groups along, about 1 minute per word, until each group has had an opportunity to respond to each word (10 minutes total).

3. Have participants return to their seats. Post the questions that you have prepared on newsprint:
- Which words do you feel comfortable using?
- Which words make you uncomfortable? What is it about these words that make you uncomfortable? What other feelings do these words bring up for you?
- Which words would you use with your teenager? A doctor? A close friend? A sexual partner? Your parents?

4. Go to each newsprint sheet in turn and ask for responses to these questions. Allow about 8 minutes for responses.

Conclude by saying that the purpose of this activity is to help our youth become knowledgeable about and conscious of their choices of language. Certain words are more pejorative than others. The words we learn have an impact on the way we view male and female sexuality.

SEXY SAFE FANTASY   30 minutes

(Adapted from Workshop 9)

1. Divide participants into groups of three or four. Invite everyone to reach into the grab bag and pull out one item. Go around the room so that one person from the first group picks something, then one person from the second group, etc., until every person has something.

2. Tell participants that you are going to have a contest to see which group can write the sexiest, hottest, most desirable fantasy. Explain that there are three rules to follow when writing their fantasies:

- The fantasy may *not* involve penetration of any kind.
- The fantasy may only include activities that are completely safe, i.e., pose no risk of sexually transmitted infections or pregnancy.
- The fantasy must incorporate each of the items the group pulled from the grab bag.

Say that as long as they follow these three rules, the groups are free to write whatever they like with the goal of making their fantasies as sexy and desirable as possible. Reiterate the need for anonymity of authorship within the group.

3. Tell participants they have about 10 minutes to write their fantasies and warn them when they have three minutes remaining. When time is up, have a volunteer from each group read the fantasy. Tell participants that they will vote for the fantasy they think is the best and that this decision will be final!

4. To help participants process this activity, ask:

- How did it feel to write these fantasies? To listen to them?
- Was anyone surprised by anything they heard?
- Were the fantasies sexy?
- Were any parts of these fantasies realistic for people who want to engage in sexual behavior but stay safe?
- Does this exercise make you think about sex any differently?

GAY RIGHTS POSTERS 15 minutes

(Adapted from Workshop 37)

1. Explain that many people tend to think that sexual orientation only encompasses the people with whom a person has sex and what they do together sexually. Explain that as in any relationship, sex is usually just a small part of what brings people together. Because our culture sees homosexuality and bisexuality as outside the norm and sometimes as wrong or perverted, people who are bisexual, gay, or lesbian face many challenges when they try to enjoy the things in life that heterosexual people frequently take for granted.

2. Divide participants into groups of four or five. Give each group a newsprint sheet and marker. Ask the groups to spend 5 minutes listing on newsprint all the issues they associate with gay rights. If necessary, offer examples such as gay parenting, gay adoption, gay marriage, sharing property, visiting partners in hospitals, sharing housing, public affection, estate planning.

3. Then ask the groups to assume that they have been asked to create placards to be carried in a gay rights demonstration or parade. Explain that each group should choose one or two of the issues on the list and think of a slogan for a placard. Write these on newsprint.

4. After 5 minutes, invite the groups to share their issues and slogans.

GUIDED IMAGERY

10 minutes

(Adapted from Workshop 37)

1. Invite participants to participate in a guided imagery about standing up for justice. Explain that a guided imagery allows them to experience in a safe, nonthreatening, and personal way a situation they might not otherwise have an opportunity to explore.

2. Dim the lights in the room and ask participants to assume comfortable positions. Explain that for the purpose of this guided imagery they are to imagine that they are teenagers in this day and time. Read the following guided imagery *slowly*, *calmly*, and *clearly*.

GAY PRIDE PARADE

Close your eyes and take several deep breaths. As you inhale, feel yourself filling with warmth and serenity. As you exhale, try to let out any stress or tension you may feel. Relax your feet and legs . . . your pelvis and lower back . . . your chest and neck . . . your jaw and forehead. Allow your arms and hands to rest comfortably. Let your mind be blank for a moment.

Imagine a brilliantly sunny day in your hometown. The air is fresh, and the sky is bright blue. It's a perfect day for a parade. A local human rights organization is having its annual parade. You hear bands playing, and you see people marching along carrying banners with all kinds of slogans and images.

Imagine that you are marching along in the parade carrying the poster you made today. Many of the people marching near you are wearing T-shirts and carrying banners representing the Gay Pride Alliance, a local gay rights group. As you turn a corner, you see a group of your friends standing outside a local store watching the parade. You are not sure if they see you or not.

What are you thinking about at this moment? How are you feeling?

Now you are home from the parade, waiting for dinner to be ready. Your family is sitting together watching the local news, and there you are on the screen holding your poster. The video freezes on you as the announcer reports on the parade.

What do you think would happen in your house? How would your family members respond to your participation in the parade? How do you think you would feel?

Assume that most of the people you know would have seen the news report— your friends, teachers, coworkers, other relatives, coaches, etc.

What responses would these people have? How would you feel about being seen by them?

Take a few more seconds to identify how you are feeling, what issues are being raised for you. I am going to ask you to bring some of those feelings back to this room with you.

Slowly begin turning up lights. Ask participants to remain silent.

3. Immediately after bringing participants back from the guided imagery, ask them to reflect on what they were thinking and feeling during the imagery. Ask:

- During what portion of the imagery did you have the most powerful response?
- If it had been your teenager who was part of the gay rights parade, how would you feel now?

Spend about 5 minutes discussing responses to these questions.

4. Conclude by saying that since we have all been raised in a homophobic culture and have been taught a great deal of misinformation about homosexuality, we are all at least a little homophobic. Point out that even gays can internalize homophobia. Say that often when we discover that we have been insensitive to or unaware of others' feelings, we feel uncomfortable. Point out that it is beneficial and useful to become conscious of one's genuine feelings and values because then we can choose to change them or hold on to them. Explain that one goal of this program is to help our youth be more aware of their feelings and values so that they can be more compassionate in their responses to others.

Permission Form

I/We give _____

child(ren)'s name(s)

permission to participate in *Our Whole Lives: Sexuality Education for Grades 10–12*, part of the

education program at _____

(name of organization)

I/We have been offered the opportunity to view these materials. I/We have attended an orientation to this program.

Signed _____ Signed _____

(parent/guardian)

Name _____ Name _____

(print)

Address _____ Address _____

_____ _____

_____ _____

Phone Number Phone Number

Daytime _____ Daytime _____

Evening _____ Evening _____

Date signed _____ Date signed _____

Handout 1

PROGRAM OUTLINE
Our Whole Lives: Sexuality Education for Grades 10–12

OPENING SESSION

SESSION ONE	*Sexual Health*	Learning About Our Bodies
Workshop 1	Language	
Workshop 2	Body Image and Feelings	
Workshop 3	Anatomy and Physiology	
SESSION TWO	*Sexual Health*	Taking Care of Our Sexual Selves
Workshop 4	Sexual Response Cycle and Sexual Functioning	
Workshop 5	Reproductive and Sexual Health Care	
Workshop 6	AIDS and Other STDs	
SESSION THREE	*Sexual Health*	Making Safer Choices
Workshop 7	Contraception	
Workshop 8	Condoms and Negotiating for Safer Sex	
Workshop 9	Sexy Safe Fantasy	
Workshop 10	*Sexual Health*	Closure
SESSION FOUR	*Lifespan Sexuality*	Exploring Our Sexual Development
Workshop 11	Gender Roles	
Workshop 12	Identity, Roles, and Orientation	
Workshop 13	Sexual Orientation	
SESSION FIVE	*Lifespan Sexuality*	Becoming a Parent
Workshop 14	Conception, Pregnancy, and Birth	
Workshop 15	Parenting License	
Workshop 16	Parenting Alternatives	
SESSION SIX	*Lifespan Sexuality*	Expressions of Sexuality
Workshop 17	Sexuality Time Line	
Workshop 18	Sexuality and People with Disabilities	
Workshop 19	Sexual Expressions and Relationships	
Workshop 20	*Lifespan Sexuality*	Closure
SESSION SEVEN	*Building Healthy Sexual Relationships*	Communication
Workshop 21	Verbal and Nonverbal Communication	
Workshop 22	What Makes a Good Relationship?	
Workshop 23	Questions of the Other Gender	

SESSION EIGHT   *Building Healthy Sexual Relationships*   Intimacy, Masturbation, and Lovemaking
Workshop 24   Defining Intimacy
Workshop 25   Masturbation Myths and Facts
Workshop 26   Sexual Behavior
Workshop 27   Images of Love and Sex in Music and Video

SESSION NINE   *Building Healthy Sexual Relationships*   Recognizing Unhealthy Relationships
Workshop 28   Power and Responsibility
Workshop 29   Power in Relationships
Workshop 30   Breaking Up and Moving On
Workshop 31   *Building Healthy Sexual Relationships*   Closure

SESSION TEN   *Sexuality and Social Issues*   Reproductive Rights
Workshop 32   Abortion
Workshop 33   New Reproductive Choices

SESSION ELEVEN   *Sexuality and Social Issues*   Power and Control
Workshop 34   Sexual Exploitation, Sexual Harassment, and Erotica
Workshop 35   Date Rape
Workshop 36   Between Consenting Adults

SESSION TWELVE   *Sexuality and Social Issues*   Equality
Workshop 37   Gay Pride Parade
Workshop 38   Gender Equality
Workshop 39   *Sexuality and Social Issues*   Closure

CLOSING SESSION

Handout 2

OUR WHOLE LIVES PROGRAM GOALS

- To provide the *accurate information* that young people need about sexuality. We believe that accurate information is essential, especially for young adults, and that holding back knowledge will hinder healthy sexual development.

- To provide a forum in which *all questions are legitimate* and appropriate.

- To provide *learning about sexuality issues* that goes *beyond factual information* and that will be useful throughout participants' lives.

- To help participants to develop the skills necessary to make good decisions that will allow for a healthy, satisfying life.

OUR WHOLE LIVES PROGRAM ASSUMPTIONS

The following statements form a bill of rights for young people.
In this program, teens have the right to

- ask any questions they have about sexuality.

- receive full and accurate information about sexuality.

- explore any issues of sexuality that interest them.

- have support in making their own decisions about sexual matters.

- express their sexuality in ways that are healthy and life-affirming.

- be treated with respect by leaders and participants in this program.

Handout 3

OUR WHOLE LIVES PROGRAM VALUES

Self-Worth

- Every person is entitled to dignity, self-worth, and his/her own attitudes and beliefs about sexuality.

Sexual Health

- Knowledge about human sexuality is helpful, not harmful. Every individual has the right to accurate information about sexuality and to have her/his questions answered.

- Healthy sexual relationships are:

  - consensual (both people consent)

  - nonexploitative (equal in terms of power; neither person pressures or forces the other into activities or behaviors)

  - mutually pleasurable (both receive pleasure)

  - safe (no or low risk of unintended pregnancy, sexually transmitted infections, and emotional pain)

  - developmentally appropriate (appropriate to the age and maturity of persons involved)

  - based on mutual expectations and caring

  - respectful (honesty and keeping commitments made to others are vital)

- Sexual intercourse is only one of many valid ways to express sexual feelings with a partner. It is healthier for young adolescents to postpone sexual intercourse.

Responsibility

- We are called to enrich our lives by expressing sexuality in ways that enhance human wholeness and fulfillment and express love, commitment, delight, and pleasure.

- All persons have the right and obligation to make responsible sexual choices.

Justice and Inclusivity

- We need to avoid double standards. Women and men of all ages, people of different races, backgrounds, income levels, physical and mental abilities, and sexual orientations must have equal value and rights.

- Sexual relationships should never be coercive or exploitative.

- Being romantically and sexually attracted to two genders (bisexual), the same gender (homosexual), or another gender (heterosexual) are all natural in the range of human sexual experience.

Leader Resource 1

TIME LINE ACTIVITY CARD LIST

Make the following Age Cards

Always	Birth
Never	Ages 1–30+
	(one card for each year)

Make the following Event Cards

Become a parent	Learn about HIV/AIDS
Cohabitate (live together)	Learn about the birth process
Drink alcohol and drive	Learn about contraception
Experiment with cigarettes	Learn about masturbation
Fall in love	Learn about pregnancy
First coed party	Choose own haircut/color
First kiss	Drink alcohol
First pelvic exam	Become engaged
Get a sexually transmitted disease (STD)	Experiment with drugs
Get ears pierced (son)	First car date
Have a baby	First date
Have sexual intercourse	First romantic kiss
Kiss/hug person of other sex	French kiss

Get ears pierced (daughter)

Go steady

Have an abortion

Kiss/hug person of same sex

Kiss/hug parent(s)

Learn about anal and oral intercourse

Learn about condoms

Learn about "how babies are made" (reproduction)

Learn about menstruation

Learn about sexual abuse

Learn about sexual orientation (homosexuality, bisexuality, heterosexuality)

Learn about transsexuals and transvestites

Learn breast self-exam

Learn about first pelvic exam

Get married or make a lifetime commitment

Mix alcohol and sex

Mutual masturbation

Own a car

Pet below the waist

See a birth

Smoke marijuana

Stay out all night

Stop showering/bathing with parent(s)

Use contraception

Use tampons

Watch MTV

Wear makeup

Learn about sexually transmitted diseases (STDs)

Learn about wet dreams

Learn proper names for parts of the body

Learn about testicular exam

Masturbate

Mix drugs other than alcohol with sex

Engage in oral sex

Pet above the waist

Become pregnant

See a nude man or woman

Start toilet training

Stop showering/bathing with sibling(s) of the other sex

Take a trip/vacation with peers

Use street drugs

Watch an "R" rated movie

Wear a bra

Wear sexually attractive underclothes

Opening Session

RATIONALE

Building group cohesion and creating a positive and comfortable learning environment are the goals of this session. The session gives participants the opportunity to discuss their concerns and hopes for the program. It also establishes ground rules for participants that will enhance their ability to learn and to take the risks necessary for personal growth.

Time Required: 1 hour

GOALS

To help participants to
- identify factors that might interfere with their ability to learn in this group.
- create ground rules that will enhance the learning atmosphere.
- learn about the goals and assumptions of the program.
- begin the process of building group cohesion.

OBJECTIVES

By the end of this session, participants will be able to
- express their concerns about being in this group.
- demonstrate an awareness of factors involved in creating a good learning environment by listing, and agreeing to, guidelines for this group.
- share one hope they have for this program.

MATERIALS

- ☐ Newsprint, markers, and masking tape
- ☐ Handout 2, Our Whole Lives Program Goals and Assumptions, from the parent orientation

PREPARATION

- Review this session and decide with your coleader how to divide leadership responsibilities.
- List the goals and assumptions from Handout 2, Our Whole Lives Program Goals and Assumptions, on newsprint.

Activities

ICE BREAKER   10 minutes

Welcome participants to the program. Explain that this hour will be spent getting to know one another and becoming familiar with the program. Encourage everyone to get as comfortable as possible. Tell the group that the first step in building a group that can work and share together is to learn one another's names. Explain that to do this, the group will play the following game: Each person will say his/her name and one activity that he/she enjoys that begins with the same letter as his/her first name. Say that after the first person is finished, the next person must repeat the first person's name and matching word and then add his/her own. Participants will continue to go around the circle, each naming all of the people who have gone before and then adding their own names, until everyone has gone. The facilitator(s) should go last.

WHAT IS SEX?   10 minutes

Ask the group, "What is sex?" Tell them to shout out anything that comes to mind. Write down all answers on newsprint. Then tell them that, technically, *sex* refers to two things: gender and sexual intercourse. Everything else that they thought of comes under the term *sexuality*. Ask the group to brainstorm some more about what they would include in the term *sexuality*. Make sure that the list includes:

- How we feel about ourselves as men and women.
- How we interact with other people in our lives.
- Cultural messages about sexual behavior.
- Part of our identity from birth to death.

Tell participants that both sex and sexuality will be part of this program.

TALKING ABOUT SEXUALITY   5 minutes

Tell the group you would like to brainstorm again, this time about the question: What makes it difficult to talk about sexuality in a group such as this? Invite participants to say anything that comes to mind and list their responses on newsprint.

GROUND RULES   15 minutes

When the group has made an exhaustive list of things that can make talking about sexuality difficult, ask: "What can we do to make this a safe and comfortable group for discussing sexuality? What ground rules should we set up?" As people call out suggestions, write them on newsprint. Allow the group to come up with as many rules as they can. If they do not agree on some, allow discussion about whether certain rules would enhance or hinder learning. Make sure that the ground rules include the following:

- *Confidentiality*—Whatever is said in this room, stays in this room. When people choose to share something personal, it is a gift and should be treated as such.

    NOTE: After the ground rules have been discussed, tell participants that, as leaders, you have a legal and moral responsibility that is greater than the rule of confidentiality. If you believe a participant's life or well-being is in serious danger because of abuse or a threat of suicide, you cannot keep that knowledge a secret. Assure the group that you would never take the step of telling others without first discussing it with the individual her/himself.

- *Right to Pass*—While group participation and discussion are important parts of this program, no one is ever required to speak on any given issue. One can simply say, "I pass."
- *No Killer Statements*—Put-downs are not acceptable. We need to respect one another.
- *Respect for Diversity*—We are not going to agree on every subject or even most subjects. We need to respect one another's views without trying to change or dismiss them.
- *Openness*—It is important to be open and honest, but participants should not disclose information about the private lives of family members, friends, neighbors, or others. It is fine to discuss general situations without using names.
- *"I" Statements*—Group members should try to share their own feelings, beliefs, or values using "I" statements such as "I believe," "I feel." People should speak for themselves and not for a whole group, such as "Girls like this" or "Boys never think that."
- *No Direct Questions*—Participants should be free to speak as much or as little about themselves as they choose and should not be put on the spot by other group members asking direct personal questions. Questions like "Are you a virgin?" or "How many times have you had sex?" are inappropriate. Participants and leaders should not direct personal questions to participants or leaders.
- *Right to call one another on ground rules*—It is the group's responsibility, as well as the facilitator's, to enforce the ground rules. Therefore, group members have a right to call one another on the rules when they feel one is being broken.

When the group has agreed to a set of ground rules, write the following statement on newsprint: "The undersigned agree to abide by the following ground rules while a member of this group engaged in this program." Then list the ground rules. Explain to the group that this is a group contract. Then ask each person to come up to the group contract and sign his/her name. When all group members, including the facilitators, have signed the contract, post it for the duration of the program. If it must be removed at the end of each session, it is important to bring it back and hang it up each time the group meets as a reminder of the rules that were established.

GOALS AND ASSUMPTIONS   10 minutes

Tell the group that you would like to explain the major goals and assumptions of the *Our Whole Lives* program. One at a time, uncover the goals that you have written on newsprint and posted. After reading each one, provide opportunity for discussion.

Tell participants that they should try to make the same assumptions as the program assumptions and keep them in mind as they participate in the program. Point out that these assumptions do not and should not carry judgments with them—there is nothing wrong with having little knowledge about sexuality, no one sexual orientation is better or more acceptable than another, and a sexually experienced person is no better or worse than a sexually inexperienced person.

Distribute copies of Handout 2, Our Whole Lives Program Goals and Assumptions. Ask participants if they have questions about what is included in this sexuality education program. Take time to address participants' concerns and questions.

CLOSING   10 minutes

Conclude by asking each person to express one hope that he/she has for this program. Leaders should also participate.

Learning About Our Bodies

1

WORKSHOP 1 Language

RATIONALE

If participants are uncomfortable with the language needed to discuss sexual issues, very little learning can take place. This workshop introduces the topic of sexual language in a fun, nonthreatening way that encourages interaction among participants. When slang and "dirty" words are out in the open, they become less powerful inhibitors to open discussion and growth.

Time Required: 45 minutes

GOALS

To help participants
* explore the language of sexuality.
* become more comfortable discussing sexuality issues.
* practice using words about sex and sexuality with other people.
* develop trust and intimacy in the group.

OBJECTIVES

By the end of this workshop, participants will be able to
* demonstrate understanding of the difficulties in discussing sexual topics by naming the words with which they are uncomfortable.
* demonstrate through group discussion their awareness that language can shape, as well as reflect, values.
* express through group discussion their understanding that sexuality-related terms often have negative connotations.
* demonstrate increased comfort with sexual terms by using the terms throughout the activity and by deciding which terms are appropriate to use for the remainder of the program.

MATERIALS

☐ Newsprint
☐ Masking tape
☐ Markers, one for each participant
☐ Handout 4, Language of Sexuality

PREPARATION

- Review this workshop and decide with your coleader how to divide leadership responsibilities.
- Write one of the following terms at the top of a sheet of newsprint: penis, vulva, sexual intercourse, breasts, oral sex, masturbation. Post the sheets on the walls around the room.
- Photocopy Handout 4, Language of Sexuality, for all participants.
- Post the ground rules from the Opening Session.

Activities

LANGUAGE BRAINSTORM   5 minutes

1. Give each participant a marker and divide the group so that the same number of people are standing before each posted term. Tell participants that they have 1 minute to write on the newsprint as many synonyms as they can think of for the term printed on that sheet. Encourage participants to think about all types of words, including slang, colloquialisms, and words used in their families, not just "proper" terms.

2. After one minute, have participants move to the next sheet of newsprint and repeat the process, adding to the list started by the previous group. Continue this process, allowing 1 minute per word, until every person has had an opportunity to respond to each word.

LANGUAGE OF SEXUALITY   15 minutes

1. Ask each participant to choose a partner, preferably someone he/she does not know very well. (If you prefer, pair the participants yourself.) Give each pair a copy of Handout 4, Language of Sexuality.

2. Invite pairs to examine each list, discuss their answers to the worksheet questions, and then write their answers on the worksheet. They are to spend two minutes at each word. Tell them when to move to the next word. The questions on the worksheet include:
- Which words do you feel comfortable using?
- Which words make you uncomfortable? What is it about these words that makes you uncomfortable? What other feelings do these words bring up for you?
- Which words would you use with parents? A child? A doctor? A sexual partner? In this room?

LANGUAGE OF SEXUALITY DISCUSSION   25 minutes

1. Bring participants together to process the activity. Use the following questions to stimulate discussion:
- What did you learn or observe from this activity?
- How did it feel to talk about these words with someone else?
- Did you have to point to words instead of saying them out loud?
- Were there any words that you and your partner differed significantly on what you would feel comfortable using in different situations?

- What words do we want to use in this group? What words do we definitely *not* want to use in this group?

NOTE: Give examples of a word or words that might inhibit learning for oneself or others. You might say, for example, "When I hear the word 'cunt,' it makes me angry—so angry that I can't concentrate on what the person using the word is saying. There are probably terms which cause similar reactions for many of you. Can we decide what kind of language we will use here that does not make members of our group see red and that does not put people down?"

2. Be sure to make the following important points during discussion:
- Different people use different words when talking about sex and sexuality. People have different feelings about different words.
- Certain words are more pejorative than others. Words associated with women's sexuality are often more negative than words associated with men's sexuality. For example, the words for penis usually reflect power ("muscle," "monster"), weaponry ("heat-seeking missile," "cannon," "sword," "hammer"), and cunning ("snake"), while the words for vulva are more likely to have unpleasant connotations ("fish," "ax wound," "black hole"). The words people learn and use have an impact on the way they view male/female sexuality. The words that people use for sexual intercourse reflect their views of sex and sexuality.
- Language both reflects and shapes values. The language that we use with different people in our lives affects the kinds of conversations we can have on different topics. The language we use with children affects their views. For example, referring to genitals as "down there" or with no language at all sends a message that sexual anatomy is something to be ashamed of or embarrassed about.
- Most people are uncomfortable talking about sexuality, in part because they lack words that they feel comfortable using in daily conversation. This discomfort reflects our society's uneasiness about sexuality in general.

Handout 4

LANGUAGE OF SEXUALITY

1. Which words do you feel comfortable using?

2. Which words make you feel uncomfortable? What is it about these words that makes you uncomfortable? What other feelings do these words bring up for you?

3. Which words would you use with parents?

A child?

A doctor?

A sexual partner?

In this room?

WORKSHOP 2 Body Image and Feelings

RATIONALE

The way we feel about our bodies is an integral part of who we are as sexual beings. For adolescents, who are undergoing tremendous change, body image is a crucial link to self-esteem. This workshop encourages participants to think about how they feel about different parts of their bodies and about gender differences in the ways in which men and women look at themselves. It demonstrates that cultural ideals for male and female bodies are unrealistic for most people and can result in poor body image in people who make them their goals. This activity is designed to give participants privacy in rating their own bodies but asks them to share two responses of their choice so that they may have the opportunity to see and hear how others see themselves. By encouraging participants to begin some risk-taking, this activity fosters trust and group intimacy.

Time Required: 45 minutes

GOALS

To help participants to
- identify how they feel about their own bodies.
- explore differences in how men and women make judgments about their bodies.
- explore differing ideals for body types.
- look at how body image is a culture-bound phenomenon.

OBJECTIVES

By the end of this workshop, participants will be able to
- show an understanding of their feelings about their own bodies by sharing with the group one part of their body they like and one that they dislike, and explaining why.
- show an awareness of the emotional connection to body image by sharing how it felt to rate their own bodies and share those ratings with the group.
- display a knowledge, through discussion and drawings, of gender differences in the ways in which people judge bodies.
- demonstrate an understanding that body ideals are culturally determined by naming as a group at least three body ideals that differ from culture to culture.

MATERIALS

☐ Handout 5, Parts of the Body, Female, and Handout 6, Parts of the Body, Male
☐ Pencils
☐ Two sheets of drawing paper for each participant
☐ Crayons, markers, and/or other drawing materials
☐ Masking tape

PREPARATION

• Review this workshop and decide with your coleader how to divide leadership responsibilities.
• Make one copy of Handout 5, Parts of the Body, Female, for each female participant, one copy of Handout 6, Parts of the Body, Male, for each male participant, and one copy of each for leaders to use as tally sheets.
• Gather drawing materials for the ideal male and female drawings.
• Post the ground rules from the Opening Session.

Activities

PARTS OF THE BODY HANDOUTS   5 minutes

1. Distribute Handout 5, Parts of the Body, Female, to each female participant, Handout 6, Parts of the Body, Male, to each male participant, and pencils. Tell participants *not* to put their names on the handouts.

2. Ask participants to rate each part of the body on the handout as either positive (+), negative (–), or neutral (0), according to how they feel about that part of their bodies. Explain that you will collect the handouts later to add up the total number of positives, negatives, and neutrals.

IDEAL BODIES DRAWING   5 minutes

When participants have finished their handouts, distribute the drawing paper, two sheets for each participant. Ask participants to use the paper to draw pictures of what they believe are the ideal male body and the ideal female body (one picture on each sheet). If participants feel that they are not good at drawing, suggest that they limit themselves to very simple line drawings or word descriptions. Have each participant put her/his gender but no name at the top of each sheet.

   While participants are drawing, collect Handouts 5 and 6. Add the total number of positive, negative, and neutral ratings for each part of the body for all females and enter the totals on one copy of Handout 5. Add the total number of positive, negative, and neutral ratings for each part of the body for all males and enter the totals on a copy of Handout 6.

SHARING RATINGS   15 minutes

Have participants put their drawings aside. Ask each participant to share with the group one part of the body he/she rated as positive and one part he/she rated as negative. Ask each participant to explain why the part was rated in that way.

RATINGS DISCUSSION

After participants have shared their ratings, lead a group discussion using the following questions:

- How did you feel rating parts of your own body and sharing some of those ratings with the group?
- How did you decide whether to rate a part as negative, positive, or neutral? Did you decide by what you *think* about it or how you *feel* about it? Did you decide by what someone else thinks about your body?
- Do you see any patterns in how people rated parts of their bodies? [Share with the group any patterns that emerge in the group tallies you have prepared.]
- Are there differences in the parts that males and females tend to like and dislike? Are there differences in the reasons they give for their ratings? [Research has shown that men tend to rank parts of their bodies based on function and women tend to rate parts of their bodies based on appearance. Share with the group any gender differences or commonalities that are revealed in the tallies. Invite discussion.]
- What about the parts that you rated neutral? Are these parts that people do not have strong feelings about? Why don't we think about certain parts? Can you imagine a time in your life when some of these parts might take on more meaning for you? For example, pregnancy can affect how a woman feels about her body; trying to conceive can affect how someone looks at his vas deferens or her ovaries.

IDEAL BODIES DISCUSSION

Collect participants' drawings of the ideal female and male bodies and redistribute them so that no one has his/her own drawings. Have participants hang the pictures in two groupings, one grouping for the ideal male body and one for the ideal female body. Use the following questions to lead a discussion with the whole group:

- What are some common elements among the drawings of the ideal female body? Are there differences between male and female perceptions of the ideal female body?
- What are some common elements among the drawings of the ideal male body? Are there differences between male and female perceptions of the ideal male body?
- How realistic are these ideals?
- Where or how do we learn what is the ideal male body or ideal female body?
- How do the males in this group feel looking at these pictures?
- How do the females in this group feel looking at these pictures?
- What does this say about how we view men and women in this culture? What do we value in men and women in our culture?
- Are body ideals different in different cultures and in different times? Can you give an example?

Handout 5

PARTS OF THE BODY (Female)

Rate each of the parts of the body below with one of the following three symbols:

+ positive, you like or feel happy with this part of your body.

– negative, you dislike or feel unhappy with this part of your body.

0 neutral, you neither like nor dislike, feel neither happy nor unhappy with this part of your body.

Please do not put your name on this sheet.

_____	Ankles	_____	Mouth
_____	Arms	_____	Neck
_____	Breasts	_____	Nipples
_____	Buttocks	_____	Nose
_____	Calves	_____	Ovaries
_____	Clitoris	_____	Skin
_____	Ears	_____	Stomach/Abdomen
_____	Eyes	_____	Thighs
_____	Fallopian tubes	_____	Uterus
_____	Feet	_____	Vagina
_____	Hair	_____	Vulva
_____	Hands	_____	Waist
_____	Knees		

Handout 6

PARTS OF THE BODY (Male)

Rate each of the parts of the body below with one of the following three symbols:

+ positive, you like or feel happy with this part of your body.

– negative, you dislike or feel unhappy with this part of your body.

0 neutral, you neither like nor dislike, feel neither happy nor unhappy with this part of your body.

Please do not put your name on this sheet.

_____	Ankles	_____	Nipples
_____	Arms	_____	Nose
_____	Buttocks	_____	Penis
_____	Calves	_____	Prostate gland
_____	Chest	_____	Scrotum
_____	Ears	_____	Seminal vesicles
_____	Eyes	_____	Skin
_____	Feet	_____	Stomach/Abdomen
_____	Hair	_____	Testicles
_____	Hands	_____	Thighs
_____	Knees	_____	Vas deferens
_____	Mouth	_____	Waist
_____	Neck		

RATIONALE

Having thought about and discussed how they feel about their bodies, participants move into an activity that helps them assess their knowledge of sexual and reproductive anatomy and function. The game adds a fun and competitive element to the acquisition of new information. Because the activity employs teams, individual participants are not forced to reveal their lack or abundance of knowledge in this area.

Time Required: 45 minutes

GOAL

To help participants to
- learn the basic reproductive and sexual parts of human bodies.
- develop an understanding of the range of normal size, shape, color, and odor and the function of each part.

OBJECTIVES

By the end of this workshop, participants will be able to
- demonstrate an understanding of reproductive and sexual body parts and functions by answering questions as teams.
- show a knowledge of the location of reproductive and sexual body parts by placing labels correctly on an anatomical diagram.

MATERIALS

☐ Index cards
☐ Leader Resource 2, Body Parts Smarts Questions and Answers
☐ Leader Resource 3, Female Sexual System
☐ Leader Resource 4, Male Sexual System
☐ Leader Resource 5, Glossary of Terms: Female Sexual System
☐ Leader Resource 6, Glossary of Terms: Male Sexual System

PREPARATION

- Review this workshop and decide with your coleader how to divide leadership responsibilities.
- Write each of the following terms on individual cards:

Female	*Male*
1 clitoris	1 penis
2 labia majora	2 foreskin
3 labia minora	3 glans
4 Bartholin's glands	4 testicle (testis)
5 hymen	5 seminiferous tubules
6 vagina	6 scrotum
7 cervix	7 vas deferens
8 uterus	8 seminal vesicle
9 Fallopian tubes (oviducts)	9 sperm
10 ovary	10 Cowper's (bulbourethral) gland
11 perineum	11 prostate gland
12 Grafenberg spot	12 urethra
13 ovum	13 bladder
14 vaginal opening	14 anus
15 urethral opening	15 rectum
16 mons	16 epididymis
17 vulva	17 urethral opening
18 urethra	
19 bladder	
20 anus	
21 rectum	

- Post the cards on the wall, so that everyone can see them.
- Photocopy to enlarge and post Leader Resource 3, Female Sexual System, and Leader Resource 4, Male Sexual System.
- Post the ground rules from the Opening Session.

Activity

BODY PART SMARTS   45 minutes

1. Divide participants into two mixed-gender teams. To add to the fun, invite the teams to come up with team names. Have each team choose one member to be the designated answerer. Flip a coin to decide which team goes first.

2. Tell participants that this is a contest to see which team knows the most about reproductive and sexual anatomy. Explain that you will ask the first team a question (use Leader Resource 2, Body Parts Smarts: Questions and Answers), the answer to which is one of the terms on the cards. Say that the team has 30 seconds to confer before the designated answerer must give the team's response. Only the team whose turn it is may respond to the question. Use the numbered lists above to determine if the answer is correct. Tell participants that if the correct response is given, the team scores one point. If the answer is incorrect, the other team gets one opportunity to give the correct answer for one point. After a team has correctly identified the part of the body, the team member who answered the question takes the card with the correct term on it and tries to locate it correctly on the appropriate diagram. If the participant correctly locates the part of the body, he/she may write the term on the appropriate line on the diagram. A successful placement earns the team an additional point. If the placement is incorrect, the other team has one try to earn a point.

3. The game continues until time is up or all the terms have been properly placed on the diagram. The team with the most points at the end of the game wins.

NOTE: Point out that both the sperm and the ovum are microscopic and not visible on these drawings. Have participants place them in the organs in which they are produced.

Alternatives

- If a group is particularly knowledgeable, do not post the cards for reference.
- Another option is to require the teams to score points by choosing the correct card and placing it correctly on the diagram. In this version, if the answer is correct but the placement is wrong (or vice versa), no points are earned.

Leader Resource 2

BODY PARTS SMARTS

Questions and Answers

Although the following questions are arranged in male and female categories, ask them in random order.

Female Anatomy Questions

1. What is the only organ in the human body with the sole purpose of sexual sensation and arousal? **Clitoris**

2. What is the smooth skin between the vulva and the anus that sometimes tears or is cut (episiotomy) during childbirth? **Perineum**

3. What membrane may partially or completely cover the opening into the vagina and, if present, may be ruptured during athletics, tampon use, or first intercourse? **Hymen**

4. What is the passageway extending from the uterus to the outside of the body? **Vagina**

5. What is the term for the female's external genitalia? **Vulva**

6. What is the soft fatty tissue that covers a woman's pubic bone and is covered with pubic hair? **Mons**

7. What is the name for the mouth of the uterus that protrudes into the uppermost part of the vagina? **Cervix**

8. What is the name of the small opening above the vagina for the passage of urine? **Urethral opening**

9. What is the pear-shaped muscular organ, about the size of a fist, that sheds its lining during menstruation and that houses a fetus during pregnancy? **Uterus**

10. What are the approximately four-inch-long passageways for the eggs, between the ovaries and the uterus? **Fallopian tubes (oviducts)**

11. What structures are responsible for the production of estrogen and progesterone, female sex hormones? **Ovaries**

12. What part is located between the urethral opening and the anus? **Vaginal opening**

13. What serves as the passageway for urine from the bladder? **Urethra**

14. What is the name of two small, round glands on either side of the vaginal opening that secrete fluid during sexual arousal? **Bartholin's glands**

15. What is the name of the female sex cell, about the size of a pinhead, that must be fertilized by a male sperm in order to produce a baby? **Ovum**

16. What is the name for the folds of fatty tissue on both sides of the vulva that are covered with pubic hair and protect the clitoris and urethral and vaginal openings? **Labia majora**

17. What is the name for the inner folds of skin surrounding the clitoris and containing sweat and oil glands as well as extensive blood vessels and nerve endings? **Labia minora**

18. What structure is located within the front wall of the vagina about one-third to one-half of the way from the vaginal opening and associated with sexual arousal and orgasm in some women? **Grafenberg spot (G-spot)**

Male Anatomy Questions

19. What is the name of the male sex cell that must fertilize a female sex cell in order to produce a baby? **Sperm**

20. What is the passageway for sperm leading from the testicles to the urethra? **Vas deferens**

21. What is the name for the two sac-like structures that are responsible for producing seventy percent of the semen? **Seminal vesicles**

22. What is the name for the two glands responsible for producing sperm and the male sex hormone, testosterone? **Testicles (also called testes)**

23. What is the gland, about the size and shape of a walnut, at the base of the bladder, that produces approximately thirty percent of the seminal fluid? **Prostate gland**

24. At the top of each testicle, what tightly coiled tube stores sperm and allows sperm to continue to mature for up to six weeks? **Epididymis**

25. What is the loose sac of skin that holds, protects, and helps regulate the temperature of the two testicles? **Scrotum**

26. What is the tube that transports urine and semen at different times out of the male body? **Urethra**

27. What is the organ that has as its main functions sexual pleasure, reproduction, and urination? **Penis**

28. What covers the glans of the penis totally or partially, unless it is removed through a procedure called circumcision? **Foreskin**

29. What is the name for the smooth head of the penis? **Glans**

30. What is the name for two pea-sized glands that secrete fluid before ejaculation (pre-ejaculate) which helps to neutralize the acidic environment of the urethra? **Cowper's glands (or bulbourethral glands)**

31. What is the organ that holds the fluid flowing from the kidneys? **Bladder**

32. What are the small tubes where germ cells are produced and developed into sperm? **Seminiferous tubules**

33. What is the name of the small opening at the tip of the penis for the passage of urine and semen? **Urethral opening**

Gender-Neutral Questions

34. What is the tube-shaped entryway into the rectum? **Anus**

35. What is the name for the eight- to nine-inch tube-like structure of smooth tissue which is the passageway for solid waste? **Rectum**

Leader Resource 3

FEMALE SEXUAL SYSTEM

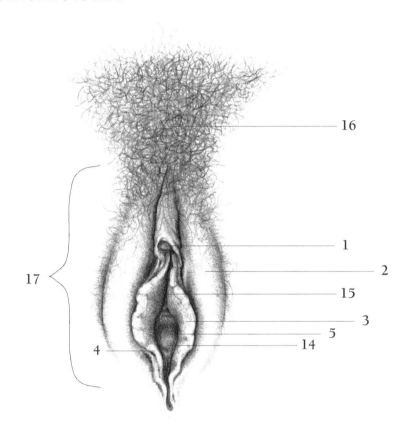

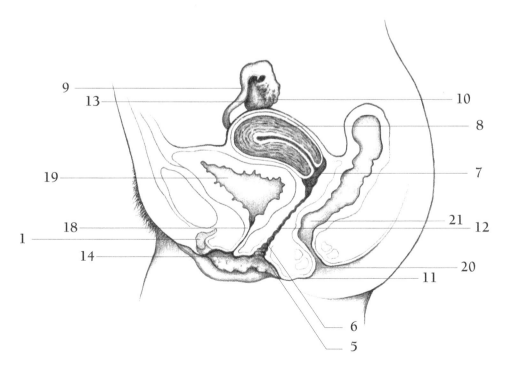

Leader Resource 4

MALE SEXUAL SYSTEM

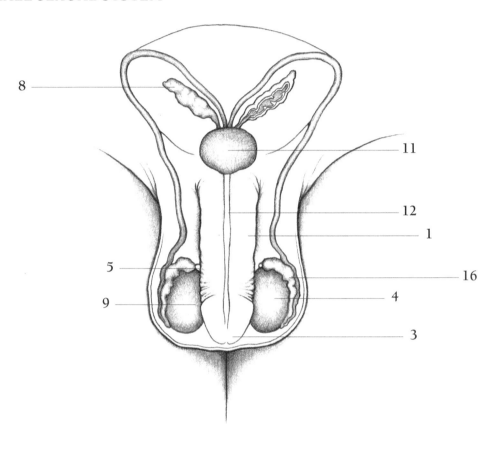

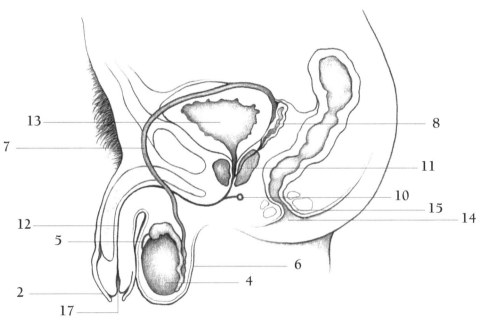

Taking Care of Our Sexual Selves

2

Sexual Response Cycle and Sexual Functioning

RATIONALE

Human sexual response is a complex physical, psychological, social, and spiritual process. No two individuals respond sexually in the same way. Each person's experience is different. Indeed, even for the same person, sexual response can vary, depending on the situation, partner, and other factors. This session helps participants understand that a range of responses is normal and thus provides individuals with the freedom to experience their sexuality without being limited to a predefined or stereotypical set of responses that may not reflect their true needs, desires, or capabilities.

Time Required: 45 minutes

GOALS

To help participants
- understand the body's physiological response to sexual arousal.
- understand the physical, emotional, and psychological components related to sexual response.
- understand the difference between a goal/orgasm-oriented model of sexual response and one in which pleasure is the only goal.
- understand the psychological and biological causes of common sexual dysfunctions and their treatments.

OBJECTIVES

By the end of this workshop, participants will be able to
- describe how each of the five senses is involved in sexual arousal.
- demonstrate an understanding of the models of sexual response by comparing and contrasting them during a discussion.
- be able to describe common sexual dysfunctions and their treatments.

MATERIALS

☐ Newsprint, markers, and masking tape
☐ Index cards

PREPARATION

- Review this workshop and decide how to share leadership responsibilities with your coleader.

- For the Five Senses activity, write each of the five senses—seeing, hearing, smelling, touching, tasting—on index cards.
- For the Sexual Response Cycle: Mini-lecture and Discussion, become familiar with the content of the mini-lecture on page 43, which is based on *Exploring Our Sexuality* by P. Koch. Prepare the following chart to summarize the first four models of the sexual response cycle. The representation of these models intentionally resembles ladders. You will draw the fifth model as a circle during your presentation.

SEXUAL RESPONSE CYCLE

Four Models

Resolution Orgasm Plateau Excitement	(Masters, William and Virginia Johnson. *Human Sexual Response*. Boston: Little Brown, 1966)
Desire	(Kaplan, Helen Singer. *The New Sex Therapy*. New York: Brunner/Mazel, 1974)
Satisfaction Peak Feeling Physiological Readiness Arousal Desire	(Zilbergeld, Bernie. *The New Male Sexuality*. New York: Bantam, 1999)
Reflection Surrender Sensations Seduction	(Reed, Walter. Model described in Koch, Patricia Barthlalow. *Exploring Our Sexuality*. Dubuque, Iowa: Kendall/Hunt, 1995)

- Post the ground rules from the Opening Session.

Activities

THE FIVE SENSES   15 minutes

1. Introduce the activity by saying, "In this workshop, we are going to learn more about how the human body responds to sexual stimuli. We will go over several different models of sexual response and determine what we like and don't like about each model. We will talk very specifically about what happens during sexual arousal, excitement, and orgasm, and we will describe what can interfere with sexual functioning. Before we talk about those specifics, however, we need to talk about the role our five senses play in sexual response."

2. Divide participants into five groups. Give each group a sheet of newsprint and a marker. Turn the five senses index cards face down and have one person from each group select a card without reading it. When all the cards have been handed out, instruct the groups to turn the cards over and take five minutes to make a list of all of the ways the sense they have selected plays a role in sexual arousal. Remind them that they are brainstorming and that all responses should be written down.

3. After five minutes, have the groups post their lists. Use the following questions to lead a 10-minute discussion with the whole group:

- What was surprising to you about this activity?
- Was it easy or difficult to think about the ways in which sense contributes to sexual arousal?
- Did you define sexual arousal primarily in terms of readiness for intercourse?
- Was the discussion male or female oriented? Heterosexually oriented?

If participants have defined arousal in terms of readiness for intercourse, ask them to describe how the senses can be used in a sexual way when no intercourse is going to take place. If participants are discussing sexual interactions in heterosexual terms only, point this out to them. If their descriptions seem sexist, ask both genders to respond to how they felt about the discussion that took place in their groups.

MINI-LECTURE AND DISCUSSION   20 minutes

1. Post the newsprint chart you have prepared and then, using the material below, *briefly* describe the sexual response cycle from a physiological perspective (Masters and Johnson).

MASTERS AND JOHNSON

This model describes four phases of sexual response that focus primarily on physical sensations. The first phase is *excitement*. During this phase, physical stimulation causes vasocongestion and myotonia. Vasocongestion is the accumulation of blood in various parts of the body. Myotonia is the tightening of muscles, or muscle tension. In this phase, a woman experiences vaginal lubrication, the vagina expands, the uterus is pulled upward, and the clitoris becomes engorged or full of blood. A man experiences erection of the penis, the scrotal skin smoothes out, and the testicles are drawn up toward the body. In both men and women, there is breast enlargement and nipple erection; muscle tension increases in the genitals and throughout the body; and heart rate, respiration, and blood pressure increase.

The second phase of the sexual response cycle in this model is called the *plateau* phase. In this phase, sexual tension usually levels off. In women, the outer third of the vagina swells, lubrication may slow, and the clitoris pulls back. In men, the testes swell and continue to elevate, and the head of the penis swells slightly and may grow darker in color. Heart rate, respiration, blood pressure, and muscle tension increase in both men and women.

The third phase in this model is called the *orgasm* phase. This includes the release of sexual tension through rhythmic contractions of the uterus and vagina in women and the prostate gland and the seminiferous tubules in men. Semen is often ejaculated at this time. Heart rate, respiration, and blood pressure are at their peak.

The final phase in this model is called *resolution*. At this time, the body usually returns to its unaroused state. Men also go through a phase called the refractory period. During this time, men are usually unable to get an erection or to ejaculate. The refractory period can last anywhere from a few minutes to a few days. The length of the refractory period gradually increases as a man gets older.

Ask participants,

- Does every sexual experience look like this one?
- What do you think of this model?
- Does it appear to be missing anything?
- What would make it a more inclusive model?
- What is the end of the model?
- What impact can this model have on how people perceive a sexual experience?

2. Now, using the following material, describe the other three models:

HELEN SINGER KAPLAN MODEL

This model includes the addition of the *desire* phase as the first part of the sexual response cycle. Desire is defined as an erotic feeling that stimulates one to seek sexual gratification. Unlike the first model, which begins immediately with physical excitement, this model begins to take into account the importance of the individual's psychological readiness, not just physical readiness, for sexual experience.

Ask participants,

- What do you think about this model?
- What, if anything, would you change or add?

ZILBERGELD MODEL

This model begins with *desire* but follows desire with *arousal*, which is defined as the subjective experience of feeling turned on. The excitement phase is replaced by a phase called *physiological readiness*, which emphasizes body changes resulting from vasocongestion and myotonia. The orgasm phase here is defined as a *peak feeling*, which is not synonymous with but often accompanies physical release. The orgasm phase is followed by a phase called *satisfaction*, which includes both emotional and physical feelings of satisfaction. In this model, a distinction is made between orgasm and feelings of pleasure and satisfaction. One can have a pleasurable and satisfying experience without having an orgasm.

Ask,

- What do you think about this model?
- Compared to the first model, how does this model change what a pleasurable sexual experience could look like?

REED MODEL

This model includes four phases that differ significantly from the phases of the first three because it is a psychological model intended to complement the physiological models. The first phase is called *seduction*. During seduction, a person is turned on to a person while trying to attract him or her. The next phase is *sensations*, during which one's senses trigger pleasurable and erotic feelings. Following the sensations phase is a phase called *surrender*. According to this model, surrender includes letting go and giving control over to the shared experience. Often orgasm is experienced during this phase, but it is not seen as the goal. In fact, giving oneself over to what is going on without feeling pressured to have an orgasm may be one way a person experiences surrender. The final phase of this model is called *reflection*. Reflection is described as how one feels immediately after the sexual experience. During reflection one might ask oneself, "Did I enjoy that? Would I do it again?"

Ask,

- What do you think about this model?
- Does it seem realistic?
- What do you like or dislike about this model?

During the discussion of the Reed model, include the following:

This model eliminates the orgasm or goal-oriented viewpoint and focuses more on how both partners feel and receive pleasure in a variety of ways. It does, however, focus on sexual encounters that include another person and does not describe a sexual response in which the individual is engaged in self-stimulation.

3. Lead a discussion comparing and contrasting all the models. To encourage discussion, ask:

- What is missing from the models?
- Do the models promote a variety of sexual experiences and outlets for sexual pleasure?

You may want to include the following points as the models are compared:

- All of these models are linear. They all describe sexual arousal as having a beginning and an end and moving forward in some sequence. Thus, these models can be described as ladder models of sexuality. [Draw a ladder on newsprint.]
- In a ladder model of sexuality, there is a series of fixed steps that represent increasingly arousing activities. The series ends with the top rung, the "goal," which is orgasm. The bottom or first rung may be a look [write "look" on the bottom rung of the ladder diagram]. Then comes an invitation [write this on the next rung], then a "touch," a "kiss," a "caress/fondle;" then "erection/lubrication;" followed by "penis into vagina;" and finally the big "O," orgasm. Usually, the goal is "O/O"—mutual orgasm.
- Ladder models are goal-oriented. They assume a male-female couple, and once the couple moves from one step on the ladder to the next, they cannot go back. They must continue up the ladder until they reach orgasm. If orgasm is not achieved, the entire experience is a failure. Ladder models do not recognize the pleasure of the activities themselves

4. Contrast the linear models with a circle model of mutual pleasure. Draw a large circle on newsprint. Tell participants, "In this model, the only goal is mutual pleasure. There can be any number of activities around the circle depending on what individual people find pleasurable. And activities can appear more than once on the circle in any order." Around the circle, in random order, write the following: caress, oral sex, invitation, kiss, massage, lubrication, talking, fondling, phone sex, touch, orgasm, erection, look, holding hands, anal sex, bubble bath, masturbation, snuggle, _____?, etc. Write some words more than once, such as kiss, orgasm, snuggle, and blanks at different points around the circle. Then say,

In this model, one can start or stop at any point, because the circle has no designated beginning or end. There is room for people to experience arousal and pleasure in many different ways. Pleasure does not always have to involve inter-course, and each activity is appreciated for the pleasure it gives rather than as a step toward an ultimate goal. This model allows for more options and more free-dom. It also acknowledges that a wide range of people—including same-sex couples, individuals, people with physical disabilities, and people of all ages—can experience sexual arousal.

Ask,

- What do you think about these models?
- Which model do you think represents the way most people think about sex?
- What are the advantages or disadvantages of these models?

SEXUAL DYSFUNCTION   10 minutes

1. To begin a discussion of sexual dysfunction, have participants brainstorm answers to this question: "What kinds of sexual difficulties or problems do you think men worry most about?"

2. List participants' responses on newsprint and go over them. Use the following in-formation to discuss various male sexual dysfunctions:

- *Premature ejaculation*: experiencing ejaculation before the individual wants to ex-perience it. It was once thought that if a man ejaculated before his partner had an orgasm, the man was experiencing premature ejaculation. We now under-stand that the majority of women are not able to experience orgasm through intercourse alone. Thus, the older definition of premature ejaculation sets up un-realistic expectations. It also assumes that orgasm for both partners is the only goal. If, however, a man is experiencing ejaculation before he penetrates the vagina, and he wants to have intercourse, then he may wish to seek treatment. There are techniques that a man can use if he decides that he would like to delay ejaculation. A qualified sex therapist can help.

- *Retarded ejaculation*: an inability to experience orgasm and ejaculation when one wishes. This condition can have biological and/or psychological causes. Alcohol, drugs, and some prescription medications can impact a man's ability to ejaculate. Men who have taught themselves to prolong orgasm and ejaculation to please a partner may have difficulty switching gears and letting go when they would like. Other psychological causes are also possible.

- *Erection difficulties*: inability to achieve or maintain an erection. Erections often come and go during a sexual encounter. The inability to achieve or maintain an erection is only a problem for the man when it interferes with his wishes. Again, drugs, alcohol, and some medications may play a role. Fatigue and some ill-nesses can also result in erection difficulties. Anxiety over pleasing a partner, fear, distraction, stress, not being fully aroused, or other psychological causes may also play a role. Most men experience this dysfunction at some time in their sexual lives. Prescription medication or sex therapy may help.

3. Ask participants to brainstorm answers to this question: "What kinds of sexual dif-ficulties do women worry about most?"

4. List participants' responses on newsprint and go over them. Use the following information to describe various female sexual dysfunctions:

- *Inability to experience orgasm* can result from a variety of factors, including inadequate or uncomfortable stimulation, fear or anxiety, stress, distraction, and other psychological causes. Drugs, alcohol, and some medications may play a role. Communication with the partner and help from a sex therapist may help with psychological factors. Women who have masturbated to orgasm often know what kind of stimulation feels best and can communicate this to their partners. Many therapists suggest that women learn to have orgasms on their own as a first step toward having orgasms with a partner.

- *Lack of lubrication* results in vaginal dryness, making penile penetration painful or uncomfortable. It is often caused by lack of full arousal, but it can also be caused by hormonal changes, drugs, and medications. Use of K-Y jelly or another water-soluble lubricant will help.

5. Finally, explain to the group that both men and women can be so self-conscious about how their bodies look or smell that they cannot enjoy themselves. Point out that both women and men can experience performance anxiety, caused by unrealistic expectations about what a sexual experience should be. Say that many people feel that partners should experience simultaneous orgasms but that this expectation is both unnecessary and unrealistic, that orgasm is not necessary for a sexual experience to be pleasurable. Tell participants that when men and women are having penis-vagina intercourse, most women do not experience enough clitoral stimulation from thrusting alone to have orgasms. Conclude by saying that feeling pressured to behave in a certain way—to look, sound, smell, or respond according to an unrealistic set of standards—makes sexual sharing uncomfortable for both partners. Sexual responding can be whatever feels good to both participants and is usually fostered by genuine caring and respect for one another and open, intimate communication.

RATIONALE

People of all ages are often uncomfortable addressing their sexual health-care needs because they feel embarrassed about or even ashamed of their sexuality and their genitals. This workshop emphasizes that sexual health is a part of an individual's overall health and that maintaining sexual health does not have to be embarrassing or difficult. By discussing the medical, social, and psychological factors involved in maintaining sexual health and by providing information about when and how to seek medical help, this workshop aims to help participants prevent problems and feel positive about taking good care of themselves.

Time Required: 45 minutes

GOALS

To help participants

- view reproductive and sexual health care as a part of their overall health care.
- understand what a breast self-exam and testicular self-exam are, how to perform these exams, how often to perform them, and what to do if there is a noticeable change or symptom.
- understand what a pelvic exam includes and what the experience is like for a young woman.
- understand what a visit to a health clinic includes and what the experience is like for a young man.

OBJECTIVES

By the end of this workshop, participants will be able to

- state reasons why they would seek the care of a regular physician and why they might seek the care of a gynecologist or reproductive health-care clinician.
- describe a breast self-exam and a testicular self-exam and explain why they are important.
- write down and share at least one feeling or thought they experienced during an imaginary field trip to a reproductive health-care clinic.

MATERIALS

- ☐ Newsprint, markers, and tape
- ☐ American Cancer Society breast self-exam and testicular self-exam brochures, videos, and/or models

PREPARATION

- Review this workshop and decide with your coleader how to divide leadership responsibilities.
- Order brochures (or video or models if desired) about breast and testicular self-examination from the American Cancer Society (see Resources).
- Post the ground rules from the Opening Session.

Activities

SEXUAL HEALTH CARE   10 minutes

1. Tell participants that today's activities will help them look at the issue of sexual health. Explain that we need to do specific activities to keep the sexual parts of our bodies healthy just as we need to brush our teeth, eat properly, and get enough exercise. Say that maintaining health begins with understanding our bodies and learning to listen to them and includes knowing how and where to get care if we need it.

2. Ask participants to brainstorm reasons why they might go to their family doctor or another general practitioner. Have participants call out their answers and list their responses on newsprint.

3. After one or two minutes, ask the group to brainstorm a list of reasons why they might go to a gynecologist or family planning clinic. Write these responses on newsprint.

4. After a minute, help the group process the activity by asking,

- How are these lists similar?
- How are they different?
- Do your parents go to the family doctor with you? Make appointments for you? Pay for your medical visits?
- Would you be comfortable having your parents do the same for a visit to an STD (sexually transmitted disease) clinic or a gynecologist?
- What is the difference between going to a clinic to get checked for a possible sexually transmitted disease symptom and going to a family doctor for an earache or a sore throat?

5. Conclude the discussion by stressing that sexual health care is important because all of the systems of the body work together. If the sexual system isn't working well, it will have an impact on other aspects of the body's health as well.

6. Using the American Cancer Society brochures, go over the breast self-exam (BSE) and the testicular self-exam (TSE). Stress the importance of doing the exams as a way of getting to know how our bodies normally feel, so that changes will be easy to spot. Explain that these exams are not looking for cancer, but looking for changes that may signal the need for medical evaluation. Point out that most breast lumps and testicular growths are not cancerous but that regular self-examination substantially improves the chances of early detection and cure when they are.

7. To help participants process the activity, ask what might make people less likely to perform a BSE or TSE. Then ask participants, "What would make you more likely to perform these exams?"

VIRTUAL FIELD TRIPS

1. Introduce this activity by saying, "We are going to take a field trip to a clinic. But since we don't really have time today to go to a clinic, we are going to do a guided imagery trip in our minds. I would like you to try to put yourself into the thoughts and feelings of our imaginary clinic visitor, Jane. At the end of the trip, I will ask you to share some of what you think she was feeling."

2. Invite participants to sit in a comfortable position and relax. Tell them they may close their eyes if they wish. Ask them to listen carefully and try to think at each step of the way what Jane is thinking or feeling. Read the clinic visit story in a calm, measured voice.

JANE'S CLINIC VISIT

Jane takes the bus downtown to the clinic. She gets off the bus and enters the front door of the clinic.

She gives her name to the receptionist and is told to have a seat in the waiting room. She sits and waits, looking at the other people in the waiting room.

A young women calls her name and asks Jane to follow her to an interview room. The young woman tells her that she is a family planning counselor and she is going to be asking Jane a lot of questions so that the clinicians can provide the best care to Jane and so that they can work with her to meet her family planning and health-care needs.

The woman asks Jane about her personal and family medical history, about her drug and alcohol use, cigarette smoking, when she got her first period and her menstrual history. She is also asked about her sexual experience, contraceptive use, and her pregnancy and abortion history. Then the woman asks Jane if she has any questions or concerns. Jane asks the counselor if it is necessary for a woman who has never had sexual intercourse with a man to seek the care of a gynecologist. The counselor tells her that all women over the age of eighteen should have annual pelvic and breast exams and Pap tests. During these visits, a woman will also have a chance to discuss changes in her needs for contraception, if any, and to discuss any other concerns she may have about sexual or reproductive health, such as menstrual irregularities or problems, infections, or sexual dysfunction.

Then the woman leads Jane to an examining room. She tells Jane to take off her clothes and put on a paper gown. She tells Jane that the doctor will be in in a minute, then she leaves Jane alone. Jane gets undressed and sits on the table, waiting.

After a few minutes, the doctor comes in, introduces herself and asks Jane why she has come here today. Jane explains that she is considering beginning a sexual relationship with a man and would like to discuss her options for STD protection and contraception.

The doctor takes Jane's blood pressure and asks Jane to lie back on the exam table. The doctor examines each of Jane's breasts and shows Jane how to feel for lumps and changes. Then the doctor asks Jane to put her feet in the stirrups. The doctor then inserts a gloved finger into Jane's vagina and presses against Jane's abdomen with her other hand. She feels for the position, size, and overall condition of Jane's cervix, uterus, and ovaries. Then the doctor inserts a speculum—an instrument used to hold the walls of the vagina apart—into Jane's vagina so that she can see Jane's cervix. She uses a long swab to take a sample of cells for a Pap test, a test to screen for cervical cancer. The doctor then removes the speculum and tells Jane to get dressed and meet her across the hall in her office. The doctor leaves the exam room, and Jane gets dressed.

In the office, the doctor discusses Jane's options for contraception and talks to her about using condoms to protect against STDs. The doctor tells her that the clinic will call her if her Pap results need further evaluation. She and Jane go over Jane's contraceptive choices, and they discuss condoms and foam as a good option if Jane decides to have sexual intercourse. The doctor thanks Jane and says good-bye.

Jane pays the receptionist, leaves the clinic, and catches the bus home.

3. Ask participants to take a minute to be aware of a thought, feeling, image, or question they had during the field trip. After a minute, invite everyone to share one of their responses to the virtual visit.

4. Allow brief discussion. Ask, "Were there any differences in the way men or women seemed to feel about the imagery?"

5. Ask participants to again sit in a comfortable position, relax, and close their eyes if they wish. Begin reading "Beating the Stats" by Brad Bailey from the Sex Etc. Web site, posted by the Network for Family Life Education (http://www.sexetc.org).

BEATING THE STATS

It's important for teenagers who are having sex or considering having sex to visit a doctor or clinic that screens for and treats sexually transmitted diseases and provides birth control, says Dr. Barbara Snyder, chief of Adolescent Medicine, University of Medicine and Dentistry-New Jersey. Young women should go at least once a year when they reach 18 or become sexually active. You should go more often if you have health problems or if you have several sexual partners. Some doctors require females to have a pelvic exam to get birth control pills and other types of contraception, but others don't. Either way, all doctors agree it's important for females to have regular pelvic exams.

For guys, the routine is a little different—but no less important. Unfortunately, most guys don't go to the doctor unless they're having problems, Snyder says. But guys should get screened routinely if they're having sex. . . .

SEX, ETC. asked a male to talk about his trip to the clinic. Here is his story.

I knew the stats.

Three million teenagers get infected with a sexually transmitted disease each year. Nearly one million teen girls get pregnant. HIV, the virus that causes AIDS, is infecting young people faster than any other group. One-half of all new HIV infections hit people under 25.

I didn't want to become another statistic. So here's what I did:

MONDAY, 9:15 A.M.

I decide against going to my family doctor because he knows me and my family too well. I figure I'll find a free clinic in Philadelphia (not far from where I live). I'll be less likely to run into someone I know.

9:30 A.M.

Call the Philadelphia City Hall to find a free clinic. They transfer me to the director of health and free clinics. The guy explains the process to me. He talks to me as if I already have a disease. Jerk. But he does give me the info I need and tells me how to get to the clinic.

WEDNESDAY, 2 P.M.

Jump into my car and head for Philly. I find the clinic, circle the block, and park. When I step out of the car, my mouth goes dry, my stomach queasy.

2:05 P.M.

Walk into the clinic and feel like everyone's wondering, "What's he got?" Feeling really nervous now and questions reel through my mind. What are they going to do? How are they going to treat me? Just get it over with, I tell myself. I head for the reception desk.

The receptionist tells me they don't take "walk-ins" 'til 4 P.M. Great. Two hours to kill. I take in a few sights.

4 P.M.

Back at the clinic. The receptionist gives me a form with two blue tickets attached to the top. They both have the same number on them. I fill out the form, which asks for basic info—name, address, etc. I give her back the form. She hands me one ticket and keeps the other. Now I'm just a number. They don't use names to track your test results.

I wait. A video about STDs plays in the waiting room.

4:45 P.M.

The nurse calls out, "163, 164, and 165, please come with me." That's me—163. I follow her into the back with two other patients. The nurse calls us into the room one at a time. She takes two vials of blood—a needle stick and it's over. The clinic will use one vial to test for HIV. The other for syphilis. Back to the waiting room.

5:10 P.M.

Another nurse calls me in. She starts asking some really personal questions. I swallow hard and tell the truth. "Do you have sex with females, males, or both? When was the last time you had sex? How many partners have you had in 30 days? Do you always, sometimes, or never practice safe sex? Have you had an HIV test in less than or more than six months?"

My answers determine which tests I'll take. I'll get four—oral, rectal, urethra, and physical. Any questions, the nurse asks. Just one, I say. That urethra test, I hear it hurts, you put a needle-like instrument in the tip of the penis? It stings, she says, but not too much. Yeah, right.

5:30 P.M.

The doctor finally comes into the room with a warm smile and says hello. I really wasn't expecting a woman, but she makes me feel comfortable. She explains all the tests, which basically tell if I have different sexually transmitted diseases, including gonorrhea (most people call it "the clap") and chlamydia. Both can cause sterility and other health problems, and you can sometimes have them without knowing it. The physical exam is to check for urinary problems.

5:40 P.M.

The tests start. First, the oral test—a simple swipe with a cotton swab on the back of my throat. A breeze. Next comes the rectal test—swiping the anus with a cotton swab. Definitely a little uncomfortable, considering the position, but not painful. Then the urethra test, which is basically what I expect. Painful, but not unbearable. Last is the physical exam. The doc pushes on the groin and testes areas and asks if there is any pain. It feels kinda like a little tummy massage.

The whole time, the doc is talking, making me feel comfortable, like all this awkward testing is totally normal. She finishes and asks if I have any questions. I thought, yeah, I have a few.

"Do condoms protect me from all STDs?"

"Condoms, as with any disease/pregnancy prevention method, are not 100 percent effective. They can break or have microscopic holes," she explains but adds that condoms are still the best protection for people who are having sex.

Is there a wrong way to use a condom?

Yup, she says, and hands me a brochure that tells me the right way. It also shows different types of condoms and when you should use them. It says to use condoms even during oral sex. Never heard that before.

5:45 P.M.

Next stop, a social worker, who explains the whole HIV testing thing to me.

5:55 P.M.

I get the results to the syphilis test. Negative.

Pheweee. The doctor tells me keep it that way. Always practice "safer sex," she says. That means using a condom every single time and choosing partners carefully. The more partners, the greater chance of getting a disease. No problem, I tell her.

We set an appointment time for me to come back to get the results of the other tests. Then she hands me a bag of about 30 lubricated, spermicidal condoms. That should last me the next 100 years.

6 P.M.

It's over. Relief. Driving home, I think about the whole experience. It was more comfortable than I expected. OK, not completely 100 percent comfortable. When the tests were being performed, I definitely felt awkward and a little embarrassed. But everyone made everything seem normal. Hey, maybe it was. It's just not something I'm used to.

I realize, too, how important it is to be responsible and healthy. I really didn't think I had a disease or anything, but there's always a slight chance. Some diseases go undetected and you may not find out about it until it's way more serious. But later, after I get my other test results, I'll know I'm OK. And that eases my mind. Not to mention my partner's.

To find a family planning clinic near you, call Planned Parenthood at 800/230-PLAN (7526), or check out their website at www.plannedparenthood.org.

6. Summarize the activity by saying something like, "Youth who are sexually active or considering having sex should visit a doctor or clinic that screens for and treats sexually transmitted diseases and provides birth control information and methods. Although teens should have regular health exams, often males do not go to a doctor unless they are having a problem. Did you notice that Brad seems to have been motivated by fear of an STD? Sometimes when we don't know what to expect, we let fear or ignorance keep us from taking good care of ourselves. I hope that you will use the information you've learned today to make good decisions about your health, including your sexual health."

AIDS and Other STDs

RATIONALE

This workshop provides important information upon which later lessons will be based. The activities in this workshop provide factual information about STDs, including AIDS; help participants understand the importance of protecting themselves; and invite participants to reconsider some of the myths that surround these topics. The information provided to participants will allow them to begin to make decisions for their own health. This workshop also gives participants the opportunity to explore the range of ideas and values held by their peers and to figure out how they themselves feel about some controversial issues.

Time Required: 45 minutes

GOALS

To help participants to
- become familiar with the most common symptoms of sexually transmitted diseases (STDs).
- become aware of the need to consult a health-care professional if they suspect they have a sexually transmitted infection and learn where they might seek such care.
- be able to assess their own risk for infection, based on their personal behaviors.
- be aware of the stereotypes, prejudices, and myths that surround the topic of HIV/AIDS.
- acquire or review a basic understanding of HIV, including modes of transmission, window period, testing issues, latency period, and current rates of adolescent infection.
- explore different values associated with STDs and understand their personal feelings and values on this topic.

OBJECTIVES

By the end of this workshop, participants will be able to
- demonstrate awareness of how STDs, including HIV, are transmitted.
- show knowledge of issues related to HIV, including window period, antibody test, and dormancy period.
- through reflection on a fictional story, articulate some of their own values about sexual behavior and discuss them with others.

MATERIALS

☐ Index cards

☐ Pencils

☐ Leader Resource 5, HIV/AIDS Quiz, and Leader Resource 6, HIV/AIDS Facts

☐ Handout 7, The Story of Jake and Nora

☐ Handout 8, Toll-free Hotlines and Local Resources

☐ Prizes for all participants (optional)

PREPARATION

• Review this workshop and decide with your coleader how to divide leadership responsibilities.

• Prepare a deck of index cards for How Serious is the Threat of an STD to Me? On the back corner of one index card, write the letter *I*; on two cards, the letter *C*; on another two cards, the letter *A*; and on one card, the letter *O*. (Note: If there are more than ten in the group, you may want to add another card with the letter *O* and one more with the letter *A* or *C*.) The letters should be written discreetly so that participants won't notice them. Approximately half of the cards in the deck should have a letter on them, and the rest should be blank. Be sure to shuffle the cards after you have prepared the deck.

• Prepare to give the STDs mini-lecture. Read Leader Resource 8, HIV/AIDS Facts, so that you will be able to answer questions that come up during the HIV/AIDS Quiz.

• Make one copy of Handout 7, The Story of Jake and Nora, for each participant.

• Identify local clinics and other resources for teens, add them to Handout 8, then photocopy the handout for all participants.

• Post the ground rules from the Opening Session.

Activities

HOW SERIOUS IS THE THREAT OF AN STD TO ME?   10 minutes

1. Give an index card from the deck you have prepared and a pencil to each participant. Ask everyone to stand up and walk around until they find a partner. When each participant has a partner, tell them they have one minute to discuss the following question: "What puts a person at risk for HIV or other sexually transmitted diseases?"

2. When the minute is up, ask everyone to sign her/his name on the partner's card. Have the group mingle again and select new partners. Give the group 1 minute to discuss this question: "How easy or difficult would it be for you, if you were sexually active, to discuss STDs with your sexual partner?"

3. After one minute, again ask each participant to sign his/her name to the partner's card. Ask the group to walk around and select new partners to discuss the following question for one minute: "If you found out that a close friend of yours was infected with HIV, what would you say or do?"

4. After everyone has signed his/her partner's cards, ask participants to return to their seats.

5. Explain that one person's card has the letter *I* written on the back of it. Tell the group that for the purposes of this exercise, they are going to pretend that the *I* means that this person has a sexually transmitted infection. (You may want to use a specific infection such as chlamydia or HIV.) Reinforce the point that this is just a game and that the cards were passed out randomly. Ask the person who is "infected" to stand up.

6. Ask, "Who has the infected person's signature on their card?" Ask those people to stand up. Tell the group that if a standing person has no letter written on her/his card, she/he had unprotected intercourse with the infected person and is now infected; if a person standing has the letter C on his/her card, the person used a latex condom when having sexual intercourse with the infected person, did not become infected, and may sit down; if a standing person has the letter A on his/her card, the person chose to abstain from risky sexual behavior, has not become infected, and may sit down; if a standing person has an O on her/his card, the person engaged in "outer-course" (sexual behavior without the exchange of bodily fluids), is also safe, and may sit down.

7. Now ask, "Who has the signature of any of the people who are standing?" Ask these people to stand up and point out that these individuals have been exposed to a sexually transmitted infection. Tell the group again that anyone with a blank card should remain standing while those with a C, A, or O may sit.

8. Continue this process until all names have been used.

9. Ask the group to look at how many people are standing. Tell the group that this is the infected group. Explain that they all became infected from one infected person. Say, "This is why we hear the phrase, 'When you have sex with someone, you are having sex with everyone they ever had sex with.' " Stress to participants that in this game, people were infected at random. Point out that in real life, people have control over their behavior. Tell participants that we are all vulnerable to the threat of a sexually transmitted infection and we all must take precautions to protect ourselves.

10. Help participants process this activity with the following questions:
   • How did it feel to discover you were infected with a sexually transmitted infection or to discover that you were not infected?
   • Were you relieved?
   • Did you feel lucky?
   • Do you think if you played the game again you would remain uninfected?

SEXUALLY TRANSMITTED DISEASES MINI-LECTURE   5 minutes

Introduce the concept of sexually transmitted infections by offering the following information:
   • A recent national survey has found that almost half of all female students and six out of ten male students in grades 9-12 has had sexual intercourse.
   • Three million teenagers every year get some kind of sexually transmitted infection, accounting for one quarter of all new cases of STDs each year.
   • Sexually transmitted diseases are passed during sexual contact between a person who has the infection and another person. Unprotected sexual contact includes oral sex, anal sex, and/or vaginal sex without the use of a latex condom with spermicide. Some STDs are passed through more casual contact as well.
   • With the exception of HIV, herpes, and genital warts, which are caused by viruses, most STDs can be treated with antibiotics and cured. Many STDs, however, have no symptoms and can go untreated for months or even years. Because a woman's

reproductive organs are all internal, it is often difficult to notice any signs of infection. STDs that remain in the body for long periods of time can damage the reproductive organs, cause infertility, and, if left untreated, even damage the brain.

- Some STDs do have symptoms, including bumps, lumps, blisters, or sores on or near the genitals, unusual or foul-smelling discharge, and pain or a burning sensation during urination. Even if the symptoms seem to go away, the disease may still be in your body, you can still pass it to another person, and it can still cause harm to your body.

- If you have a sexually transmitted disease and you have sexual contact with another person, the other person may become infected. You must tell anyone you have had sexual contact with to go to a doctor or clinic and get treatment.

HIV/AIDS QUIZ   10 minutes

1. Explain to participants that you are going to see how much they know about the most serious sexually transmitted disease, AIDS. Divide participants into teams of four or five. Ask the questions on Leader Resource 7, HIV/AIDS Quiz, alternating evenly among groups. Score one point for each right answer. If a team answers incorrectly, give the next team the opportunity to respond.

2. As you are asking questions or after the quiz is over, answer any questions the participants have.

Alternatives

- If the group does not enjoy competition, conduct the game in a collaborative rather than competitive format and do not keep score.
- If your group believes it already has extensive knowledge about HIV/AIDS, have participants divide into teams, write their own questions and answers, and quiz each other.

THE STORY OF JAKE AND NORA   20 minutes

1. Give each participant a copy of Handout 7, The Story of Jake and Nora. Have each person read the story silently and then rank the characters according to the instructions at the bottom of the handout.

2. After everyone has finished, divide participants into groups of four. Ask the members of each group to work together to achieve a group consensus ranking. Remind them that consensus means that although not everyone agrees with the answer, everyone is willing to accept the group's decision.

3. When time is up, have each group present its consensus to the large group. Look for the following issues as each consensus is discussed:
- The criteria the groups used to make their judgments
- The meaning of friendship
- The importance of trust in relationships
- How alcohol affects behavior
- Identifying how one can be assured of being "safe"
- How sexual experiences "just happen" and how to prepare oneself
- A definition of "faithful" and a discussion of how realistic monogamy may be
- The issue of rape or coercive sexual behaviors

4. Help participants process the activity with the following questions:
   - What did you think of this activity?
   - What was the most difficult part?
   - What issues did you find most complicated or confusing?
   - How realistic was the situation?

Handout 7

THE STORY OF JAKE AND NORA

Jake and Nora met during the first week of school when Jake was starting his senior year in high school and Nora was starting eleventh grade. They fell in love over the course of the school year, first becoming good friends and then falling deeply in love. Although both of them had had steady partners, neither of them had had sexual intercourse. When they decided to have sex for the first time, they went to the clinic together, and Nora went on the pill. They felt confident that they did not need to use condoms since both of them were virgins.

The following fall, Jake left to go to college about one hundred miles away. He and Nora vowed to remain faithful. Since they would see each other about twice a month, Nora kept taking the pill so that they could have sex without worry during their visits.

Before Jake left, he asked his best friend Chris to keep Nora company while he was away. Chris was staying in town to work at his father's restaurant. Chris said he'd be glad to hang out with Nora, and even got her a job at the restaurant after school and on weekends.

Chris and Nora spent a lot of time together. Chris was always asking Nora's advice about his girlfriends, and Nora was glad to have the company because she missed Jake very much. Jake's visits were becoming less frequent as his workload became heavier and he became more involved in school events. Sometimes if Chris did not have a date, he and Nora would raid the bar after the restaurant closed and sit at a booth talking and drinking until very late. One Friday evening, when Jake had canceled his plans to visit, Nora was very upset. She and Chris ended up drinking more than usual. As she was crying on his shoulder, Chris told her that she should dump Jake because he probably was seeing other people anyway. Chris also told her that he had always envied Jake because he thought Nora was really hot. Then he began touching her breasts and trying to undress her. Although Nora initially protested, she and Chris ended up having sex on the floor of the restaurant.

The next day, when Chris's father discovered that Chris had been stealing liquor and partying in the dining room, he fired him. Chris left town without a word to Nora. Two weeks later, he called to tell her that he had an STD and that she needed to get checked. Nora was completely confused and upset. Jake was planning to come home that evening, and her parents were going out of town. She knew that if she asked Jake to wear a condom he would be suspicious because she had promised to be faithful. But if she had the STD and Jake did not wear a condom, she might give it to him. She called her best friend Trisha and asked her what she should do. Trisha said, "Only you can make that decision."

As her mother packed for her trip, Nora told her the story, saying that it had happened to a friend of hers. Her mother said, "Well, it just goes to show that all men are scum."

Eventually, Nora left to pick up Jake at the bus station. All the way back to her house, she agonized over what to do. She just couldn't bear to hurt him by telling him that she'd had sex with his best friend. That evening, they had sex without using a condom, and Nora prayed that she didn't give him anything.

Later that weekend Jake told Nora that although he really loved her, he thought that maybe they should date other people while they were separated.

Rank the following characters from the story from the person you admire, respect, or like the most (1) to the person you admire, respect, or like the least (5).

Jake _____   Nora's mother_____   Trisha _____

Nora _____   Chris _____

Handout 8

TOLL-FREE HOTLINES AND LOCAL RESOURCES

National Toll-Free Hotlines

American Social Health Association	1-919-361-8400
CDC National HIV & AIDS Hotline	1-800-342-AIDS
TTY (M–F, 10 AM–10 PM, EST)	1-888-232-6348
CDC National HIV & AIDS Hotline	
for Spanish-speaking people	1-800-344-7432
(7 days, 8 AM–2 AM, EST)	
CDC National Prevention Information Network	1-800-458-5231
Emergency Contraception Hotline	1-800-584-9911
http://opr.princeton.edu/ec	1-888-NOT-2-LATE
Gay and Lesbian National Hotline	1-888-843-4564
HIV/AIDS Treatment Information Service	1-800-HIV-0440
National AIDS Hotline	1-800-342-AIDS
Hearing Impaired	1-800-AIDS-TTY
Spanish-speaking	1-800-344-7432
National Center for Youth With Disabilities	
Adolescent Health Program	1-800-333-6293
National Child Abuse Hotline	1-800-422-4453
(United States, Canada, and Carribean)	
National Herpes Hotline (not toll-free)	1-919-361-8488
National Resource Center on Child Sexual Abuse	1-800-543-7006
National Sexually Transmitted Disease (STD) Hotline	
(8 AM–11 PM, EST, M–F)	1-800-227-8922
National Venereal Disease Hotline	1-800-227-8922
Planned Parenthood Federation of America	1-800-220-PLAN
Rape, Abuse, Incest National Network	1-800-656-HOPE
Rape Victim Assistance	1-800-422-3204
Safer Sex Hotline	1-800-FOR-AIDS
Youth Only AIDS Line by Teens for Teens	1-800-788-1234

Resources in Your Organization

_____   _____

_____   _____

_____   _____

Local Resources

Leader Resource 5

HIV/AIDS QUIZ

A. Viral STDs

1. Can you name two STDs that are caused by a virus?
HIV, herpes, genital warts

2. How are viral STDs different from bacterial STDs in treatment?
They cannot be cured, only controlled.

3. (a) What do the letters H-I-V stand for?
Human Immunodeficiency Virus

(b) What is it?
It is a virus that causes the immune system to become less and less effective.

4. (a) What do the letters A-I-D-S stand for?
Acquired Immune Deficiency Syndrome

(b) What does it mean?
The person has a reduced ability (deficiency) to fight off infections (immunity)—a deficiency she/he wasn't born with (acquired).

5. (a) What are the symptoms of HIV?
There are none.

(b) How do you know if you have HIV?
The only sure sign is the presence of antibodies in a blood test.

6. (a) What are the symptoms of AIDS?
A variety of symptoms that are characteristic of opportunistic infections, e.g., fever, fatigue.

(b) How do you know if you have AIDS?
The only sure sign is a lowered T-cell count in the blood.

7. Can a person die from AIDS?
Yes, indirectly. A person with AIDS will die of another infection the body cannot fight off.

8. Can HIV be cured?
No. It is a virus, and viruses cannot be cured by medication. The only protection against a virus is vaccination.

B. HIV Transmission

1. There are four body fluids that can hold HIV in high enough concentration to infect another person by direct contact. Can you name three?
blood, semen, vaginal fluid, breast milk

2. How can an infected person infect another person?

By commingling receptive body fluids: semen to vaginal fluid, semen to blood, or blood to blood

3. In what three sexual activities can HIV be transmitted?

anal intercourse without a latex condom; vaginal-penile intercourse without a latex condom; oral-genital sex without a latex barrier

4. (a) Is saliva a transmitter of HIV?

Although it was not thought to be, recent research suggests it may be.

(b) Why is oral-genital sex risky behavior with an HIV-infected partner?

Infected semen or vaginal fluid can enter the bloodstream through cuts or sores in the mouth.

5. To which partner—man or woman—is vaginal-penile intercourse most risky?

The woman. Her vagina, by virtue of its construction, acts as an incubator for the virus. Women are 20 times more likely to contract HIV than men this way.

6. There are at least three ways other than sex that HIV can be transmitted. Can you name two?

sharing needles with an infected person; mother to baby during birth (perinatal transmission); breast-feeding

7. In what activities can needle-sharing convey HIV?

drug injections (whether drugs are legal or illegal); ear or skin piercing; tattooing

C. Risky or Risk-Free?

1. Can HIV be contracted by donating blood?

No.

2. Can HIV be contracted through hugging, kissing, or shaking hands?

No.

3. (a) Can HIV be transmitted through toilet seats, doorknobs, water fountains, or eating utensils?

No.

(b) Why not?

HIV does not survive long enough in open air (wet or dry) for infection. It must be in receptive body fluid to survive, and it must travel from receptive fluid to receptive fluid, with no gap.

4. Is HIV spread through mosquitoes or other animal bites?

No.

5. Can HIV be contracted through caring for a person with HIV?

No. Casual contact cannot transmit the virus.

6. Can HIV be contracted through receiving a blood transfusion?

No. Blood is heated to inactivate the virus.

7. In viral diseases, the time between infection and the development of antibodies that can be detected by a blood test is called the "window" period. What is the "window period" for HIV?

3 to 6 months

8. If a person became exposed to HIV today, would infection show up in a blood test tomorrow?

No.

Next week?

No.

Next month?

No.

9. If a person became infected today, could he/she transmit the virus to someone else tomorrow?

Yes.

10. Could a person who tested negative for HIV transmit the disease?

Yes, if transmission occurred in the "window" between contracting the virus and testing positive for the virus.

11. Is there any time when a person infected with HIV cannot transmit the virus?

No.

12. For viral infections, the latency period is the time between a person's contracting the infection and the time he/she shows symptoms. In HIV/AIDS, when the latency period is over, a person goes from being HIV-positive to having AIDS. What is the latency period for AIDS?

2 to 10 years or more

13. How is it determined that a person has moved from being HIV-positive to having AIDS?

The T-cell count falls below 200; symptoms appear of opportunistic infections that are rare in the general population, such as Kaposi's sarcoma.

14. Do all people with HIV become sick and die?

We don't know for sure.

15. What two behaviors put you at risk for contracting HIV?

Unprotected sex; sharing needles for any reason

16. In sexual behavior, how do you avoid getting an STD?

Condom-protected sex; abstinence

D. HIV/AIDS and You

1. How many people in the United States were infected with HIV as of January, 2006?

Between 992,000 and 1.2 million, or about 1 in every 250 people

2. What percentage of that group were infected as adolescents?

20 percent

3. What is one of the leading causes of death among people 25 to 44 years of age?

Opportunistic infections contracted due to AIDS

Leader Resource 6

HIV/AIDS FACTS

AIDS—acquired immune deficiency syndrome—is caused by a virus called HIV, an acronym for human immunodeficiency virus. Scientists believe that HIV attacks a person's immune system, those cells in the body that fight infection and keep a person healthy. Attacked by the virus, the helper T-cells, which normally fight invading viruses, become factories for producing HIV and eventually die. Over a period of time, as the T-cells die, the individual's immune system becomes severely weakened and is unable to fight off infection and disease. Eventually, a person with AIDS will die from an illness that a person with a healthy immune system could fight off or would never contract in the first place.

I. **Transmission.** There are four bodily fluids in which HIV is found in high enough concentrations to allow for transmission from one person to another: blood and blood products (for example, plasma), semen, vaginal fluids, and breast milk.

   A. Sexual Transmission

   1. *Anal intercourse without the use of a latex condom with a person who is infected with HIV.* Because the lining of the rectum ruptures easily, exposing blood vessels to infected semen, receptive anal intercourse with an infected man who is not using a latex condom is the riskiest form of sexual contact for both men and women. The insertive partner can also contract HIV from anal intercourse with an infected partner.

   2. *Vaginal-penile intercourse without the use of a latex condom with a person who is infected with HIV.* This kind of intercourse is more risky for women than for men, because HIV is found in higher concentrations in semen than it is in vaginal secretions. Also, because of its make-up, the vagina is a more likely receptor of infection than is the man's urethra. Therefore, women having unprotected vaginal-penile intercourse with an infected man contract HIV at a rate twenty times that of men having unprotected intercourse with an infected woman. (Padian, N., Shiboski, S., and Jewell, N. (1991). Female-to-male transmission of human immunodeficiency virus. *Journal of the American Medical Association, 266,* 1664–1667.)

   3. *Oral-genital sex without a latex barrier with a person who is infected with HIV.* Infected semen or vaginal fluids can enter the body through oral-genital sex, especially but not always through cuts or sores in the mouth. Because people often have cuts and sores in their mouths (cold sores, herpes sores, cuts from biting tongues or cheeks) of which they are unaware, and because recent research suggests that HIV can enter the body from the mouth even if cuts or sores are not present, oral-genital sex without a latex barrier such as a condom or a dental dam is risky.

   B. Nonsexual Transmission

   1. *Sharing needles with a person who is infected with HIV.* Sharing needles used to inject drugs, vitamins, or steroids; to make tattoos; or to pierce ears or

skin can transmit HIV. In fact, because HIV-infected blood is being injected directly into the bloodstream, sharing needles is an extremely easy way to become infected. It only takes a tiny bit of blood left on a needle or syringe, smaller even than can be detected by the naked eye, to transmit the virus. Needles must be disinfected or used only once and then discarded.

    2. *Perinatal transmission.* A mother who is infected with HIV can pass the virus to her unborn child through the placenta during pregnancy or during the process of childbirth. A baby born to a mother who is infected will usually test positive for HIV initially because it is born with its mother's immunities and antibodies. A baby who is not actually infected, however, will later test negative for HIV.

    3. *Breast-feeding.* Because HIV is found in breast milk, it is possible for a mother who is infected to transmit the virus to her infant through breast-feeding.

C. No Risk of Transmission

    1. *Donating blood.* In the United States, the needles used to draw donated blood are sterilized and are discarded after one use. Therefore, they cannot transmit HIV.

    2. *Casual contact.* HIV is not spread through hugging or shaking hands with an infected person. Because HIV cannot survive in the open air, it cannot be transmitted through toilet seats, door knobs, water fountains, eating utensils, etc. Unlike the virus that causes the common cold, which is very resilient, HIV is a relatively delicate virus that must be in one of the four body fluids in which it is found in order to survive.

    3. *Mosquitoes.* HIV is not spread through any kind of insect bite or contact with any animals.

    4. *Caring for a person with HIV infection.* Studies that have looked at the families and households of people infected with HIV have shown no evidence that HIV can be transmitted through living with or taking care of an infected person. (Fischl, M., Dickinson, D., Scott, G., Klimas, N., Fletcher, M., and Parks, W. (1987). Evaluation of heterosexual partners, children, and household contacts of adults with AIDS. *Journal of the American Medical Association,* 257, 640–644.)

    5. *Blood transfusion.* In the United States, donated blood is screened for HIV and then heat-treated to inactivate the virus if it is present. The chance of being infected with HIV through a transfusion of donated blood is estimated to be 1 in 40,000 to 225,000 units of blood. (Dodd, R. The risk of transfusion-transmitted infection. *New England Journal of Medicine,* 327, 419–421.) Donated organs and semen for artificial insemination are also screened, making infection from these sources extremely rare.

II. **Testing.** The current test for HIV detects only antibodies to the virus, not the virus itself. Antibodies are the cells in your immune system that develop to fight off specific viruses, bacteria, or other threats. The most common test for HIV is the ELISA (enzyme-linked immunosorbent assay) blood test. If the ELISA test is positive, meaning that antibodies to HIV have been found, a more specific test, called a Western Blot blood test, is performed. If a person wishes to be tested for HIV, there are test centers that do not ask or record the person's real name. The test and its results are linked to a fictional name or to a number that is known only to the person taking the test.

A. Window period.

    1. Because antibodies to an invading virus take some time to develop, there is a "window" period—three to six months for most people—between the time of infection and the time that antibodies can be detected in a blood test. This means that if someone becomes infected today and is tested tomorrow, the test results in all likelihood will be negative. The test cannot detect the infection because it looks for antibodies which will not have developed yet. For this reason, if someone thinks he/she may have been at risk for contracting HIV, he/she should be tested. If the results are negative, the person should wait six months, avoiding any behaviors that may put him/her at risk for infection or infecting others during that time, and then be retested. If the person believes he/she may have been exposed to HIV again during the six-month wait, it will be necessary to wait an additional six months from the latest exposure before being retested. Once a person is infected with HIV, he/she can transmit the virus to other people for the rest of his/her life.

III. Latency period. The latency period of an illness is the time during which a person is infected *and can infect other people* but has no symptoms or illness. The person may feel healthy. The latency period for AIDS can be anywhere from two to ten years or longer; scientists do not yet know how long a person's latency period can be. The length of time between becoming infected and getting sick seems to depend to some extent on age, general health, stress, access to medical care, mode of transmission (people who acquire HIV from infected needles tend to become ill and die more quickly than people who acquire HIV through sexual contact), and other characteristics, such as gender and race. We also do not know for sure whether every person who is infected with HIV will eventually develop AIDS and die.

IV. AIDS diagnosis. To have a diagnosis of AIDS, a person must have a positive result on an HIV-antibody test and a T-cell count below two hundred per cubic milliliter of blood. A healthy person's T-cell count is between five hundred and sixteen hundred. If a person tests positive for HIV antibodies but has a T-cell count above two hundred, a diagnosis of AIDS will be made if he/she suffers from one or more specific conditions listed by the Centers for Disease Control as being associated with AIDS. These conditions are typically opportunistic infections that are extremely rare in people with healthy immune systems but found in people with compromised immune systems due to AIDS or other immune disorders.

V. Who is at risk. Men, women, and children of all races, ages, and sexual orientations can get HIV/AIDS. Anyone who engages in the risky behaviors previously discussed puts him/herself at risk for HIV infection. As of 2006, more than 900,000 cases of AIDS were reported in the United States alone. (Centers for Disease Control (2008) HIV/AIDS Statistics and Surveillance Reports, Table 14: Cases of HIV Infection and AIDS in the United States and Dependent Areas, 2006), including 56,000 new cases reported in 2006. Update: Acquired immunodeficiency syndrome-United States, 1994. *Morbidity and Mortality Weekly*, 44,

64–67.) Today, it is estimated that 1 in every 250 Americans is infected with HIV; many do not know they are infected because they are asymptomatic.

VI. **Adolescents and HIV/AIDS.** AIDS is a leading cause of death among people twenty-five to forty-four years old. Currently, one in five AIDS cases diagnosed is among twenty to twenty-nine year olds. Since the latency period between infection and AIDS diagnosis is about ten years, most of these people became infected with HIV as teenagers. Many teens engage in behaviors that put them at risk for HIV. (Centers for Disease Control (2008). Trends in HIV-and STD-related Risk Behaviors Among High School Students—U.S. 1991–2007.) More than 60 percent of twelfth graders have engaged in vaginal-penile intercourse. Twenty percent have had more than four sexual partners in their lifetimes. Only half report using condoms consistently. Many are under the influence of alcohol or other drugs that impair their judgment and thus their ability to make decisions about how to protect themselves when they engage in sexual behaviors.

Making Safer Choices

3

WORKSHOP 7 **Contraception**

RATIONALE

To prevent unintended pregnancy, young people not only need to know the facts about contraception—the available methods, how they work, and their effectiveness, cost, and proper use—they also need to understand how to select a method that fits their individual lifestyles. Contraception can work only if it is used, and it will be used, especially by young people, only if it meets their needs and they are motivated to use it. This activity treats the factual material presented as a review and focuses on exploring how contraception fits an individual's health, sexual history, and present sexual lifestyle. The activity is also designed to explore the decision-making process.

Time Required: 45 minutes

GOALS

To help participants
- review methods of contraception.
- develop an understanding of the factors involved in selecting a method of contraception.

OBJECTIVES

By the end of this workshop, participants will be able to
- identify the pros and cons of each method of contraception based on cost, availability, use, and effectiveness.
- demonstrate an understanding of the factors involved in selecting a method of contraception by selecting one for a fictional individual/couple.

MATERIALS

☐ Samples of contraceptive methods (optional)
☐ Leader Resource 7, Contraception Scenarios
☐ Leader Resource 8, Contraception Scenarios Hints and "Answers"
☐ Handout 9, Contraceptive Facts

PREPARATION

- Review this workshop and decide how to share leadership responsibilities with your coleader.
- Photocopy Handout 9, Contraceptive Facts, for each participant.
- Familiarize yourself with Leader Resource 8, Contraception Scenarios Hints and "Answers."
- Determine the number of small groups (at least three to a group) you can make.
- Select and photocopy one contraception scenario from Leader Resource 7 for each of the small groups.
- Post the ground rules from the opening session.

Activity

CONTRACEPTION SCENARIOS   45 minutes

1. Introduce the activity by saying,

> Many of you have had the opportunity to learn about methods of contraception in other situations. We are not going to focus on learning the facts about each method today. However, I will be happy to answer any questions you have about all aspects of contraception as we go along. What I want you to begin thinking about now is how a person chooses a method of contraception. Each person is different, and there is no one method that will suit every individual's needs throughout life. What suits you at one time in one situation may not suit you in a different situation or at a different time in your life. There are many factors to consider. This activity will help us look at all of those factors and evaluate methods based on the needs of the people using them.

2. Divide participants into small groups. Each group should have at least three participants; four or five is optimal. Give each participant a copy of Handout 9, Contraceptive Facts. Then say,

> I am going to give each group a situation, and it will be the group's job to decide which method of contraception is the best choice for the person or persons in the scenario you have. You must look at each method and evaluate not only which one would be *best* but also *why* the other methods would not be the best choice for the situation. Think about the people in your scenario. Would the person(s) actually use the method you selected for them? Use the information in your fact sheets to help make choices. You will be presenting your situation and your choices to the rest of the group.

3. Hand out the scenarios and have the participants work together in their groups for 15 minutes. During this time, the facilitators should circulate throughout the room to offer assistance and answer questions.

4. When time is up, bring the whole group together. Ask someone from each small group to read their scenario aloud, then have members of each small group explain, method by method, why some were rejected and why one was chosen. Take about 15 minutes for the small groups to present their decision-making processes. Drawing on

Leader Resource 8, share with participants appropriate methods for each couple if the group has not already identified them.

5. After the groups have presented their conclusions, use the following questions to process the activity for about 10 minutes.

- What was participating in this activity like for you?
- Did you learn anything you did not already know?
- Was it is easy or difficult to make decisions about the methods?
- Did you sometimes need more information to make a good decision? What kind of information did you need? Where would you get more information?
- How realistic did this seem to you?
- What method(s) of contraception could be right for all of the couples?

6. Summarize the activity by saying,

Making good decisions about contraception or any other important issue takes time and effort. You need to be sure you have all the relevant information, and you need to be sure you understand all the facts. Sometimes people think that if they do nothing, they have avoided making a difficult decision. In reality, doing nothing is making a decision to let someone else or something else control your life. If a decision is difficult to make give yourself time to get more information, weigh the options, and feel right about the decision before you act.

Handout 9

CONTRACEPTIVE FACTS*

1. Abstinence (No Sexual Intercourse)

How abstinence works: Excludes sexual intercourse of any type—penis in vagina, penis in anus, or oral-genital contact. Still allows for expression of sexual feelings or release of sexual tension through behaviors that do not include intercourse. Prevents sperm release into the vagina.

How abstinence is used: Mutual agreement or an independent decision by either partner.

How effective abstinence is: 100 percent when used consistently. However, many people have not acquired the skills they need to follow through with a decision to abstain from intercourse, so the method fails.

Myths about abstinence: Causes "blue balls" in males. A female who abstains is hung up or frigid. A male who abstains is a wimp.

Additional information: Abstinence is a method without cost, medical side effects, or physical risks. It can, however, have emotional risks such as frustration and possible strain on a relationship.

A person who has had sexual intercourse in the past may decide to abstain at any time in any relationship.

2. Male Condom (Rubber)

How the condom works: Prevents sperm passage into the vagina.

How the condom is used: Before there is any contact between the penis and vagina, place the condom over the erect penis. Space *must* be left at the end to collect the sperm (some condoms have a special tip for sperm collection). After ejaculation, the condom should be held in place while removing the penis from the vagina, so sperm do not spill into the vagina.

Condoms must be used for each act of intercourse and thrown away after one use.

How effective the condom is: 86 percent in actual use. With correct and consistent use, this rate is 98 percent. Effectiveness rates are also increased when the condom is used with spermicidal foam.

Where to obtain the condom: Drugstores, family planning clinics, the Internet and some public rest rooms. It is best to buy latex condoms that are lubricated with nonoxynol-9.

Additional information: Vaseline and heat will destroy a condom. Condoms may deteriorate over time, especially if stored in a tight space such as a wallet. The condom is a relatively inexpensive contraceptive method and the only nonpermanent method that is for males. Condoms prevent the spread of most sexually transmitted diseases and should be used for this purpose in addition to any other choice of birth control.

3. Contraceptive Foam

How the foam works: Temporarily blocks the opening into the uterus and kills sperm.

How the foam is used: The can is shaken about 20 times before filling an applicator with the foam. Depending on the foam brand, one or two applicators of foam should be inserted into the vagina immediately before intercourse. If intercourse is repeated, more foam must be inserted.

How effective foam is: 74 percent in actual use.

NOTE: The effectiveness rate increases to 97 percent if used with condoms (based on actual use). COMBINED USE IS RECOMMENDED.

Where to obtain foam: Drugstores, the Internet, and family planning clinics.

Additional information: Foam must be available and used each time intercourse occurs. Foam dissolves in the vagina; douching is unnecessary but, if used, should be delayed at least six to eight hours after intercourse. Different brands of foam may have different instructions. It is important to be aware of brand-specific instructions in order to use foam effectively.

Foam is an inexpensive method but causes irritation in some women and can be fairly messy. It also provides little or no protection against STDs.

4. Vaginal Contraceptive Film (VCF)

How VCF works: Dissolves in the vagina and produces foam, which acts like contraceptive foam applied with an applicator to block the opening into the uterus and to kill sperm.

How VCF is used: VCF is a very thin film, about two inches square, that is made of dehydrated (dried) spermicide. When moisture such as that in the vagina comes in contact with VCF, it begins to dissolve into a foamy substance. VCF must be inserted quickly with a *dry* finger all the way to the back of the vaginal wall and up against the cervix. A couple using VCF must wait five minutes after insertion before having intercourse. If intercourse is repeated, additional VCF must be used.

How effective VCF is: 74 percent in actual use.

Where to obtain VCF: Drugstores, the Internet, and family planning clinics.

Additional information: VCF can be kept readily available because of its small size and portability. It provides some protection against STDs, including HIV, but should be used with a latex condom to maximize its effectiveness.

5. Female Condom

How the female condom works: Prevents semen from entering the woman's body and protects the male partner from contact with vaginal fluids during intercourse.

How the female condom is used: The female condom is a polyurethane sheath like a condom but with the addition of a flexible ring at either end. Before sexual intercourse begins, it is inserted into the vagina. One of the rings is used to insert the device and hold it in place against the cervix, much like a diaphragm. The other ring stays outside of the vagina and covers the vulva.

The female condom must be removed immediately after intercourse and thrown away after one use; it should never be washed and reused.

How effective the female condom is: 79 percent, based on actual use for six months.

With correct and consistent use, this rate is 95 percent. Effectiveness rates are also increased when used with spermicidal foam.

Where to obtain the female condom: Family planning clinics; the Internet; drug, grocery, and some convenience stores.

Additional information: The female condom helps to prevent the spread of most sexually transmitted diseases, including HIV. It provides women with a way to protect themselves if they are with a partner who refuses to use another form of protection.

6. Oral Contraceptives (Pills)

How the pill works: Prevents release of an egg from the ovary (ovulation). Prevents implantation of the fertilized egg in the uterus (if ovulation should occur).

How the pill is used: One type is taken daily for 21 days and stopped for 7 days before starting a new package. The most popular type is taken continuously for a 28-day cycle; the last seven pills are placebos designed to keep the woman in the habit of taking a pill every day. Pills should be taken in order at a convenient and consistent time each day.

If a woman misses a pill, she should take the one she missed as soon as possible and take the next pill at the regular time. If two pills are missed, the woman should take the two pills, and continue with her cycle of pills, but she must use a backup contraceptive method to prevent pregnancy through the rest of the month. The backup is necessary for most women because of the low dosages of estrogen in the pill today. A woman should ask her doctor for specific instructions for using the pill.

How effective the pill is: 95 to 98 percent, based on actual use, including those who skip days.

Where to obtain the pill: Private physician or family planning center.

Myths about the pill: Pills "mess you up," cause physical pain, sterility, deformed babies. You take the pill only on the days that you have intercourse.

Additional information: Today's birth control pills can be used safely by most healthy nonsmoking women from their teenage years until menopause. Modern pills contain only a small amount of female hormones. Possible mild side effects include minor breakthrough bleeding (bleeding between periods), breast tenderness, headaches, slight weight gain, and nausea. Serious but rare side effects include hypertension, stroke, and blood clots. The pill also has other important health benefits, such as lighter menstrual flow, less menstrual pain, and more regular cycles. It can also help reduce the risk of endometrial and ovarian cancers, benign breast disease, ovarian cysts, and ectopic pregnancy. The pill provides no protection against STDs, including HIV, and should therefore always be used with a latex condom and spermicide.

7. Diaphragm

How the diaphragm works: Prevents sperm from entering the uterus.

How the diaphragm is used: Can be inserted as early as two hours before intercourse. The woman places a sperm-killing cream or jelly in the cap and around the rim of the diaphragm, then puts the diaphragm into the vagina, completely covering the cervix. After intercourse the diaphragm should be left in place for six to eight hours; if intercourse is repeated, the diaphragm must be left in and more jelly inserted into the vagina with an applicator. After each use, the diaphragm should be washed with soap and water, dried, and stored in its case.

How effective the diaphragm is: Approximately 80 to 85 percent, based on actual use. Studies have shown wide differences in effectiveness rates for users of the diaphragm. One study has shown that the diaphragm can be 98 percent effective if used carefully and properly.

Where to obtain the diaphragm: Private physician or family planning clinic.

Myths about the diaphragm: It always destroys the spontaneity of sex. It is uncomfortable to wear for six to eight hours. It can get lost in the body.

Additional information: The diaphragm must be kept readily available and used each time intercourse occurs. If the diaphragm is inserted incorrectly, it may not protect the woman from conceiving.

The diaphragm has minimal side effects. The spermicidal cream or jelly can cause irritation and some people find it messy or feel uncomfortable touching themselves.

Petroleum or heat destroys the diaphragm.

The diaphragm does not protect against STDs, including HIV, and therefore should always be used with a latex condom and spermicide.

8. Intrauterine Device (IUD)

How the IUD works: There are several theories; some medical professionals hypothesize that the IUD prevents the fertilized egg from implanting in the uterus. Also, depending on the type of IUD, copper or progesterone, a hormone is released and appears to interfere with conception.

How the IUD is used: The IUD is a T-shaped device that is inserted into the uterus by a trained medical practitioner. Today's IUDs release either copper or progesterone. The copper-releasing version can stay in place up to eight years. The IUD has an attached string that is left hanging into the vagina so that a woman can check it every month (after her period) by feeling deep inside her vagina.

How effective the IUD is: 95 to 98 percent, based on actual use.

Where to obtain the IUD: Private physician or family planning clinic.

Myths about the IUD: An IUD can travel to the heart and cause a stroke. The IUD string can cut a man's penis.

Additional information: The IUD is one of the easiest birth control methods to use but is not recommended for women who have never had a child.

Possible side effects include cramps, heavier menstrual flow, irregular bleeding, infection, dislodging or expulsion, and rarely, uterine perforation. Occasionally, the partner can feel the string during intercourse.

IUDs have been linked to an increased risk of pelvic inflammatory disease (PID), a serious infection of the female reproductive organs most common in women with more than one sexual partner. Because of the increased risk of PID, IUDs are rarely prescribed for teenagers.

In the past, many IUDs were taken off the market because of lawsuits brought by patients who had suffered complications. Problematic types of IUDs have been removed from the market. The cost of insurance to protect manufacturers from liability has become too expensive for some companies to make profits from the sale of IUDs.

The IUD does not protect against STDs, including HIV, and therefore should always be used with a latex condom and spermicide.

9. Depo-Provera (Injectable Contraceptive)

How Depo-Provera works: An injection of the hormone progestin stops the release of eggs from the ovaries for three months and thickens cervical mucus, thus blocking sperm that are released into the vagina during intercourse from the uterus.

How Depo-Provera is used: Depo-Provera is injected into the muscle of the arm or buttock by a trained practitioner. The first shot is usually given during the first five days of a woman's menstrual cycle to ensure that she is not pregnant. Shots must be repeated every 12 weeks.

How effective Depo-Provera is: 95 to 99 percent, beginning within 24 hours of the first injection and lasting for 12 weeks.

Where to obtain Depo-Provera: Health practitioner's office or family planning clinic.

Additional information: Depo-Provera provides very effective pregnancy prevention for 12 weeks with minimal side effects. Any side effects, however, will continue for some time after effectiveness has ended and linger until the last traces of the chemicals have disappeared. It may be difficult to become pregnant in the months immediately following the termination of Depo-Provera use. Depo-Provera does not provide any protection against STDs, including HIV, and therefore should always be used with a latex condom and spermicide.

10. Natural Family Planning (NFP)

Types of Natural Family Planning: Calendar (rhythm), basal body temperature, and cervical mucus.

How NFP works: Avoids the release of sperm into the vagina during the time when the egg can be fertilized.

How NFP methods are used: The time of ovulation is determined by changes in the woman's body temperature and cervical mucus. Intercourse is then avoided for a specific number of days before and after ovulation.

How effective NFP is: 75 to 85 percent based on actual use. The rates of effectiveness are much lower, however, for women in their teens or early 20s.

Where to obtain NFP instructions: Physician or family planning clinic.

Additional information: NFP is difficult for some couples to use. It requires training from a qualified professional. It is often unreliable, particularly for teenage girls whose cycles may be irregular. NFP requires the couple to refrain from intercourse for several days during each cycle and therefore requires self-motivation and control.

NFP may be used with another method of contraception if intercourse occurs close to the time of ovulation.

* Actual effectiveness rates were taken from Robert A. Hatcher, et al., *Contraceptive Technology*, 16th rev. ed. (New York: Irvington Publishers, Inc., 1999).

CONTRACEPTIVE FAILURE RATES

Method	User Failure Rate* (Percentage of women experiencing an unintentional pregnancy within the first year of typical use.)
Abstinence (consistent)	0
Depo-Provera (injection)	1
IUD (depending on type)	.1–2
Birth control pills	5
Male condom with vaginal spermicide	5
Male condom without spermicide	14
Withdrawal ("pulling out")	19
Diaphragm and spermicidal jelly	20

Method	User Failure Rate* (Percentage of women experiencing an unintentional pregnancy within the first year of typical use.)
Contraceptive sponge (for women who have never had a baby)	20
Cervical cap (for women who have never had a baby)	20
Female condom	21
Fertility awareness (rhythm, ovulation, etc.)	25
Foam, cream, jelly, or vaginal contraceptive film	26
No method of birth control used	85

NOTE: Typical use or actual use refers to how people use a method in real life, not always consistently and perfectly.

* Robert A. Hatcher, et al., *Contraceptive Technology*, 16th rev. ed. (New York: Irvington Publishers, Inc., 1999).

Leader Resource 7

CONTRACEPTION SCENARIOS

1. Rita and Paul are both nineteen, have been dating for three months, and have decided that they would like to begin a sexual relationship that includes intercourse. Paul is very concerned about Rita becoming pregnant and wants her to use a highly effective method of birth control. His girl-friend last year had a pregnancy scare, and it really frightened him. Rita is also concerned about becoming pregnant, but she knows that her high blood pressure may be a problem with some kinds of birth control. Rita also feels that since they both live with their parents and neither of them drives a car, they probably won't have many opportunities to have sex. Which method(s) do you think will best suit their needs? Which methods would not be appropriate?

2. Jamal and Carly have been a couple since they met in the tenth grade, and their romance is two years strong. They were both virgins until last month when, on their second anniversary, they had sexual intercourse for the first time. They have vowed to be faithful to each other and plan to marry after they have finished college. Until then, they want to focus on their education and do not want to worry about unintended pregnancy. They will be attending the same college and will live in the same dorm room. Which method of contraception makes the most sense for this couple? Which methods would not be appropriate?

3. Ariel is seventeen and the only daughter of two college professors. She has been raised to feel good about her body and to appreciate all of its potential. She has been sexually active for the past year and has had many sexual encounters, although she has had intercourse only twice, once with a steady boyfriend and once with a guy she met at a Greenpeace rally. She did not use any contraception either time and has been feeling pretty dumb ever since. Now she would like to find a method to accommodate her erratic and varied sex life. What method would be a good choice for her? Which methods would not be appropriate?

4. Tony and Deena have been married for six years and have three children under the age of five. Tony is working two jobs to support them, but most of their money goes to pay for the medication Deena needs to treat her re-curring pelvic infections. Tony and Deena do not want to have any more children in the near future. Which method(s) of contraception would be the best for this couple? Which method(s) would be inappropriate?

5. Ruth is a thirty-year-old executive who has been dating Irving steadily for about six months. They are considering marriage as both feel that they have found the right partner. She smokes a pack of cigarettes a day, although she plans to quit after they have married, bought a house, and are trying to have a baby. Both have been tested and neither is HIV+. Which method of contraception is most appropriate for this couple? Which method(s) would not be appropriate?

6. Nancy is a high-school junior who is going to Europe for the summer to study art history. She knows she is going to want to experiment in a variety of ways, possibly sexually. She is a virgin. She has no idea how the men she meets will feel about condoms and is afraid she won't be able to communicate well with them. She wants to be protected from pregnancy and STDs. What should she take with her?

Leader Resource 8

CONTRACEPTION SCENARIOS HINTS AND "ANSWERS"

1. *Rita and Paul.* Because of Rita's high blood pressure, any of the methods that rely on hormones (Depo Provera and birth control pills) would not be a good choice. As Rita and Paul may not have many opportunities to have sexual intercourse they probably do not need "round the clock protection." That is, their sexual encounters will probably be somewhat more planned and predictable. Since we know Paul has had at least one previous sexual partner and we know nothing else about Rita's and Paul's sexual pasts, we should assume that condoms are necessary, which makes condoms and contraceptive foam, cream, or jelly an excellent choice for them. A diaphragm or cervical cap would not provide enough protection from STDs.

2. *Jamal and Carly.* Because this couple has a history of monogamy and abstinence and because they will have many chances to have sexual intercourse with each other in the next year, a method such as the pill or Depo Provera would work well for them. *However*, if their relationship stops being monogamous, neither of them is protected from STDs. Thus, condoms and contraceptive cream, foam, or jelly would also be appropriate for this couple. (A diaphragm or cervical cap would also work well if Carly keeps it with her and takes the time to insert it before having intercourse.)

3. *Ariel.* Ariel's sex life is unpredictable and with a variety of partners. She certainly needs to use condoms to protect herself from STDs, but she may also want the added protection of a back-up method such as the pill or Depo Provera. Using both methods together or just condoms and contraceptive cream, jelly, or foam would work well for her. Although a diaphragm or cervical cap would offer pregnancy prevention, it may be more difficult for a person with an unpredictable sex life to carry it with her at all times and to take the time necessary to insert it every time she has intercourse. Furthermore, for STD protection, she would still need condoms.

4. *Tony and Deena.* Depo Provera and the pill are moderately expensive, and some antibiotics, such as those Deena may be taking for her pelvic infections, can interfere with their effectiveness, making these poor choices for her. Two possible choices for this couple are condoms and spermicide or a diaphragm or cervical cap with a spermicidal cream, jelly, or foam. If Deena and Tony decide they do not want to have more children, they may wish to consider sterilization.

5. *Ruth and Irving.* Because Ruth smokes, she should not use any methods of contraception that rely on hormones (the pill or Depo Provera). She and Irving do not need to use condoms, given their HIV status and an assumption of monogamy. They need an easily reversible method since they are planning to try to have a baby in the near future. Condoms are certainly an option for pregnancy prevention. The diaphragm or the cervical cap would also be a good choice.

6. *Nancy.* Nancy needs to take assertiveness with her on her trip. Because she may have sex with people she does not know well, she needs to be protected from STDs. Although she could get a prescription for birth control pills and have it filled if she decides to become sexually involved with someone who was willing to wait until they become effective, she still would need STD protection. A box of condoms and the willingness and ability to insist that any partner use them is her best protection from both pregnancy and STDs.

RATIONALE

Latex and polyurethane condoms for males and females are the best defense against sexually transmitted infections for adolescents who engage in sexual intercourse. They are also a reliable method of contraception. Because condoms are the only contraceptives that provide disease protection, it is important to spend time learning about them and becoming comfortable touching them, using them, and negotiating with a sexual partner about using them. The activities in this workshop provide fun, hands-on opportunities for participants to become comfortable with all aspects of condom use.

Time Required: 35 minutes

GOALS

To help participants to
- become more comfortable looking at and touching condoms.
- learn about the female condom and the dental dam.
- learn the correct ways to use a male and a female condom.
- understand the necessity for using a condom in almost all sexual situations in which adolescents take part.
- negotiate with a sexual partner about always using a condom for sexual activity.

OBJECTIVES

By the end of this workshop, participants will be able to
- demonstrate the ability to negotiate with a sexual partner about condom use by writing responses that encourage condom use with hesitant partners.
- show an understanding of the importance of condom use.
- demonstrate ability to put a condom on a penis model properly.

MATERIALS

☐ Male latex condoms (at least one per participant)
☐ Two penis models. Although a penis model is preferable, you may supplement with other items such as cucumbers or bananas so that every person can practice putting a condom on a model. Large test tubes also make good models.
☐ Female Reality® condom
☐ Dental dam. If no dental dam is available, make one, using scissors and either plastic wrap or an extra condom. You may wish to show the class how to do this.
☐ Newsprint, markers, and tape
☐ Writing paper
☐ Pens or pencils

☐ Leader Resource 9, Reasons for Not Wanting to Use a Condom
☐ Prize for winner of the Condom Use Contest (optional)

PREPARATION

- Review this workshop and decide how to share leadership responsibilities with your coleader.
- Read Leader Resource 9, Reasons for Not Wanting to Use a Condom, and choose four of the reasons (or make up some of your own). Write a different reason at the top of each of four sheets of writing paper.
- Practice putting a condom on the model while explaining what you are doing.
- Post the ground rules from the opening session.

Activities

CONDOM USE BRAINSTORM   5 minutes

Have participants brainstorm situations involving adolescents and sexual intercourse (vaginal-penile, anal, oral) in which using a condom is *not* appropriate or necessary. When they have finished, they should find that there are very few if any situations involving adolescents and sexual intercourse in which condoms are not appropriate or necessary. Point out that clearly condoms are an essential component to safer sexual activity that involves intercourse.

CONDOM DEMONSTRATION   5 minutes

Give a condom to each participant. Encourage participants to open the packets, touch the condoms, inspect them, play with them, stretch them, smell them, etc. Explain that you are going to demonstrate the appropriate way to put on and use a latex condom and that anyone who wishes will have the opportunity to practice after the demonstration. As you go through each step, explain what you are doing and thinking so that participants can follow the steps.

Before you begin, be sure to emphasize that the condom should always be latex or polyurethane. Lambskin or natural skin condoms, while effective for preventing pregnancy, do not offer protection from sexually transmitted infections.

1. Check the expiration date on the packet to make sure the condom is good. Tell participants that if the condom is past its expiration date, it may tear or have holes. Mention that it is important not to keep condoms in a very warm spot (such as a glove compartment, wallet in a back pocket) for a long period of time because the latex can dry out.

2. Open the packet. Explain that you should never use your teeth to open a condom packet because you run the risk of tearing the condom with your teeth.

3. Check the condom to see which way it unrolls. Explain that if you try to unroll it the wrong way you'll get stuck.

4. As you place the condom on the penis model, make sure to pinch the tip of the condom with the forefinger and thumb of one hand. Explain that it is necessary to leave room for the semen when the man ejaculates. If there is an air bubble or no extra space at the tip, the condom could break. Explain that some condoms come with what is called a *reservoir tip* for capturing semen, which can make it easier to leave room.

5. Roll the condom down to the base of the penis model. Tell participants to make sure there is enough natural or artificial lubrication before penetration as a condom may tear if the vagina or anus is dry. Many condoms come already lubricated, often with a spermicide for extra protection. The spermicide nonoxynol-9 is particularly recommended because it has been shown to kill HIV in a test tube. Extra lubrication can also come from products such as water, K-Y jelly, or various spermicidal creams, jellies, or foams but that oil-based lubricants such as petroleum jelly, baby oil, cooking oil, massage oil, or shortening should never be used for lubrication as oil can cause the latex to deteriorate or tear.

6. Tell participants that after the man ejaculates, he needs to withdraw or pull out of his sexual partner right away. Because a man does not typically lose his erection immediately after ejaculating, withdrawing while he still has a partial erection makes it less likely that the condom will fall off his penis and stay in his partner or spill semen into or onto his partner. If the male stays inside his partner until his penis is completely flaccid (soft), it is much more likely that the condom will fall off or spill semen. When withdrawing his penis from his partner, the man should hold the rim of the condom against the base of the penis to keep the condom from slipping off and to prevent semen from spilling.

7. Say that once the condom is removed, the man should throw it away. Tell the group that a condom should never be reused. Say that the man may want to wash himself.

8. Tell the group that once the condom is removed, the man may relax with and hold his partner, or continue to pleasure his partner without further penetration with the penis.

Invite anyone who wants to to practice putting a condom on a penis model. Encourage participants to describe aloud what they are doing and thinking at each step.

CONDOM USE CONTEST   5 minutes

1. Tell the group you are going to have a contest to see who can put a condom on a penis model correctly in the shortest amount of time. Ask for two volunteers to take part in the contest. (A small prize for the winner can add to the fun.)

2. Give each contestant a penis model and a condom. Explain that because sex often takes place with the lights off, it is important to be able to put on a condom without seeing what you are doing. Tell the group that the volunteers will be blindfolded for the contest but that each contestant will have a coach. Ask for two volunteers to be the coaches. The coaches are to stand behind the contestants and tell them what to do but they are not allowed to touch the condom or the penis model.

3. Tell the remaining participants that they are to be the judges. Divide them into two groups and assign each group to one team. Explain that the judges are to watch to make sure that the person follows the steps in putting on a condom and are to call out if they see an infraction.

4. Give the "GO" signal. The only people who may give directions are the coaches. The first team to put a condom on a penis model correctly wins the contest.

5. Help participants process the activity by asking, "How did being blindfolded affect your ability to put on the condom? Was it difficult? Did you have to rely on other senses to complete the task?"

FEMALE CONDOM AND DENTAL DAM
DEMONSTRATION   5 minutes

1. Show the group a female condom. They have information about how it works in Handout 9, Contraceptive Facts, from a previous activity. Reinforce the point that the female polyurethane condom, like the male latex condom, offers protection from sexually transmitted infections as well as pregnancy. An additional benefit is that the female condom may be inserted up to eight hours before vaginal-penile intercourse, which means sex play does not need to be interrupted to put it in. Like the male condom, it is available over the counter, although it is a bit more expensive. A female condom makes it unnecessary to rely on the male to be responsible for using one, which may be particularly helpful for some women who find it difficult to negotiate condom use with a partner. Pass the female condom around the group and encourage participants to look at, touch, smell, study, and ask questions about the Female Reality® condom.

2. Hold up a dental dam for the group to see. Pass it around and encourage participants to feel, smell (if there are enough for each person to have one, taste), and study the dental dam. Say,

> The dental dam is a six-inch square of latex that is used by dentists when working on people's teeth. It provides protection from sexually transmitted infections during oral-genital or oral-anal sex. By covering the vulva or anus during oral stimulation, the dental dam prevents body fluids from being exchanged. Although dental dams can be difficult to obtain, they are available in some drugstores or in specialty stores that sell safer sex items. You can make a dental dam by cutting a nonlubricated condom lengthwise. Nonmicrowavable plastic wrap is also effective as a dental dam. The male condom can be used for oral stimulation of a penis.

NEGOTIATING CONDOM USE
WITH A SEXUAL PARTNER   15 minutes

1. Divide participants into four groups. Tell the groups they are going to be writing a dialogue between two sexual partners negotiating condom use: One partner does not want to use condoms and one does. The goal is to end the dialogue with a successful resolution.

2. Give each group a piece of paper with a reason a person might give for not wanting to use a condom. (see Preparation). Each group should have a different reason for not using a condom. Each group has two minutes to think about and then respond to the line with a comment aimed at getting the partner to use a condom.

3. After two minutes, have the groups pass their sheets of paper to the left so that each group has another group's initial comment and response. Tell the groups to continue the dialogue with a line that makes a new argument for not using a condom in response to the previous group's argument in favor of using a condom.

4. After two minutes, have the groups pass their sheets to the left again and receive a dialogue that has been started by two previous groups. By this time the papers will have three lines of dialogue on them, starting with the original argument against using a condom and two responses. Tell the groups to continue the dialogue on their new sheet with an argument for condoms that follows logically the line of the dialogue on their new sheet.

5. Groups continue to pass their sheets to the left every two minutes until they get their original paper back, which should have five lines of dialogue, pro and con. Have the groups respond one last time with a pro-condom argument on their original sheets. This last argument should attempt to reach a final resolution of the conflict over using condoms.

6. Have a participant from each group read the group's entire dialogue out loud.

7. Help participants to process the activity with questions such as these:
   - Which arguments were the most difficult to counter?
   - Did you find yourself becoming combative when you did not want to?
   - How difficult do you think it would be to have this conversation with a real sex partner?
   - Are there any valid arguments for not using a condom?
   - How did it feel to argue against using a condom?
   - Which resolutions do you think were successful?

Leader Resource 9

REASONS FOR NOT WANTING TO USE A CONDOM

"If you really loved me, you wouldn't ask me to use a condom."

"I love you, and if we have a baby, that would be great."

"Are you suggesting that I might have a disease or something?"

"It ruins the spontaneity of sex."

"I don't get any feeling when I use a condom."

"It's like taking a shower with a raincoat on."

"They don't make condoms big enough for me."

"I've never been with anyone else but you, so we don't need to use a condom."

"If we love each other, nothing should come between us."

"They are uncomfortable."

"Condoms are so un-sexy."

"I'm on the pill, so we're safe."

RATIONALE

This is a fun way for participants to use all the information they have to think about how to have a sexy experience while staying healthy and safe from pregnancy and disease. The Sexy Safe Fantasy encourages participants to use their imaginations to explore the many ways in which they can express their sexuality and have their sexual needs met without putting themselves at risk. It reinforces an important theme of this program: Sex is a lot more than intercourse. Working together in groups allows a measure of anonymity, which encourages participation and creativity.

Time Required: 30 minutes

GOALS

To help participants to
- explore the range of sexual behaviors that do not put them at risk for pregnancy or disease.
- define sex as much more than intercourse.
- think about safer sex as fun and sexually fulfilling.

OBJECTIVES

By the end of this workshop, participants will be able to
- demonstrate an understanding that sex is more than intercourse by describing, through written fantasies, sexually exciting and fulfilling behaviors that do not involve penetration.

MATERIALS

☐ Writing paper
☐ Pens or pencils
☐ A large bag of items to be used in the fantasies, for example, a telephone, a feather boa, candles, music tapes, radio, massage oil, nightgown, scarf, honey, flowers, teddy bear, silk underwear, book of erotica, book of poetry, chocolate syrup. Just about anything will do.
☐ Candies or other simple prizes for all participants (optional).

PREPARATION

- Review this workshop and decide how to share leadership responsibilities with your coleader.

- Gather a variety of items as described in the Materials listing and place them in a large grab bag. Be sure there are at least as many items as there are participants. NOTE: This activity is designed as a contest among small groups. If you feel that competition would be inappropriate for your group, follow the procedure described but omit the competitive dimension.
- Post the ground rules from the opening session.

Activity

SEXY SAFE FANTASY   30 minutes

1. Divide participants into groups of three or four. Have each group choose one person to be the group's official scribe. Then ask each person to reach into the grab bag and pull out one item. Move around the room so that one person from group one picks something, then one person from group two, etc., until every person in every group has an item.

2. Tell participants that you are going to have a contest to see which group can write the sexiest, hottest, most desirable fantasy. There are three rules they must follow when writing their fantasies:

- The fantasies may *not* involve penetration of any kind.
- The fantasies may only include activities that are completely safe, that is, pose no risk of sexually transmitted infections or pregnancy.
- The fantasy must incorporate each of the items the group pulled from the grab bag.

Say that as long as the groups follow these three rules, they are free to write whatever they like with the goal of making their fantasies as sexy and desirable as possible. Encourage participants to think about the circle model of pleasure they talked about in Workshop 4 as a model for their fantasies. They will have fifteen minutes to write their fantasies, and then point out that individual contributions will remain anonymous—each fantasy is a group effort.

3. Warn participants when they have 3 to 4 minutes remaining. When time is up, have a volunteer (someone other than the scribe) from each group read the fantasy. Let the participants vote for the fantasy they think is the best.

4. Help participants process the activity with questions such as these:

- How did it feel to write these fantasies? To listen to them?
- Was anyone surprised by anything he/she heard?
- Were the fantasies sexy?
- Were any parts of these fantasies realistic for people who want to engage in sexual behavior but stay safe?
- Did this exercise make you think about sex any differently?

RATIONALE

After people have experienced, learned, and processed a great deal of information on both cognitive and affective levels, it is important for them to find a way to organize their significant thoughts and feelings so that they can learn from them and use them. Understanding what you have learned and being able to identify its importance in your life are critical parts of the learning process but not automatic, especially for young people. Closure activities address an individual's need to put new learning and new insights in their place and move on.

Time Required: 10 minutes

GOALS

To help participants
- find meaning in the materials they have learned in Sessions 1–3.
- identify how they will use what they have learned in their own lives.

OBJECTIVES

By the end of this workshop, participants will be able to
- identify two health-related behaviors they promise to change, continue, or start as a result of their participation in Sessions 1–3.
- share at least one insight, thought, feeling, or idea that was surprising, helpful, or meaningful to them.

MATERIALS

☐ Paper
☐ Pencils or pens
☐ An envelope for each participant

PREPARATION

- Review this workshop and decide how to share leadership responsibilities with your coleader.
- Post the ground rules from the opening session.
- Decide when you will return the envelopes to the participants. The suggested time interval is six months after the end of the program.

Activities

LETTER-WRITING ACTIVITY

5 minutes

1. Introduce this activity by saying,

> We have spent a great deal of time learning about our bodies, how they work, what they can do, and how we can take care of them, love them, and trust them. We have learned about things that can hurt us and things that we can do to keep our bodies strong and healthy. Now we need to find a way to think about what we have learned and move on to learn more.

2. Hand a piece of paper, an envelope, and a pencil to each participant. Instruct participants to write down two promises they will make to themselves about their health behavior that are related to what they have learned. Tell them they may write down something they already do that they feel empowered to continue doing, a promise to start a new behavior, or a pledge to change a behavior that does not feel right anymore. Let them know that they will seal their written promises into the envelope they have and no one else will see them. Have them write their names on the outside of the envelope only, and explain when the envelopes will be returned to them. Collect the envelopes and set them aside.

GROUP DISCUSSION

5 minutes

Go around the group and ask each participant to share something about his/her participation to date. Tell them they may share anything that was meaningful, important, or surprising to them. Thank each participant for his/her comment and participation in the group.

Lifespan Sexuality
Exploring Our Sexual Development

WORKSHOP 11 **Gender Roles**

RATIONALE

During adolescence conformity within same-gender peer groups and a reliance on stereotyped notions of gender offer young people a "safe" way of relating to others. This workshop helps participants explore the concept of gender-role stereotyping, how prevalent it can be and how constraining it may ultimately be on their relationships with others. Participants consider how gender roles affect the ways they lead their lives and the decisions they make about their lives in the present and for the future. This activity may also begin to break down some of the barriers to open communication and empathy among young women and men.

NOTE: This session focuses on male and female gender identities; the next workshop will introduce the idea of transgender identities.

Time Required: 45 minutes

GOALS

To help participants

- become familiar with the idea of gender roles and their impact on our daily lives.
- clarify their own ideas about their gender and other genders.
- explore the range of perceptions and misconceptions people have about each gender.
- gain insight into the similarities as well as the differences between females and males.

OBJECTIVES

By the end of this workshop, participants will be able to

- demonstrate an understanding of the influence of gender roles on their lives by describing how they believe their lives would change if they were a different gender.
- show empathy for people of other genders by naming what they believe is hard about having other gender identities.
- demonstrate an understanding of misconceptions about their own gender by naming the aspects of the stories written about their gender they believe to be inaccurate.
- show an understanding of the similarities between females and males by describing the ways their lives would stay the same if they were another gender.

MATERIALS

☐ Writing paper
☐ Pens or pencils

PREPARATION

• Review this workshop and decide how to share leadership responsibilities with your coleader.
• Choose one of the various approaches to the Writing Stories activity.
• Post the ground rules from the opening session.

Activities

WRITING STORIES   15 minutes

1. Introduce this activity by explaining that we don't often think about how our gender affects the way we lead our lives—the people with whom we interact, the activities in which we become involved, and the decisions that we make on a daily basis. Tell participants that this exercise is an opportunity to examine gender and gender expectations by imagining what their lives would be like if they were another gender.

2. Hand paper and a pen or pencil to each participant. Explain that participants are to imagine that they wake up one morning and discover they are a different gender. Ask them to write a story about what the day would be like. Tell them they should assume they would be the same people they are now with the same interests, strengths, and personalities, just a different gender. Give them 15 minutes to write the story. Be sure to warn them when they have about 3 minutes remaining so that they can write an ending to their stories.

Alternatives

Depending on the age and ability of your group, you may decide to conduct this activity differently.

• Rather than write a story, have participants describe the thoughts, feelings, ideas, and images they have when thinking about being another gender.

• If the group is young or members seem unable to work on their own for 15 minutes, consider using question prompts to aid and direct their stories.

• Use the prompts that follow to engage the group in a guided imagery exercise. Ask participants to get comfortable and close their eyes while ideas, situations, and images are suggested to them. Ask them to picture, as best as they can, the images that come to them. Begin by saying, "Imagine that one morning you wake up to discover that you are the other gender." Then ask,

  • What would your morning ritual be like?
  • What would your interactions with friends be like?
  • Would interactions with teachers be any different?
  • Would people treat you differently than they do now? Would your teachers, parents, friends?
  • Would your best friend still be your best friend?

- What about your life would stay the same?
- What new hardships might arise for you that do not exist now?
- What difficult aspects about your life now might get easier if you were the other gender?

To process the imagery, ask participants to share some of their reactions, thoughts, and feelings to the different images and questions posed.

SHARING STORIES   10 minutes

When the group has finished writing, ask for four volunteers, two female and two male, to read their stories aloud. Ask participants to listen for similarities to their own stories as well as differences. Also ask them to think about whether the perceptions about being their gender seem accurate or inaccurate.

NOTE: This activity may generate feelings and thoughts that are extremely negative, particularly in young men who are asked to imagine themselves as females. If this occurs, it is important to spend some time talking about why there is such a negative association with being a female for some males. How do these negative feelings affect the way girls and young women think of themselves? The way boys and men think of themselves? Do you think that society values males more than females? Why? Engage the group in a discussion of how they feel when they hear negative feelings expressed about their own or another gender.

GENDER REVERSAL DISCUSSION   20 minutes

1. Ask the group to talk about their own stories as well as the ones read aloud. Encourage the discussion with questions like these:

- Was anyone surprised by anything he/she wrote?
- What was hard about being another gender?
- What was easy about being another gender?
- What was difficult for you to imagine?
- What aspects of being another gender would you keep, if you could?
- Which gender do you think has it easier in this society? Why?
- Ask females: What in the stories you heard from males do you think was accurate? Why? Inaccurate? Why? How did you feel listening to the males' perceptions of life as a female?
- Ask males: What in the stories you heard from females do you think was accurate? Why? Inaccurate? Why? How did you feel listening to the females' perceptions of life as a male?
- As you imagined being a different gender, did you find there were more things that would be different or more things that would stay the same?
- In general, do you think that men and women are more similar or more different?

2. Conclude by defining the term *gender role* as the way we behave in our lives and interact with other people based on the expectations of the ways males and females ought to behave, feel, and think. Tell participants that although we often depict males and females as opposites (e.g., the "war of the sexes," "the opposite sex"), men and women are really much more alike than different. Point out that society's expectations

of how each gender should behave and think have a very powerful influence over our lives. Explain that some argue that by adhering to strict gender roles, both genders lose the opportunity to express the parts of themselves that do not match stereotyped beliefs about their gender. Tell participants that what we believe about how people of each gender should behave can have a stronger impact on our thoughts and behaviors than our biology does. Say that they will investigate this more in the next workshop.

RATIONALE

This workshop explores the development of gender identity, gender roles, and sexual orientation. The mini-lecture explains these concepts in ways that encourage the acceptance of individual differences and diversity in the expression of sexual orientation and gender. Participants are also encouraged to examine the extent to which biology and socialization influence sexual development.

Time Required: 30 minutes

GOALS

To help participants
- understand and be able to differentiate between biological sex, gender identity, gender roles, and sexual orientation.
- develop an understanding of the extent to which our culture and our biology influence our sexual development.

OBJECTIVES

By the end of this workshop, participants will be able to
- differentiate between biological sex, gender identity, gender roles, and sexual orientation.
- identify ways in which culture influences gender roles.

MATERIALS

☐ Leader Resource 10, *X*

PREPARATION

- Review this workshop and decide how to share leadership responsibilities with your coleader.
- Prepare to give the two mini-lectures: Biological Sex, Gender Identity, and Gender Roles, and Sexual Orientation.
- Post the ground rules from the opening session.

Activities

MINI-LECTURE ON BIOLOGICAL SEX, GENDER IDENTITY, AND GENDER ROLES
10 minutes

Tell participants that you want to share some information on sexual development. Then explain the points that follow.

- Sexual development starts at the very beginning of life. When a sperm cell and an egg cell join, a process begins that determines not only what genitals we will have but also how we feel about who we are, how we are treated by our culture, and how we think about other people in our lives.

- The most basic component of sexual development is an individual's biological sex, which develops before birth. In normal development, chromosomes determine an individual's biological sex, genitals, and reproductive organs. A person with two X chromosomes (XX) is female, and a person with an X chromosome and a Y chromosome (XY) is male. All egg cells carry an X chromosome, but there are both X-bearing sperm and Y-bearing sperm. Thus, the kind of sperm that fertilizes the egg determines whether the fetus will develop into a boy or a girl. Our sex chromosomes influence how our bodies develop in the womb. Male and female embryos start out with the same body structures, but when these body structures are exposed to male sex hormones, they become the penis, scrotum, testicles, and vas deferens for a boy. When they are not exposed to male sex hormones, they become the clitoris, vagina, labia, ovaries, Fallopian tubes, and uterus for a girl.

  Not everyone's body follows this pattern. Some people are born with either extra or missing sex chromosomes. Females with *Turner's Syndrome* are missing one X chromosome (XO). Males with *Klinefelter's syndrome* have an extra X chromosome (XXY). Some males are born with an additional Y chromosome (XYY). Hormonal irregularities are also possible: a female embryo may be exposed to an unusually high level of androgens (male hormones), or a male embryo may be exposed to an unusually low level of androgens. Tissue disorders, in which the fetal body structures do not respond to sex hormones, are a third kind of irregularity that can affect biological sex. Some babies with these kinds of chromosomal, hormonal, or tissue disorders are born with genitalia that are difficult to identify as male or female. The biological sex of these children is a question at birth. The medical term for this condition is *pseudohermaphroditism*. People whose biological sex at birth included both male and female elements sometimes use the term *intersexual* to describe their biological sex.

- Our sexual gender continues to develop after we are born. *Gender identity* refers to a person's experience of feeling either male or female. When we answer the question, "Do I feel male or female?" we are talking about gender identity. The sensation that we are one gender or another develops very early in our lives and is probably very much influenced by our biological sex. For example, most people who are biologically male (that is, have XY chromosomes and a penis and testicles), *feel* that they are male and identify themselves as male. However, a person may be born as one biological sex and develop the sexual identity of the other sex. For example, some people with XX chromosomes and female genitalia grow up feeling that they are really boys trapped in girls' bodies. These people are biologically female but have a male gender identity. This is one example of a *transgender* identity. No one knows for sure what causes transgender identity, but it is clearly something that develops early in a person's life and he/she has very little control over the feeling of somehow being in the wrong body. Sometimes, but not often, a transgender or transsexual person will seek sex reassignment surgery so that the biological sex and the gender identity match.

While most people do not experience a conflict between their biological sex and their gender identity, those who do experience such a conflict may be described as transgender. Transgender is an umbrella term that includes transsexuals, intersexuals, and people whose gender identity is neither male nor female but who may describe themselves as "two-gender" or "two-spirit," or use other terms that incorporate both male and female attributes.

- Another aspect of our sexual development is the *gender role* we take on. Gender roles are the ways in which we behave and are treated based on our perceived biological sex and gender identity. A person who identifies himself as male will act the way he believes males should act, and a person who identifies herself as female will act the way she believes females should act. What is considered masculine or feminine behavior? A great deal of research has attempted to establish whether gender roles are biologically determined or learned during socialization. While there do seem to be some innate or biologically determined differences between males and females that affect behavior, the vast majority of behaviors are learned as we grow up. Men and women are much more alike than they are different. What frequently happens in society, however, is that men and women learn to behave in gender stereotypical ways and to reject behaviors that do not conform to these stereotypes even when they are naturally inclined to do otherwise. Strict gender role stereotyping can be both inhibiting and limiting for people in many ways.

STORY: X BY LOIS GOULD   15 minutes

Explain that you are going to read a story about gender role development and that the group will talk about it afterward. Read aloud Leader Resource 10, X, or have participants take turns reading sections of the story aloud. Then, use the following questions to discuss the story:

- What did you think about the story?
- Do you recall anything from your own childhood that was either very stereotypical or counter-stereotypical?
- Do you think our culture has changed in the ways in which we treat male and female children?
- Do you think it is more difficult to treat a boy or a girl in nonstereotypical ways? For example, is it more acceptable for an eight-year-old girl to play with trucks or for an eight-year-old boy to play with dolls?
- How do you think you will treat your own child?
- Do you think that how you treat a child has an impact on his/her gender role?
- How much of gender role do you think is nature (biology, heredity) and how much nurture (culture, learned behavior)?

MINI-LECTURE ON SEXUAL ORIENTATION   5 minutes

Explain to participants that you are going to give them some information on another aspect of sexual development, sexual orientation. Then relate the following information:

- Another aspect of sexual development is sexual orientation. Sexual orientation refers to the gender of the people to whom one is romantically and/or sexually attracted. A person who is primarily attracted to people of another gender is considered *heterosexual*. A person who is primarily attracted to people of the same gender is considered *homosexual*. A person who is attracted to people of both male and female genders is considered *bisexual*.

- How a person's sexual orientation is determined has been a matter of much study and controversy. What is known is that sexual orientation is determined early in a person's life and cannot be changed.

- A number of years ago, the scientist Alfred Kinsey proposed a way of defining a person's sexual orientation by using a scale that ran from 0 to 6. According to Kinsey's scale, if someone has sexual experiences primarily with people of another gender, that individual is considered a heterosexual and is rated 0 on the scale. If a person has sex primarily with people of his/her own gender, that person is considered a homosexual and is rated a 5 or 6 on the scale. Kinsey's model is useful in some ways but limited in others because it considers only behavior, not feelings. People can have sexual and erotic feelings and not act on them, or they can participate in sexual behaviors without having erotic feelings. Therefore, behavior alone is not a good indicator of sexual orientation.

- A more recent way of classifying sexual orientation is Klein's Sexual Orientation Grid, which uses seven different categories: sexual attraction, sexual behavior, sexual fantasies, emotional preferences, social preference, lifestyle, and self-identification. By looking at her/his past and present experiences and future goals, Klein's model also considers how these aspects of a person's life change over time. Thus, in the Klein model, sexual orientation is defined as a somewhat more fluid aspect of a person's personality that may change during a person's lifetime but that is not controlled or determined by a person's will.

Conclude the mini-lecture by saying that our sexual development may be determined by a variety of factors and that much of who we are cannot be changed. Point out that we can, no matter who we are, learn ways in which to experience and express our sexuality that are healthful, pleasurable, and loving. Tell the group that they will learn more about sexual orientation in Workshop 13.

Leader Resource 10

X

by LOIS GOULD

Once upon a time, a baby named X was born. It was named X so that nobody could tell whether it was a boy or a girl.

Its parents could tell, of course, but they couldn't tell anybody else. They couldn't even tell Baby X—at least not until much, much later.

You see, it was all part of a very important Secret Scientific Xperiment, known officially as Project Baby X.

The parents had to be selected very carefully. Thousands of people volunteered to take thousands of tests, with thousands of tricky questions.

Almost everybody failed because it turned out, almost everybody wanted a boy or a girl, and not a Baby X at all.

Also, almost everybody thought a Baby X would be more trouble than a boy or a girl. (They were right, too.)

Finally, the scientists found the Joneses, who really wanted to raise an X more than any other kind of baby—no matter how much trouble it was.

The Joneses promised to take turns holding X, feeding X, and singing X to sleep.

The day the Joneses brought their baby home, lots of friends and relatives came to see it. And the first thing they asked was what kind of baby X was.

When the Joneses said, "It's an X!" nobody knew what to say.

They couldn't say, "Look at her cute little dimples!"

On the other hand, they couldn't say, "Look at his husky little biceps!" And they didn't feel right about saying just plain "kitchy-coo."

The relatives all felt embarrassed about having an X in the family.

"People will think there's something wrong with it!" they whispered.

"Nonsense!" the Joneses said cheerfully. "What could possibly be wrong with this perfectly adorable X?"

Clearly, nothing at all was wrong. Nevertheless, the cousins who had sent a tiny football helmet would not come and visit anymore. And the neighbors who sent a pink-flowered romper suit pulled their shades down when the Joneses passed their house.

Ms. and Mr. Jones had to be Xtra careful. If they kept bouncing it up in the air and saying how *strong* and *active* it was, they'd be treating it more like a boy than an X. But if all they did was cuddle it and kiss it and tell it how sweet and dainty it was, they'd be treating it more like a girl than an X.

On page 1654 of the *Official Instruction Manual*, the scientists prescribed: "plenty of bouncing and plenty of cuddling, *both*. X ought to be strong and sweet and active. Forget about *dainty* altogether."

There were other problems, too. Toys, for instance. And clothes. On his first shopping trip, Mr. Jones told the store clerk, "I need some things for a new baby." The clerk smiled and said, "Well, now, is it a boy or a girl?" "It's an X," Mr. Jones said, smiling back. But the clerk got all red in the face and said huffily, "In that case, I'm afraid I can't help you, sir."

Mr. Jones wandered the aisles trying to find what X needed. But everything was in sections marked BOYS or GIRLS: "Boys' Pajamas" and "Girls' Underwear" and "Boys' Fire Engines" and "Girls' Housekeeping Sets." Mr. Jones went home without buying anything for X.

That night he and Ms. Jones consulted page 2326 of the *Official Instruction Manual*. It said firmly: "Buy plenty of everything!"

So they bought all kinds of toys. A boy doll that made pee-pee and cried "Pa-Pa," and a girl doll that talked in three languages and said, "I am the Pres-i-dent of Gen-er-al Mo-tors."

They bought a storybook about a brave princess who rescued a handsome prince from his tower, and another one about a sister and brother who grew up to be a baseball star and a ballet star, and you had to guess which.

The head scientists of Project Baby X also reminded the Joneses to see page 4529 of the *Manual*, where it said, "Never make Baby X feel *embarrassed* or *ashamed* about what it wants to play with. And if X likes climbing rocks, never say, "Nice little Xes don't get dirty climbing rocks."

Likewise, it said, "If X falls down and cries, never say, "Brave little Xes don't cry." Because, of course, nice little Xes *do* get dirty, and brave little Xes *do* cry.

But then it was time for X to start school. The Joneses were really worried about this, because school was even more full of rules for boys and girls, and there were no rules for Xes.

Teachers would tell boys to form a line, and girls to form another line.

There would be boys' games and girls' games, and boys' secrets and girls' secrets.

The school library would have a list of recommended books for girls, and a different list for boys.

There would even be a bathroom marked BOYS and another one marked GIRLS.

Pretty soon boys and girls would hardly talk to each other. What would happen to poor little X?

The Joneses spent weeks consulting their *Instruction Manual*.

Finally, X was ready.

But nobody could help X with the biggest problem of all—other children.

Nobody in X's class had ever known an X. Nobody had even heard grown-ups say, "Some of my best friends are Xes."

What would other children think? Would they make Xist jokes? Or would they make friends?

You couldn't tell what X was by its clothes. Overalls don't even button right to left, like girls' clothes, or left to right, like boys' clothes.

And did X have a girl's short haircut or a boy's long haircut?

As for the games X liked, either X played ball very well for a girl, or else played house very well for a boy.

When X said its favorite toy was a doll, everyone decided that X must be a girl. But then X said the doll was really a robot, and that X had computerized it, and that it was programmed to bake fudge and then clean up the kitchen.

After X told them that they gave up guessing what X was. All they knew was they'd sure like to see X's doll.

After school, X wanted to play with the other children. "How about shooting baskets in the gym?" X asked the girls. But all they did was make faces and giggle behind X's back.

"How about weaving some baskets in the arts and crafts room?" X asked the boys. But they all made faces and giggled behind X's back, too.

"Boy, is *she* weird," whispered Susie to Peggy.

That night, Ms. and Mr. Jones asked X how things had gone at school. X tried to smile, but there were two big tears in its eyes. "The lessons are okay," X began, "but ...

"But?" said Ms. Jones.

"The other children hate me," X whispered.

"Hate you?" said Mr. Jones.

X nodded, which made the two big tears roll down and splash on its overalls.

Once more, the Joneses reached for their *Instruction Manual*. Under "Other Children," it said:

"What did you Xpect? Other Children have to obey silly boy-girl rules, because their parents taught them to. Lucky X—you don't have rules at all! All you have to do is be yourself.

"P.S. We're not saying it'll be easy."

X liked being itself. But X cried a lot that night. So X's father held X tight, and cried a little, too. X's mother cheered them up with an Xciting story about an enchanted prince called Sleeping Handsome, who woke up when Princess Charming kissed him.

The next morning, they all felt much better, and little X went back to school with a brave smile and a clean pair of red and white checked overalls.

There was a seven-letter-word spelling bee in class that day. And a seven-lap boys' relay race in the gym. And a seven-layer cake baking contest in the girls' kitchen corner.

X won the spelling bee. X also won the relay race.

And X almost won the baking contest, Xcept it forgot to light the oven. (Remember, nobody's perfect.)

One of the Other Children noticed something else, too. He said: "X doesn't care about winning. X just thinks it's fun playing boys' stuff and girls' stuff."

"Come to think of it," said another one of the Other Children, "X is having twice as much fun as we are!"

From then on, some really funny things began to happen.

Susie, who sat next to X, refused to wear pink dresses to school anymore. She wanted red and white checked overalls—just like X's.

Overalls, she told her parents, were better for climbing monkey bars.

Then Jim, the class football nut, started wheeling his little sister's doll carriage around the football field.

He'd put on his entire football uniform, except for the helmet.

Then he'd put the helmet *in* the carriage, lovingly tucked under an old set of shoulder pads.

Then he'd jog around the field, pushing the carriage and singing "Rockabye Baby" to his helmet.

He said X did the same thing, so it must be okay. After all, X was now the team's star quarterback.

Susie's parents were horrified by her behavior, and Jim's parents were worried sick about his.

But the worst came when the twins, Joe and Peggy, decided to share everything with each other.

Peggy used Joe's hockey skates, and his microscope, and took half his newspaper route.

Joe used Peggy's needlepoint kit, and her cookbooks, and took two of her three baby-sitting jobs.

Peggy ran the lawn mower, and Joe ran the vacuum cleaner.

Their parents weren't one bit pleased with Peggy's science experiments, or with Joe's terrific needlepoint pillows.

They didn't care that Peggy mowed the lawn better, and that Joe vacuumed the carpet better.

In fact, they were furious. It's all that little X's fault, they agreed. X doesn't know what it is, or what it is supposed to be! So X wants to mix everybody *else* up, too!

Peggy and Joe were forbidden to play with X anymore. So was Susie, and then Jim, and then *all* the Other Children.

But it was too late: the Other Children stayed mixed-up and happy and free, and refused to go back to the way they'd been before X.

Finally, the parents held an emergency meeting to discuss "The X Problem."

They sent a report to the principal stating that X was a "bad influence," and demanding immediate action.

The Joneses, they said, should be forced to tell whether X was a boy or a girl. And X should be forced to behave like whichever it was.

If the Joneses, refused to tell, the parents said, then X must take an Xamination. An Impartial Team of Xperts would Xtract the secret. Then X would start obeying all the old rules. Or else.

And if X turned out to be some kind of mixed-up misfit, then X must be Xpelled from school. Immediately! So that no little Xes would ever come to school again.

The principal was very upset. X a bad influence? A mixed-up misfit? But X was an Xcellent student! X set a fine Xample! X was Xtraordinary!

X was president of the student council. X had won first prize in the art show, honorable mention in the science fair, and six events on field day, including the potato race.

Nevertheless, insisted the parents, X is a Problem Child. X is the Biggest Problem Child we have ever seen!

So the principal reluctantly notified X's parents.

At Xactly 9 o'clock the next day, X reported to the school health office. The principal, along with a committee from the Parents' Association, X's teacher, X's classmates, and Ms. and Mr. Jones, waited in the hall outside.

Inside, the Xperts had set up their famous testing machine: the Superpsychiamedicosocioculturometer.

Through it all, you could hear the Xperts' voices, asking questions, and X's voice, answering answers.

I wouldn't like to be in X's overalls right now, the children thought.

At last, the door opened. Everyone crowded around to hear the results. X didn't look any different, in fact, X was smiling.

"What happened?" everyone began shouting.

"In our opinion, young X," said one Xpert, "Is just about the *least* mixed-up child we've ever Xamined!"

"Yay for X!" yelled one of the children. And then the others began yelling, too. Clapping and cheering and jumping up and down.

The Parents' Committee was angry and bewildered. How could X have passed the whole Xamination?

Didn't X have an identity problem? Wasn't X mixed up at all? Wasn't X any kind of a misfit?

How could it *not* be, when it didn't even *know* what it was?

"Don't you see?" asked the Xperts. "X isn't one bit mixed up! As for being a misfit—ridiculous! X knows perfectly well what it is! Don't you, X?" The Xperts winked. X winked back.

"But what is X?" shrieked Peggy and Joe's parents. "We still want to know what it is!"

"Ah yes," said the Xperts, winking again. "Well, don't worry. You'll all know one of these days. And you won't need us to tell you."

"What? What do they mean?" Jim's parents grumbled suspiciously.

Susie and Peggy and Joe all answered at once. "They mean that by the time it matters which sex X is, it won't be a secret anymore!"

Needless to say, the Joneses were very happy. The Project Baby X scientists were rather pleased, too. So were Susie, Jim, Peggy, Joe, and all the Other Children. Even the parents promised not to make any trouble.

Later that day, all X's friends put on their red and white checked overalls and went over to see X. They found X in the backyard playing with a very tiny baby that none of them had ever seen before.

The baby was wearing very tiny red and white checked overalls.

"How do you like our new baby?" X asked the Other Children proudly.

"It's got cute dimples," said Jim. "It's got husky biceps, too," said Susie.

"What kind of baby is it?" asked Joe and Peggy.

X frowned at them. "Can't you tell?" Then X broke into a big, mischievous grin. "*It's a Y!*"

—"X" by Lois Gould. (New York: Stonesong Press, 1978)

RATIONALE

The topic of sexual orientation arouses a great deal of curiosity, anxiety, fear, and prejudice in our society, and these feelings are especially pronounced among adolescents. As young people begin to explore their sexuality and to define their identities, the issue of sexual orientation becomes prominent. Lesbian, gay, and bisexual teens may feel isolated, anxious about being different, and afraid of being ostracized. Others who are unsure of their orientation may have many questions with no apparent place to get answers.

In this workshop, participants talk with a panel of speakers who have identified themselves as gay, lesbian, or bisexual. The discussion with panel speakers forces participants to confront their misconceptions, to face prejudices they may have learned, and to see that gay, lesbian, and bisexual people are very similar to other people they know. Faced with actual people, it becomes very difficult to maintain myths about a group. The panel also allows gay and lesbian youth to interact with people who are like them and to know that they are not alone.

For those classes unable to arrange a panel of speakers, alternative activities expose participants to personal stories of lesbian, gay, and bisexual youth, and provide opportunities for participants to look at their own values regarding sexual orientation, listen to different perspectives among their peers, and decide whether they want to change or keep the values they hold.

Time Required: 45 minutes

GOALS

- To understand that sexual orientation is not a choice.
- To understand that sexual orientation may have both biological and learned components.
- To recognize that sexual orientation is not just about behavior.
- To understand that sexual orientation is not just about with whom we have sex but also about with whom we become friends and with whom we identify.
- To clarify personal values about sexual orientation.

OBJECTIVES

By the end of this workshop, participants will be able to

- express one misconception they have had about sexual orientation that they no longer have.
- demonstrate an understanding that people of different sexual orientations have much in common.

- demonstrate an understanding of the difficulties many gay, lesbian, and bisexual youth experience by stating ways in which the life of a gay, lesbian, or bisexual adolescent may be different from that of a heterosexual youth.
- state and support their positions on various issues related to sexual orientation.

MATERIALS

☐ Leader Resource 11, Stories of Gay, Lesbian, and Bisexual Adolescents
☐ Leader Resource 12, Statements for Forced Choice Exercise

Optional

☐ *Two Teenagers in Twenty*, edited by Ann Heron (Boston: Alyson Press, 1995).

PREPARATION

- Review this workshop and decide how to share leadership responsibilities with your coleader.
- Invite a panel of gay, lesbian, and bisexual people to speak to your group about their experiences growing up gay, lesbian, or bisexual and, in particular, their experiences as adolescents. An adolescent guest who is comfortable speaking about his/her experiences is ideal. It is also desirable to include a twentysomething adult who can discuss adolescent concerns and experiences with the advantage of hindsight.

  When putting together the panel, strive for diversity of age, race/ethnicity, socioeconomic status, and other categories so that participants have the opportunity to meet and to talk with people from many walks of life. Use this opportunity to break down preconceptions. For example, homosexuals are often thought of as younger people. Having someone on the panel in his/her sixties or seventies would be extremely educational. Gay men, especially, are most often depicted as upper middle class Caucasians. Someone with a different profile would challenge stereotypes.

  The most important attribute for panelists, however, is comfort speaking openly to adolescents about their lives and sexual orientations. For help in finding appropriate guests, see the resources section, "Resources for Bisexual, Gay, Lesbian, Transgender, and Questioning Youth," at the end of this book.

- If you are not presenting the speaker's panel, you will be leading two alternative activities. Read the stories at the end of this workshop, or seek out others to use and prepare to present and discuss them for the alternative activity, Stories of Gay, Lesbian, and Bisexual Youth.

- For the Forced Choice activity, you may want to make two signs, AGREE and DISAGREE.

- Post the ground rules from the opening session.

Activity

SPEAKERS PANEL   30 minutes

1. Welcome your guests and invite introductions from panelists and participants.

2. Ask each member of the panel to speak for about five minutes about growing up gay, lesbian, or bisexual. When did they first realize they were gay, lesbian, or bisex-

ual? How did friends, family, and others react if and when they came out? How do they perceive their lives to be different from those of "straight" people? How do they perceive their lives to be the same? Be sure to leave time for panelists to answer questions from the group.

3. Invite questions from participants. Encourage them to ask any questions they may have.

4. When time is up, thank your guests and say goodbye to them.

PROCESSING THE SPEAKERS PANEL 15 minutes

1. Help participants process the panel discussion with the following questions:
- Was there anything that you heard today that surprised you?
- Did any of the speakers change the way you feel about lesbian, gay, or bisexual people?
- Do you think our guest speakers are very different from people who are heterosexual?
- In what ways did you find their experiences to be similar to those of people who are heterosexual?
- Did you learn anything new from this experience?
- How did you feel listening to their stories?
- Was there a general theme in the stories you heard?

2. Ask the group to think about how easy it is for us to think in terms of differences between people or groups of people when, in fact, we have much more in common with one another than we have differences. Remind the group that gender identity, gender role, and sexual orientation are three distinct aspects of sexual development and that while they are related, one cannot predict one from the others. Tell them that there are many gay men who adopt traditional masculine gender roles and many lesbians who follow traditional female gender roles. Heterosexuals also fall along the entire continuum of gender roles. Conclude by saying,

> The debate about whether different components of our sexuality are biologically based or learned is for the most part unimportant. We need to look at the goals, dreams, and desires that we share, and to recognize that diversity in sexuality, as in all other aspects of human life, is natural.

Alternatives

STORIES OF GAY, LESBIAN, AND BISEXUAL ADOLESCENTS 20 minutes

If a panel of speakers is not possible, read the firsthand accounts of two or three lesbian, gay, or bisexual adolescents to the group or have participants take turns reading them aloud. The stories may be from Leader Resource 11, Stories of Gay, Lesbian, and Bisexual Adolescents, from the book *Two Teenagers in Twenty* (see Materials for publication information), or from other sources. Process the stories with the questions and concluding points listed for Processing the Speakers Panel.

FORCED CHOICE

25 minutes

1. A forced choice exercise presents values-based statements and requires each person to take a position either in favor or against each statement. Explain to the group that you are going to read a statement having to do with sexual orientation. Each person is to decide whether he/she agrees or disagrees with the statement and then move to the appropriate spot. Designate one end of the room "Agree" and the opposite end of the room "Disagree." (You may want to post signs to avoid confusion.) Tell participants that they are not allowed to stand in the middle. There is no middle ground; they must pick one side or the other.

2. Read the first statement out loud to the group: If my best friend told me that he/she was gay, it would not affect my friendship with him/her at all. Ask participants to move to one or the other side of the room.

3. After they have chosen their positions, invite participants to take two minutes to talk with those who are on their side to find out why they are there. Point out that people may agree with a statement for different reasons or with different parameters.

4. After two minutes, ask for a volunteer from one group to explain why he/she agrees (or disagrees) with the statement. Then ask for other comments from people in that group. While one group is explaining its position, the other group should listen but not speak.

When the first group has had an opportunity to speak, invite members of the other group to explain their positions.

5. After both sides have presented their ideas, you may choose to invite discussion between the sides, or you may disallow further discussion and move on to the next statement.

Select statements that deal with the range of issues that you believe are most appropriate to your group.

6. Bring the group back together and ask:
- What was difficult about doing this exercise?
- Did you learn anything new about yourself during this activity?
- What surprised you?
- How do you think a gay or lesbian person in our group would feel while doing this activity?

7. Conclude the session with the comments listed under Processing the Speakers Panel.

STORIES OF GAY, LESBIAN, AND BISEXUAL ADOLESCENTS

KYLE DALE BYNION, 18
Baltimore, Maryland

All my life I've known I was different. But if someone were to ask me how I feel different, I wouldn't be able to answer them. The best way to explain it would be to say that being attracted to the same sex is as natural to me as being attracted to the opposite sex is for heterosexuals.

I have probably known I was gay since I was twelve. I don't think I knew that there was such a thing as "gay" until then. I used to go down in the cellar with other boys. We'd touch and kiss each other. I know it's natural for children to "experiment" with the same sex, but I knew, even then, that that was what I wanted. When I finally figured out what I was, I honestly don't remember feeling any different. I guess being gay just felt natural to me. Of course, I didn't realize back then how hard and frustrating it was going to be.

I have a twin brother, Chad, who is also gay. I figured out Chad was gay at about the same time I figured myself out. I don't remember how I knew. I just knew. When I was seventeen, I came out to my brother and his lover. We were all away on vacation. They were in bed, and I just came in and blurted it all out. I'd known about them for a long time, but they had no clue that I was gay. I'd been very active sexually since I was twelve, and I had lots of stories to tell them. I felt great. And, of course, nothing changed between us.

Then my parents found out about Chad. My mother found a letter from his lover in his drawer. They were devastated. My mother wondered what she'd done wrong. She was afraid my little sister would be a lesbian. My stepfather immediately suspected that I was gay too. At the time, I wasn't ready to admit it to them, so I adamantly denied it. But my stepfather wouldn't stop harassing me. Finally, I just yelled, "Shut up! I'm gay. You're right!" Finally. It was off my chest and I felt good.

But two weeks later, I found out my mom thought I was kidding. She hadn't thought I meant it. When I saw the hope in her eyes, I couldn't tell her that I'd been serious. She'd be crushed. I decided I'd tell her after she accepted my brother.

In the meantime, I made a mistake. I told someone I thought I could trust about me and Chad. It turned out he wasn't really a friend. He told everyone. All of our friends at work found out. Chad felt a lot of resentment toward me.

Then my mom found out about me. Apparently, she went through my drawers and found some gay literature. She confronted me, and I told her the truth. I though it would feel great to have this burden off my shoulders, but it didn't. It did feel good that I didn't have to hide anymore. But her heart was broken. She blamed herself, my father, me. I tried to convince her that it's no one's fault. But she was too wrapped up in her religion to listen to me. She thought her prayers could make me straight.

I was a wreck. I began considering suicide. Just the thought of me tormenting her for the rest of her life tore me up inside. I didn't know if I was strong enough to handle it. I never wanted to hurt her.

I have often been asked (or overheard others being asked, about themselves) if I would go "straight" if I could. Though I have never honestly answered the question, I'd like to now. If I could change my sexuality, I would. I know I'll probably offend a lot of people by saying that, but let me explain. My family has literally been uprooted by this. I know that my brother and I, and our friends, and everyone else has a right to be gay and enjoy anything that a heterosexual would. It shouldn't matter whom we go to bed with, but it does. That is why I would change my sexuality if I could— because I don't like hurting people I love. But I can't. And I'm not going to suppress my wants and desires just to please some narrow-minded people.

Thank you for giving me and others an opportunity to express ourselves. In this world where gays are so oppressed, it's good to be able to have a voice.

Source: Ann Heron, ed., *Two Teenagers in Twenty* (Boston: Alyson Press, 1995).

RACHEL CORBETT, 16
Madison, Wisconsin

Throughout and since childhood, I've been a "tomboy." In my second-grade picture, I was wearing a plaid shirt with rainbow suspenders and jeans. I hated dresses and nylons. I thought they were uncomfortable and never understood why I should have to wear uncomfortable clothes. My hair has almost always been cut short. Once, I tried to grow it out, only to get sick of it and chop it off. To this day, I've had more male friends than female friends. As a child, I chose the He-Man figurine or Matchbox cars over the Strawberry Shortcake doll or Barbie. I was always outside on my dirt bike skinning my knees instead of inside playing house.

My mother had a couple of gay and lesbian friends when I was growing up. That's the first place I learned about being gay or lesbian. When I was young, I don't think I saw any difference between heterosexual and homosexual relationships. I was young and was brought up to believe love is love, whether it involves people of the opposite sex or people of the same sex. It wasn't until I started Catholic school in the sixth grade that I became aware of homophobia. Kids would always make comments about effeminate men and say that all the nuns at the school were lesbians. It was at that school where I learned that there is a great deal of opposition to homosexuality.

That same year, some new people moved into the neighborhood. After they had settled in, I went over to see if they had any children I could be friends with. Luckily for me, they had two boys. They were a little younger than me, but I wasn't about to be fussy. (Most of the other kids in my neighborhood were either infants or in high school.) The boys in the house were being raised by two women. As time went on, I realized that they were probably lesbians. The two women never told me that they were gay, and neither did their sons. When they moved in, the boys were about seven and eight, and I'm not sure if they knew about their moms. I can understand why the women wouldn't tell me. I was eleven at the time, and they probably weren't sure what my parents would think. I'm pretty sure they were gay, though: they shared a bedroom, and one time I heard them talking about the bills together. The boys' dads were the only men I ever saw around the place. (And recently, I saw the two women at a documentary about lesbians; I guess that pretty much confirms it!)

The two women and their children made me aware of a new type of lifestyle that I really hadn't known existed. I began to realize that I wanted to live a life like theirs . . . not like the one my parents lived. Before they moved in, I could never picture myself being a housewife while my husband went out and earned the money for our family. I realized that I could relate more to them than to my parents. Over the years, I have lost touch with them, and I regret that. But they are still very important role models in my life. They made me aware of my sexual orientation, and I thank them.

Last October, I was downtown walking around with a friend. We saw all these people marching down State Street chanting. One chant went like this: "Two, four, six, eight, how do you know your mother's straight?" I asked my friend what was going on. She told me it was a gay pride march. We watched for a while, and I was so happy to see gays, lesbians, and bisexuals unafraid to show their affection for one another. They were standing up for their rights and demanding more. That night I returned home feeling very proud and decided that it was time for me to come out to my mother.

I was scared about what my mother would say. I was worried that she wouldn't accept me. I knew she supported homosexual rights, because whenever hatemongers were on the talk shows saying that homosexuals should be killed, my mother stood up for the homosexuals. She even yelled obscenities at the TV screen! But even though I knew she was for homosexual rights, I wasn't sure how she'd feel about her daughter being a lesbian. She had always talked about me having a big marriage ceremony in a Catholic church, and a huge reception with a big cake. I didn't want to disappoint her; I wanted to live up to all the expectations I thought she had of me. After thinking about it, I realized that it wouldn't be fair for me to hide my sexual orientation from her. After all, she was my best friend and she would be able to accept it. She had always been there for me no matter what, and I hoped she still would be after I told her.

That night, I was feeling bold, so I started on my way up the stairs to her bedroom. I went in and sat on her bed like I've done many times before when I had something to talk about. She sat up and asked, "What's up, kiddo?" I sat in the dark silence. I tried to speak, but instead I began to cry.

"Rachel, what's the matter? I can't help you unless you tell me what's wrong."

I looked her in the eyes, wishing she could read my mind. It would be so much simpler that way. No chance of that happening. I began to cry harder and wanted to back down. But there was no way I could just tell her that I'd had a nightmare. I had to tell her the truth; I had to get it over with.

"Mom?"

"Yes, Rachel. Go ahead. You can tell me anything."

"Mom." Tears rolled down my face. "Mom, I'm . . . "

"Go ahead, honey, it's okay."

"Mom. . . ." I took a deep breath and decided this was it. "I'm a . . . a . . . a . . . lesbian." I cried again.

"Go ahead, honey. Tell me the rest. You can trust me."

"Mom, that's it. I'm a lesbian."

"So why are you so upset?"

"I thought you would be upset, because I'm never going to have a husband and a big wedding."

Mom began to chuckle as she surrounded me with a hug. "I'm so proud of you." A tear rolled down her cheek. "You're my daughter and I love you. I will always love you, no matter what you are. I will always support you in everything that you do. As long as you're happy, I'm happy. You sure are silly, though," she said to me with a smile on her face.

I smiled and began to cry again, because I was filled with so much joy. We talked for a long time. She asked me if I minded if anyone else in our house knew. I told her it would be okay with me, and within three days my father, grandmother, and brother knew. They all took it very well. They are proud of me.

In the weeks that followed, my mother and I talked more than ever before. She was and still is extremely supportive of me. I thank her so much. If she didn't accept me, I don't know if I'd still be around.

Now, at the age of sixteen—one year after coming out to my mother, and many books and movies later—I have learned a lot more about myself. If I had a choice, I wouldn't change my sexual orientation. I am angry, because I find it hard to meet other gays my age. But in a year and a half, I will be in college and there will be more people to meet.

Inside, I'm proud of what I am, but I'm not out to the general public. I believe that coming out is an ongoing process. Since I've told my mother, I've also told a few close friends. I have begun to speak up for homosexual rights in my private Catholic school and soon will deal with gay issues in my photography. I've also spoken to groups about what it's like to be a gay teenager. In college I'm hoping I'll be able to step further and further out of the closet, because I'll be in a more diverse group of people. And, hopefully, they will be more accepting than the five hundred students at my school.

So far, my coming-out experiences have been very positive. Again, I would like to express my thanks to the two women on the corner raising their sons, and to my best friend, who happens to be my mother. I admire you all.

Source: Ann Heron, ed., *Two Teenagers in Twenty* (Boston: Alyson Press, 1995).

LIZ

The first inklings of my sexuality came when I was at secondary school. I was very close to a girl there and I knew it was more than just a friendship. Although I didn't verbalize it to anybody, not even to her, I was sure that there was more there than society accepted. But even from that early point it didn't worry me; I knew it wasn't going to be a problem as I was happy to be in the mainline heterosexual mold for most of the time.

Just before I went to college, I stayed with a friend whom I'd known for quite a few years—we'd met every so often in the course of group meetings. She was very responsive to my friendship and I realized that this could be a physical thing, not just an emotional attachment. Although it was very brief, I realized this was a new direction that was open to me, and that was lovely.

By the time I got to college, and met my boyfriend, D, I was beginning to wonder how being a bisexual would fit into my life. For example, how would a male partner react to it? I also didn't know how I would find female lovers, apart from the friend I'd been to stay with. She was living in London, so I didn't see her very often, and as she was involved in a heterosexual relationship as well, it was difficult to fit in more than the odd cuddle.

Source: Sue George, *Women and Bisexuality* (London: Scarlet Press, 1993), pp. 152–153.

Leader Resource 12

STATEMENTS FOR FORCED CHOICE EXERCISE

If my best friend told me that he/she was gay, it would not affect my friendship with him/her at all.

It would bother me if my college roommate were gay.

I would approve of my sister or brother bringing home a gay partner for the holidays.

Bisexual people are confused about their sexual orientation, unable to make a choice.

I think gay people should not be allowed to be elementary school teachers.

It would be okay with me if my girlfriend or boyfriend was bisexual.

Gay couples should be allowed to adopt children.

If I found out my doctor was gay and the same gender as I, I would stop going to him/her.

If a gay person had a good straight lover, he/she would become straight.

It wouldn't bother me if my son or daughter were gay or bisexual.

It would be okay with me if my father told me he was gay.

Becoming a Parent

5

RATIONALE

To make informed decisions about if and when they want to become parents, it is important for participants to have some idea of what pregnancy and parenting are like. Knowing how conception takes place is also important, not only so that they will know how to become pregnant or to impregnate a partner when the time comes but also so that they will make wise choices about contraception. This workshop encourages participants to think about the role that the male partner can play after conception, throughout the woman's pregnancy, during childbirth, and afterward as a parent. It attempts to take some of the mystery and fear out of the process while providing accurate information that will help participants make healthful choices for their own lives.

Time Required: 1 hour

GOALS

To help participants learn about
- the physiological processes of conception, pregnancy, and childbirth.
- the importance of prenatal nutrition and health care to babies' health.
- the factors that may contribute to positive and negative experiences of pregnancy and childbirth.
- the psychological, social, emotional, and economic impacts of parenting.
- the importance of the father/partner in the process of parenthood.

OBJECTIVES

By the end of this workshop, participants will be able to
- demonstrate a knowledge of the process of human conception by correctly identifying the order of events.
- think about the experience of pregnancy and birth by brainstorming the positive and negative aspects of these.
- display an understanding of what a pregnant woman's partner can do to be supportive and helpful during pregnancy and childbirth.

MATERIALS

☐ Large index cards
☐ Newsprint, markers, and tape
☐ Leader Resource 13, Events of Conception
☐ Leader Resource 14, Pregnancy and Fetal Development
☐ Optional: prizes for teams

PREPARATION

- Review this workshop and decide how to share leadership responsibilities with your coleader.
- Prepare two sets of index cards for the Conception Game by making two photocopies of the steps on Leader Resource 13, Events of Conception, and cutting and pasting each step onto a large index card.
- Familiarize yourself with the information on fetal development and pregnancy provided in Leader Resource 14, Pregnancy and Fetal Development.
- Post the ground rules from the opening session.

Activities

CONCEPTION GAME   25 minutes

1. Tell participants that they need to know the steps in human conception and fetal development in order to make good decisions about family planning, contraception, having a healthy baby, and becoming a parent. Explain that this game will test their understanding of human conception. It will be a contest to see which team can figure out the correct order of the steps involved in conception first.

2. Divide participants into two teams. Give each team a set of the index cards you have prepared. Tell the teams that members need to work together to put the index cards in the correct order. Explain that in the correct order, the cards form a Y, with one line for the route of the ovum and one line for the route of the sperm. Say that at some point, these two lines need to converge for conception to occur. The line from the point of convergence represents the steps in fertilization. Tell the teams that when they think they have the right order, they may ask you and you will tell them whether or not they are correct. (Decide in advance how much coaching to give.) The correct order for the cards is indicated on Leader Resource 15, Events of Conception. The first team to arrange the cards in the correct order wins the game. You may choose to have prizes to add to the fun.

3. Take some time to answer questions participants may have as a result of this activity. Acknowledge that this game represents conception as the result of sexual intercourse between a male and a female. Point out that reproductive technologies make conception possible without intercourse. As time and interest allow, explore with the group what they know about other methods of fertilization.

PREGNANCY AND BIRTH BRAINSTORM   20 minutes

1. Tell the group that the experience of pregnancy and childbirth varies from one woman to another, from one pregnancy to another, and from one couple to another. Say that there are some aspects of pregnancy that are beyond our control and many over which we have some control. Explain that you would like them to think about what they know, what they have heard, and what they think about the experience of pregnancy and childbirth. Ask them to brainstorm ideas on the topic of the positive aspects of pregnancy and childbirth. Write their comments on newsprint.

2. When the group has exhausted its ideas, ask participants to brainstorm ideas on the negative aspects of pregnancy and childbirth. Write these ideas on newsprint.

3. Invite participants to look at both lists and consider the following questions:

- Are there aspects that you think are universal for all women/couples? Are there others that may be specific to some people's experiences?
- What aspects of pregnancy and childbirth do you think are within your control? What aspects are out of your control?
- What factors might affect how positive or negative a pregnancy/childbirth experience is for an individual or couple?

PREGNANCY AND FETAL DEVELOPMENT
MINI-LECTURE   15 minutes

1. Explain that the nine months of pregnancy are divided into three sections called *trimesters*. Each trimester has specific hallmarks for the mother and the developing fetus. A partner or support person can be helpful to the pregnant woman in a variety of ways during each stage of pregnancy. Use the information in Leader Resource 16, Pregnancy and Fetal Development, as a mini-lecture.

2. Ask participants to share their thoughts and feelings about pregnancy and birth in response to the mini-lecture. Use the following questions to stimulate discussion:

- Do you think pregnancy is something you would like to experience at some point in your life?
- What reasons would you have for wanting to experience pregnancy? For not wanting to experience pregnancy?
- How would you feel about your partner's pregnancy? What would your role be?

Leader Resource 13

EVENTS OF CONCEPTION

Sperm

Sperm produced in testicles.
Starting at puberty, a male produces sperm for the rest of his life.

Sperm travel through vas deferens to the seminal vesicle.
In the seminal vesicle, sperm mix with fluids that make up semen.

A small amount of fluid is secreted from the Cowper's gland into the urethra.
The alkaline makeup of the fluid neutralizes the acidity of the urethra. Sperm need an alkaline environment to survive.

Semen with sperm enters into a woman's vagina.
An average ejaculate contains approximately 200 to 300 million sperm. Semen's alkaline environment protects sperm from acidic environment of the vagina.

Many sperm die, some enter the uterus through the cervix.

Sperm travel up through the uterus.
Sperm can survive for approximately 72 hours in the female body. This is why it is possible for a woman to become pregnant even if intercourse occurs during or immediately after her period.

Sperm travel up the Fallopian tubes.
About half of the sperm will enter the wrong Fallopian tube (the one without an egg) and will die.

Egg

Ovaries produce estrogen, which helps develop the eggs (ova).
A female is born with all the eggs in her ovaries she will ever have, about 400,000.

Ova grow bigger inside ovaries throughout the month.

One ovum in only one of a woman's ovaries becomes fully mature each month.

A mature ovum breaks out of the ovary. (This is called *ovulation*.)
The ovum must be fertilized within 24 hours.

The ovum is swept into a Fallopian tube.

The ovum moves down the Fallopian tube toward the uterus.

Fertilization

Several hundred sperm reach the ovulated egg.
The journey from ejaculation to the egg in the Fallopian tube takes approximately 1–1 1/2 hours.

One sperm penetrates the egg.
After penetration, a chemical reaction takes place on the outside of the egg, making the egg impenetrable to any other sperm.

The new cell, called a *zygote*, splits into two identical cells, each with 46 chromosomes, and travels slowly down the Fallopian tube toward the uterus.
When it reaches the uterus it is called a blastocyst and consists of about 100 cells.

The blastocyst implants in the endometrium of the uterus.
Approximately a week after fertilization, the blastocyst secretes a hormone that helps it to implant in the wall of the uterus.

The pregnancy is established, the placenta starts to form.

Leader Resource 14

PREGNANCY AND FETAL DEVELOPMENT

THE FIRST TRIMESTER

Changes in the Fetus

After conception, the fertilized egg travels through the Fallopian tubes into the uterus and embeds in the uterine lining. The cells divide, change, and become an embryo. The amniotic sac and placenta form during this time. The amniotic sac is a fluid-filled sac in which the fetus and placenta live within the uterus. The placenta is a structure that forms along the inside of the mother's uterus and becomes the life support system for the fetus. Nutrients and blood travel through the placenta and into the fetus through the umbilical cord. The placenta also filters out many harmful chemicals so that they cannot reach the developing fetus. The placenta cannot, however, filter out all harmful elements. If a pregnant woman smokes cigarettes, drinks alcohol, uses drugs, or takes medications without a doctor's advice, the fetus may be harmed.

During the first trimester, the fetus develops its brain, heart, nervous system, and bones. By the end of the third month, a fetus looks like a completely formed tiny human, but it has a long way to go before it can survive outside its mother's body.

Changes in the Mother

The first thing a woman usually notices when she is pregnant is a missed menstrual period. Her breasts may become tender and swollen, and she may feel somewhat bloated. As the pregnancy becomes more firmly established, a woman may also experience nausea and unusual fatigue. Pregnant women are often more hungry than usual, and sometimes they have cravings for certain types of foods. Some women experience nausea and vomiting during early pregnancy and find it difficult to eat. Some foods, even the odor of certain foods, increase the nausea, making it difficult to consume all the nutrients that pregnant women need. During this time, it is extremely important that a woman eat enough nutritious food because the fetus needs the nutrients to make bones and blood. The average woman will gain about five to ten pounds during the first trimester.

Physically and psychologically, every woman experiences pregnancy in a different way. Indeed, a woman may experience each of her pregnancies differently. Some women feel stronger and more healthy than ever before, while others feel weak and vulnerable. Fear, apprehension, excitement, anxiety, joy, and ambivalence are just some of the things women feel during pregnancy. Whether or not the pregnancy was planned also affects how a woman feels. Supportive friends and family, adequate nutrition, and rest make all of the changes of pregnancy easier.

A supportive partner can help a pregnant woman by making sure that she gets good prenatal medical care. Accompanying her to prenatal medical appointments, if the woman agrees, is a good way for the partner to get involved in the pregnancy. Since a pregnant woman needs to eat a very nutritious diet, a partner can be supportive by helping to prepare healthful meals and by keeping non-nutritious foods out of the house. A partner can also help by decreasing a pregnant woman's workload. Helping to care for other children, assuming household chores, and providing opportunities for rest and relaxation are good ways to help.

THE SECOND TRIMESTER

Changes in the Fetus

During the second trimester, the fetus undergoes a great deal of development and growth. All of the major body systems develop and begin to operate. Hair and fingernails develop. The fetus grows and begins to move about inside the amniotic sac.

Changes in the Mother

During the second trimester, a pregnant woman begins to "show" as the fetus grows. Some women feel off-balance as their center of gravity shifts and changes. Nausea and fatigue usually lessen, and some women experience a sense of renewed energy. Hormones secreted during pregnancy sometimes make a woman's skin and hair look more healthy, and thus, a pregnant woman may feel more attractive. Some women, however, may develop acne and skin irritations due to hormonal changes. As the fetus grows and presses on a woman's internal organs, a woman may need to urinate more often and may become constipated. Many women have difficulty with heartburn, gas, and indigestion during pregnancy. During the second trimester women often gain an additional ten to fifteen pounds.

Some women will experience the second trimester as the best part of pregnancy. Looking pregnant, for some women, is very fulfilling and exciting. Other women feel fat and unattractive. Toward the middle of the second trimester a woman will begin to feel fetal movements, small and gentle at first, then becoming much stronger as the fetus grows. This movement confirms the pregnancy for many women and can cause a great many emotional reactions from fear to elation.

A partner can continue to encourage the pregnant woman's good nutrition and health care. In addition, a partner can appreciate the changes in the woman's body as the pregnancy progresses and reassure her that she is still attractive. Shopping for maternity clothes, reading baby name books, and attending childbirth classes are fun ways to celebrate the pregnancy. Many couples plan special trips or events that may have to be curtailed after the baby is born.

THE THIRD TRIMESTER

Changes in the Fetus

During the last three months of pregnancy, the fetus, which is now fully formed, develops some body fat to keep it warm outside the uterine environment. Its skin becomes thicker, and the fetus practices sucking, swallowing, and using its muscles. The fetus can respond to sound outside the woman's body.

Changes in the Mother

During the last three months of pregnancy, the woman's body must grow to accommodate the fetus' growth. The woman's abdomen swells considerably, and she may become clumsy and find it difficult to move around. Heartburn, gas, indigestion, constipation, and frequent urination are common during the last trimester. Many women find it difficult to sleep and may feel very tired due to size and restricted mobility. Some women experience edema, or swelling due to water retention. The uterus begins practicing the tightening and releasing, called contractions, that will push the baby out. Some contractions may be strong enough to be mistaken for "the real thing." As a woman's breasts prepare to make milk, they often become larger, deep blue veins become visible through the skin, and the nipples and areolas become darker. Many women feel even more beautiful and strong as their bodies prepare for childbirth. Other women find the last months of pregnancy uncomfortable and long. The average woman gains an additional ten to fifteen pounds during the third trimester.

As the baby's due date approaches, many women begin to feel both excited and apprehensive about childbirth. Some women are anxious to have the pregnancy over with. Many women become worried about their baby's health, as well as what kind of mother they will be. Often, women daydream about the baby and are anxious to meet him/her.

As birth approaches, a partner needs to be understanding and supportive of the pregnant woman's changing emotions, fatigue, and discomfort. Offering foot or back rubs, helping with lifting or carrying, and generally trying to be helpful will be beneficial. Arranging the baby's room or space, attending childbirth classes, and making the last few weeks of baby-free time special are loving ways to celebrate the impending arrival of a new person.

WORKSHOP 15 **Parenting License**

RATIONALE

In this workshop, participants explore the values they consider important for becoming parents. Young adults frequently have unrealistic ideas about what it takes to be a good parent. The activity provided here gives participants the chance to think about what criteria they would actually require before awarding a "license to parent."

Time Required: 35 minutes

GOALS

To help participants
- understand the many factors involved in being a parent.
- clarify their values about what parents should be, do, and have.

OBJECTIVES

By the end of this workshop, participants will be able to
- choose factors that should be considered in the decision to become a parent.
- identify which of these factors are most important.

MATERIALS

☐ Newsprint, markers, and tape
☐ Pencils or pens
☐ Handout 9, Parenting Criteria

PREPARATION

- Review this workshop and decide how to share leadership responsibilities with your coleader.
- Photocopy Handout 10, Parenting Criteria, for all participants.
- Post the ground rules from the opening session.

Activity

PARENTING LICENSE   35 minutes

1. Tell participants that this activity explores the variety of factors involved in becoming a parent. Ask participants to imagine that, because of the serious overcrowding problem, a law has been passed requiring any person or couple wishing to become a parent to obtain a parenting license. It is the job of this group to determine the criteria for obtaining this license.

2. Distribute Handout 10, Parenting Criteria. Ask participants to look it over and add any factors they believe are missing.

3. Divide participants into small groups. Ask the groups to review the list and determine as a group which would be the *five* most important factors in granting a parenting license. Let participants know that they will be asked to justify their choices to the whole group. Give them 10 minutes to choose the factors.

4. After 10 minutes, even if the groups have not completed the task, have them present their top five criteria to the large group and explain their selections. List the criteria on newsprint.

5. Facilitate discussion in the large group with the following questions:

- What did you think of this activity?
- What was difficult about it?
- What was easy about it?
- Were you surprised by anything you discussed?
- Do you think people should have to have licenses to become parents?
- How do you feel about the fact that in reality there are no requirements for parenthood?
- Did anything you learned in this activity make you rethink your own parenting plans?

6. Summarize by making the following points. Becoming a parent is a serious decision that requires a great deal of thought. It is important to realize that most people would not be able to live up to the criteria the group established in this activity. In fact, many of our own parents probably would not have been able to pass the licensing criteria we created. While there is no perfect time to become a parent and no parent is perfect, it is worth considering the factors we have discussed before taking on the challenge of parenthood.

Handout 10

PARENTING CRITERIA

Instructions

- Read this list.
- Add any factors involved in becoming a parent that you think are missing.
- As a group, identify your top five and write them in order on the lines below.

Financial status

Marital/partner status

Education

Age

Childcare knowledge or experience

Health status

Availability of extended family or other support network

Criminal record

Sexual orientation

Quality of relationship between parents

Number of children already existing

History of divorce

Should both parents have same religion?

Should both parents be same race?

Physical disabilities

History of genetic disorders

Physical attractiveness

Plans for one parent to stay home and raise children vs. plans for both parents to work full-time

The Most Important Criteria for Our Group

1._____

_____

2._____

_____

3._____

_____

4._____

_____

5._____

_____

RATIONALE

This workshop provides participants with information about two alternative kinds of families: adoptive families and child-free marriages. Not all people are able to or choose to create offspring from their own bodies. This workshop helps young people understand that there are other legitimate options for family life.

Time Required: 25 minutes

GOALS

To help participants
• become aware of alternatives to heterosexual marriage with biological children.
• identify the issues and concerns associated with adoption and child-free marriage.
• clarify values concerning adoption and child-free marriage.

OBJECTIVES

By the end of this workshop, participants will be able to
• identify issues and concerns related to adopting a child.
• discuss their feelings about choosing to be child-free.

MATERIALS

None

PREPARATION

• Review this workshop and decide how to share leadership responsibilities with your coleader.
• Post the ground rules from the opening session.

Activity

STORIES ABOUT FAMILIES   25 minutes

1. Introduce the activity by saying that although society emphasizes getting married and having children, not all families are created this way. Point out that sometimes a heterosexual couple cannot have children for biological reasons, and sometimes gay or lesbian couples or single people wish to become parents. Tell participants that there are many reproductive technologies that provide options for couples wishing to have a baby and these will be discussed in a later session. Explain that in this session, they are going to discuss two other choices: adoption and child-free marriages or partnerships.

2. Read the following stories to the group:

ADOPTION STORY

My husband and I found out we might become prospective parents in April. That gave us about seven to eight weeks to think about this. I had many things going through my mind. So many things could happen in the interim. The birth mother could still change her mind. I wondered what the child would be like. The baby's looks, personality, health—everything is unknown. . . .

I thought a lot about bonding. I wondered what I'd feel like when someone put an infant in my arms saying, "Congratulations! You're a mother. This is your child." Who is this stranger? How am I supposed to love someone I do not even know? How am I supposed to feel? I believe these are healthy feelings, but still it is frightening to think about. . . .

I believe couples facing adoption go through the same feelings that biological parents go through—the fears, insecurities, the great change of lifestyle. The only problem is that you do not have nine months to work your feelings through. It is like being told you are eight months pregnant.

Source: Boston Women's Health Collective, *The New Our Bodies, Our Selves* (New York: Simon & Schuster, 1992), p. 510.

SUZANNE

Bekah's birth mother, Suzanne, and I write each other once a year at Bekah's birthday time, sending photos and news, and Suzanne always sends a birthday present. One gift, a handpainted plate with the picture of a young girl that looks a lot like Bekah, became a particular treasure. Bekah kept it in her room, then in the kitchen, then in the attic with her baby things, then on the dining room table. She was searching, it seemed, for an area in the house that was special enough, but could never find quite the right place.

Bekah always cried and spoke about missing Suzanne after she got a present, and, on her fifth birthday, when a photo of Suzanne's new baby arrived, she begged to go see them. Someday, I promised her, we would. When she became literate, Bekah decided that she too, was going to write Suzanne yearly. In careful printing with purple marker, she wrote her first letter:

> Dear Suzanne,
>
> I am 6 now. I can ride a two wheel bike.
> This is my first time I lost my tooth.
> I want to see my half-sister.
>
> Love, Bekah

Source: Wendy Lichtman, "Visiting Suzanne" in *The Adoption Reader*, ed. Susan Wadia-Ells (Seattle: Seal Press, 1995), pp. 123–125.

3. After you have read the stories, use the following questions for discussion:

- Would you ever consider adoption?
- Even if you had biological children or knew that you could, would adoption be an option to consider? Why or why not?
- What do you think are some of the concerns of adoptive parents? What do you think it would feel like to be handed a child? How different do you think it is from being handed a baby you just gave birth to or helped create?
  NOTE: Explain to the group that although the woman in the adoption story felt like she just found out that she was eight months pregnant, adoption involves a long process (and often great expense) of filling out forms, participating in interviews and home visits, obtaining references, etc.
- Would you want your adopted child to know his/her birth parents?
- If you are adopted, how did it feel to find out that you were? If you are not adopted, how do you think it would feel?
- If you are adopted, do you want to find your birth parents someday? If you are not adopted, do you think you would? Why or why not?

4. Read the following story aloud to the group:

There are some couples who choose, for a variety of reasons, to remain child-free. Whether it is the desire to pursue careers that leave little time to devote to childrearing, or it is a genuine lack of desire to parent, it is legitimate for people to not wish to become parents. Our culture tends to believe that if you are in a committed relationship and you have some financial security, then most people have a "drive" to reproduce. There is a stigma attached to being childless by choice. Outsiders often assume that a childless couple "cannot" have children. People with children often try to influence those who do not have them to "jump on the bandwagon." Some people do not really feel the desire or the need to parent. Parenting is a monumental and life-altering challenge, which people need to feel free to choose. Here is a story of one such couple:

ON NOT HAVING KIDS

Before we left Boston for San Jose last fall, we had dinner with two couples we've known for years. We used to spend hours with them discussing the pros and cons of starting a family. Within a few months, both couples had children. We thought it was going to be a bittersweet good-bye dinner, but they ganged up on us about having children as soon as we got our coats off. They kept telling us we didn't know what we were missing. We suggested they were missing a lot too. That, they didn't like. "Well people are having children later these days," one proud mother said. "There's still time. It's a matter of maturity. When you're ready, you'll know it."

That, I didn't like. Why should maturity be equated with having children? Before I could react, they hit us rapid-fire with a series of questions that probed like a scalpel. One new father, a psychiatrist, wondered it we might be just a bit narcissistic. His wife, a clinical psychologist, asked if we were perennial adolescents, afraid of the responsibility that comes with parenthood. She suggested that our relationship was too fragile for the strains of raising kids. They were as obnoxious as could be. We had two choices: laugh it off or tell them off.

Ann and I are not narcissistic. Our relationship has endured worse strains than the "terrible twos." It's not that we do not like children either. We have loved several. We have friends here who have a wonderful 2-year-old daughter, so I catch glimpses of what I'm missing. The point is, I've chosen to miss it. We do not have children because we do not want any. If we did, we would have them.

I have no deep biological urge to reproduce myself. The world will get along fine without my kids, just as it will get along fine without me when I'm gone. I lack the drive to love, to nurture, and to shape another human being. . . .

I worry about money like most of us do, but if we had kids, I'd really worry about money. I don't want to spend money on Gerber's and Pampers and life insurance. I don't want to save for a college education. . . .

Source: John Hubner, "On not having kids," *San Jose Mercury News*, 1982.

5. Use the following questions to discuss issues raised in the excerpt:

- How do you feel about this statement?
- What do you think about child-free couples?
- Do you believe that people *should* have children?
- Is there anything wrong with not wanting to be a parent?
- Are all people meant to be parents?

6. Summarize by saying that it is important to realize that there are many different ways to create families and that it is not a good idea to get married and have children just because our culture expects us to do so. Point out that choosing to remain child-free and choosing to adopt a child are both good options for many people. Just as there are many issues to consider when deciding to become parents, there are many issues to consider in determining how and/or whether to become a parent.

Expressions of Sexuality

6

RATIONALE

Although media images might lead us to believe that only adolescents and young adults are sexual beings, sexuality is part of our lives from birth until death. This workshop encourages participants to broaden their view of sexual expression and to recognize that people of all ages are sexual, although they may express sexuality differently at different times in their lives.

Time Required: 45 minutes

GOALS

To help participants
• explore various expressions of sexuality among people of different ages.
• recognize that people are sexual beings throughout their lives.

OBJECTIVES

By the end of this workshop, participants will be able to
• demonstrate an understanding that people of all ages are sexual by listing ways in which people at various stages of life express their sexuality.
• show a knowledge of the range of sexual expression by discussing the various choices available to people at different stages of their lives.

MATERIALS

☐ Newsprint, markers, and masking tape
☐ Leader Resource 15, Sexual Being

PREPARATION

• Review this workshop and decide how to share leadership responsibilities with your coleader.
• At the top of each sheet of newsprint write one of the following headings: Infancy; Childhood; Adolescence; Young Adulthood; Middle Age; Old Age. Post the newsprint sheets on the walls around the room in chronological order.
• Become familiar with Leader Resource 15, Sexual Being.
• Post the ground rules from the opening session.

Activity

SEXUALITY THROUGHOUT THE LIFE CYCLE   45 minutes

1. Tell the group that they are going to explore the many ways that people express their sexuality at different stages of life. Divide participants into six small groups. (If there are fewer than twelve people, make fewer groups so that there are at least two people per group.) Give each group a marker. Ask each group to stand by one of the pieces of newsprint corresponding to a life stage.

Tell the groups you are going to give them three minutes to brainstorm and list all of the ways that people might express their sexual selves at the life stage written on the newsprint. Remind participants that brainstorming does not require consensus. All ideas are to be written down.

Encourage participants to include more than sexual behaviors in their concept of being sexual by reviewing Leader Resource 17, Sexual Being, which is summarized below:

Sensuality: accepting and enjoying your own body and its ability to respond sexually as well as enjoying the body of a sexual partner.

Intimacy: the basic human need to be emotionally close to another person and to have that closeness returned.

Sexual identity: a person's understanding of who they are sexually, including their sense of being male or female.

Sexual health and reproduction: the most familiar aspect of sexuality; includes all of the behaviors and attitudes that have to do with reproduction and keeping the sexual parts of the body healthy.

Sexualization: using sex or sexuality to influence, manipulate, or control other people.

2. After 3 minutes, have the groups move to the next life stage sheet so that each group is moving chronologically. (The group that started at Old Age should move to Infancy.) Allow the groups 3 minutes to add their own ideas to the lists.

3. Continue to rotate every three minutes. In the later rounds, groups will have fewer new ideas to add, but they can use the time to read and discuss the growing lists.

4. After every small group has had the opportunity to brainstorm for each of the six life stages, bring all participants back together to discuss the lists in chronological order starting with infancy. For each stage, ask:
- Are there any ideas here with which you disagree or which you do not understand?
- Is there anything particularly interesting among the items on this list?
- Is there anything surprising to you?
- Is sexuality just about what people do in bed?
- Did this exercise change your understanding of sexuality? Your understanding of any age group? How?

In addition, at the appropriate stages, include the following questions and points:

INFANCY

- When infants touch their genitals, do you think they are being sexual in the way that adults are when masturbating?
- How is touch a sexual expression?

Point out that male fetuses have been observed with erections in utero and that female fetuses in utero are known to lubricate vaginally.

CHILDHOOD

- How can the reactions of parents and other adults to childhood sex play affect the sexuality of a child? Think about their reactions to finding a child masturbating, playing doctor with a friend, asking an adult questions about sex.

Explain that this is a stage at which guilt about exploring sexuality can first be felt.

ADOLESCENCE

- What distinguishes this list from the others? [Typically, it has the most items on it.] What does this say about how we view adolescent sexuality?
- Is abstinence on this list? Is the choice of abstinence an expression of one's sexuality? How?

Tell participants that during adolescence, people ask themselves "Who am I?" In their search for self-identity, adolescents often engage in a lot of exploration and experimentation, sexual and otherwise. They try different behaviors, different groups of friends, and different ideas to figure out which feel comfortable and where they belong.

YOUNG ADULTHOOD

- How does this list differ from the adolescence list? Is sexual behavior still the main focus?
- Does the list have any expressions in common with the Infancy list?
- What are the major changes that begin to occur?
- What are the choices people are facing at this stage?

Point out that young adulthood often involves finding a permanent mate, establishing long-term intimate relationships, and thinking about whether and how to have children. These major decisions will affect sexual expressions in the following stages of life.

MIDDLE AGE

- What distinguishes this age?
- What does this stage have in common with previous stages?
- What is unique to this stage?

Say that in middle adulthood, many people spend a great deal of their time raising families. Explain that for these people, parenthood becomes the paramount form of sexual expression. For those who choose not to parent, sexual expression may involve further self-exploration and the development of other kinds of meaningful relationships. In this stage people may be divorced or widowed and may search for new partners. Typically, women go through menopause, meaning they are no longer able to become pregnant. Ask, "How do you think events such as divorce and menopause could affect a person's expression of his/her sexuality? What do you think about the sexual lives of people who are their parents' ages?"

OLD AGE

- What is unique about this stage?
- Are there biases about old people as sexual beings? Do we think of them as sexual?
- How many people in this group would like to be sexual when they get old?
- When does a man go from being a "stud" to being a "dirty old man?"

Say that in old age, many people find a reawakening of their sexual selves. Spouses often find that their sexual encounters are more enjoyable and more frequent when their children are grown and out of the house. For both men and women, the more sexually active they have been throughout their lives, the more sexually active they are likely to be now. Although sexual arousal may change and may become less important, other aspects of sexuality, such as touch, take on great importance. We tend not to touch older people as much as we touch younger adults and children, yet it is a critical component of sexual expression. Our culture does not tend to share a positive, healthy view of old age. Most people do not think about the sexual needs of older people; even old people themselves frequently do not feel entitled to sexual outlets. Nursing homes often separate couples and forbid sexual expression between residents. As people age, we stop treating them as if their feelings, needs, and opinions mattered. In other cultures, people revere and respect their elders. Our culture is ageist; it sees the world as belonging to the young, with little room for the elderly.

5. When all of the stages have been discussed, ask,

- Are there any patterns that emerge among the stages?
- Are there glaring consistencies or differences?
- Are there any expressions of sexuality that you believe are essential or important at every stage of life? What are they?

Make the point that although the ways in which we express our sexual selves may change at different times in our lives, we always have sexual needs and ways of expressing them.

Leader Resource 15

SEXUAL BEING

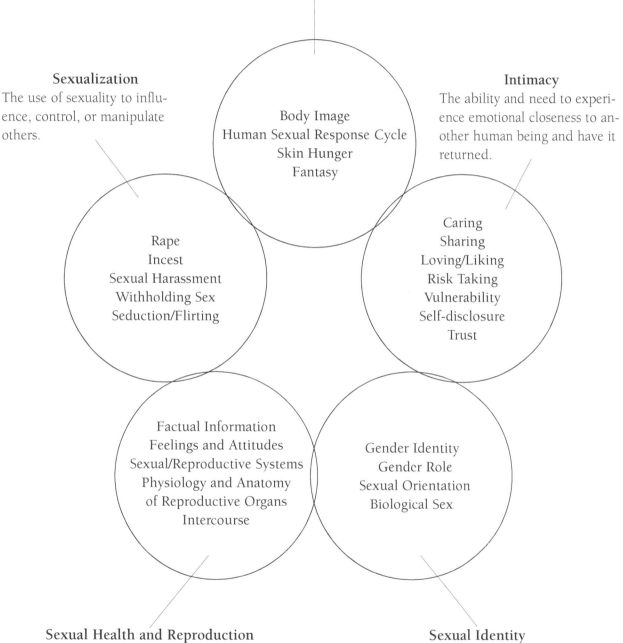

Sensuality
Awareness, acceptance of, and comfort with one's own body; physiological and psychological enjoyment of one's own body and the bodies of others.

Sexualization
The use of sexuality to influence, control, or manipulate others.

Intimacy
The ability and need to experience emotional closeness to another human being and have it returned.

Body Image
Human Sexual Response Cycle
Skin Hunger
Fantasy

Rape
Incest
Sexual Harassment
Withholding Sex
Seduction/Flirting

Caring
Sharing
Loving/Liking
Risk Taking
Vulnerability
Self-disclosure
Trust

Factual Information
Feelings and Attitudes
Sexual/Reproductive Systems
Physiology and Anatomy
of Reproductive Organs
Intercourse

Gender Identity
Gender Role
Sexual Orientation
Biological Sex

Sexual Health and Reproduction
Attitudes and behaviors related to producng children, care and maintenance of the sex and reproductive organs, and health consequences of sexual behavior.

Sexual Identity
The development of a sense of who one is sexually, including a sense of maleness and femaleness.

UNDERSTANDING THE COMPONENTS OF HUMAN SEXUALITY

1. Sensuality means accepting and enjoying your own body and its ability to respond sexually, as well as accepting and enjoying the body of a sexual partner.

Sensuality has to do with our bodies—how we feel about the body, how it looks, feels, and what it can do. Sensuality involves being aware of and in touch with the pleasure of our own bodies and the bodies of others.

The way that people experience sensuality changes as they grow and mature. For example, babies are sensuous in the way they explore their whole bodies, get pleasure from being touched and experience different textures against their skin. A nursing baby enjoys touching his/her mom's skin and is soothed by sucking her breasts. Mother and infant share a sensual experience, but they are certainly NOT having sex together. This component encompasses issues such as:

- *Understanding anatomy and physiology*—learning about the way our bodies work and gaining comfort with functions such as menstruation, wet dreams, or erections.

- *Body image*—our attitudes and feelings about our own bodies; concepts of what is and is not attractive, perceptions influenced by the media and culture.

- *Pleasure and release from sexual tension*—the human body was created to respond in certain ways to touch and pleasurable feelings. People begin to become aware of these feelings at different times. Some begin as young children; others at puberty; others not until later in adolescence or adulthood. Sexual feelings can range from feeling "turned on," or sexually interested, all the way to orgasm, either alone or with a sexual partner.

- *Skin hunger*—the human need to be touched, stroked, and held; skin-to-skin contact makes people feel connected, comfortable, relaxed, and/or physically stimulated.

- *Feeling physical attraction or desire*—strong physical and emotional reactions to particular people (sometimes real people, other times movie stars, famous athletes, or singers); often described as feeling excited, warm, quivery, or tingly; wanting to be close to, hug, kiss, or be sexual with someone, either because of the way he/she looks or because of the way he/she makes us feel.

- *Fantasy as a means of sexual expression*—thoughts, dreams, imaginary stories with a sexual theme; a safe way of exploring feelings; thoughts that do not necessarily turn into actions.

2. Intimacy is the basic human need to be emotionally close to another person and to have that closeness returned.

Intimacy focuses on emotional closeness to others while sensuality suggests a physical closeness. Relationships—friendships, family relationships, or romantic relationships—provide the vehicle for creating intimacy and give us a sense of belonging, connection, and affection. Romantic relationships may or may not include sexual contact, and sexual behavior can happen without emotional connections, but when it does, it is not nearly as fulfilling. Some aspects of intimacy include:

- *Liking or loving another person*—having a strong emotional attachment, or connection, to another.

- *Emotional risk-taking*—being open and honest; taking the risk to tell someone your true feelings, concerns, attitudes in spite of the possibility of being laughed at or rejected.
- *Reciprocity*—giving back to a person who gives to you.

As sexual beings, we have the opportunity to have intimacy with or without engaging in sexual behavior. A mature expression of sexuality often includes both intimacy and sexual behavior as two people express the fullness of their relationship with one another. However, sexual intimacy is often achieved through behaviors other than sexual intercourse.

3. Sexual identity is a person's understanding of who he/she is sexually, including his/her sense of being male or female.

Sexual identity can be thought of as having four different components that fit together to make one whole component that is a part of sexuality. Although each component is important in and of itself, the four components interact to affect how each person sees himself/herself:

- *Biological gender*—the physical package you are born with; females have a vulva, uterus, ovaries, XX chromosomes, and estrogen (hormone); males have a penis, testicles, XY chromosomes, and testosterone (hormone).
- *Gender identity*—your strong belief that you are either male or female; usually gender identity matches biological gender (the "physical package").
- *Gender role*—behaving in certain ways because of what you have been taught is appropriate for a male or female; what a female or male can or cannot do because of his/her gender; pressures to be "macho" or "feminine" affect a person's gender role behavior. These are learned behaviors.
- *Sexual orientation*—the direction of your romantic and sexual attractions: whether to persons of the same gender (gay/lesbian), the other gender (heterosexual), or both genders (bisexual); people do not choose their sexual orientation.

All youth struggle with sexual identity and need acceptance regardless of their gender identity or sexual orientation. They also need support and skills to resist the societal messages that seek to trap them in stereotypical roles and limit their future dreams and options.

4. Sexual health and reproduction, the most familiar aspects of sexuality, include all the behaviors and attitudes regarding reproduction and keeping the sexual systems of the body healthy.

While human sexuality is much more than just having sexual intercourse, it does include sexual intercourse and the human capacity to reproduce, although many individuals—the very young, the very old, some gay men and lesbians, people who do not desire children, infertile couples, for example—will not utilize that capacity. This component includes:

- *Facts about reproduction*—how the male and female reproductive systems work, how conception occurs, and how the fetus develops inside its mother.
- *Feelings and attitudes about sexual behavior*—values and opinions about sexual behavior and reproduction, especially pregnancy, parenthood, STDs, including HIV infection, use of contraception, etc.

- *Sexual intercourse*—having sexual intercourse of any kind—oral, anal, or vaginal—and dealing with the health risks related to each.
- *Contraception and risk reduction*—using effective methods of contraception to prevent pregnancy; taking steps to prevent STDs, including HIV infection; making decisions about forms of protection and discussing the subject with sexual partners; seeking preventative care from doctors, health clinics, and family planning centers as needed.

5. Sexualization is using sex or sexuality to influence, manipulate, or control other people.

These various forms of exploitation range from harmless manipulation to extreme violence.

- *Flirting*—sexualization when the flirt's intention is to manipulate or control; otherwise flirting can be a wonderful way of letting someone know you're attracted to them.
- *Seduction*—subtle (or not so subtle) pressure for sexual activity ("If you really loved me, you would . . ."). When it is mutual, seduction can be an aspect of intimacy.
- *Withholding sex or refusal of sexual activity*—sexualization when used as a negotiating or bargaining tool.
- *Sexual harassment*—any unwelcome sexual advances, requests for sexual favors, or other verbal or physical conduct of a sexual nature.
- *Rape/sexual assault*—sexual contact of any kind forced on one person by another, either using physical or psychological threats or brought about by taking advantage of someone who is unable to give his/her consent (for example, someone impaired by alcohol or other drugs).
- *Incest*—sexual intercourse between persons too closely related to legally marry.
- *Sexual abuse*—sexual contact between an adult and a minor child. Sexual abuse is sexual activity that is harmful or unwanted. Sexual abuse of a child is harmful sexual activity by an adult or significantly older child.

Sexualization is a reality in society, but using sexuality to manipulate or influence others is unhealthy and unethical. One of the goals of this program is to help youth avoid being exploited or exploiting others. Unfortunately, this experience is extremely common in our society. There are people in almost any group who have been abused or exploited in a sexual way. Encourage group members to feel free to talk privately with you about the issue of abuse or any other issues that they wish to discuss.

WORKSHOP 18 Sexuality and People with Disabilities

RATIONALE

People who have never experienced a physical or mental disability tend not to think about how such a condition might affect sexual expression. People with disabilities are invisible as sexual beings in this culture. If we live long enough, however, all of us will one day have a physical or mental disability. By asking participants to imagine how they would interact with other people if they had a disability, this workshop encourages participants to think about people with various disabilities as sexual beings.

NOTE: If your group includes participants with disabilities, this lesson should be carried out in such a way as to give these participants permission and safety to talk about the issue of disability and sexuality personally or not to do so as they choose. Well before this meeting, share with them the workshop design and elicit their input.

Time Required: 30 minutes

GOALS

To help participants
- explore their own values and attitudes regarding sexuality and disabilities.
- recognize that people with disabilities have sexual needs and expressions.
- think about how one could interact with a person with a disability in a sexual way.

OBJECTIVES

By the end of this workshop, participants will be able to
- demonstrate their understanding of the difficulties some people with disabilities face expressing their sexual needs and desires.
- demonstrate their understanding that people with disabilities are sexual beings by imagining themselves having a disability and wanting to express romantic or sexual interest in someone.
- show a recognition of the fact that people tend to discount those with disabilities as sexual beings by comparing how they think a person would respond to their overtures if they had a disability compared to how they would like that person to respond to them.

MATERIALS

None

PREPARATION

- Review this workshop and decide how to share leadership responsibilities with your coleader.
- Post the ground rules from the opening session.

Activity

IMAGING DISABILITIES   30 minutes

1. Tell the group that one group of people who are largely ignored in discussions of sexuality and in media images of sexuality, in addition to the elderly, are people with disabilities—a group that may include people they know. When people with disabilities are not ignored, their disabilities and their sexuality are often the subject of jokes. Laughter is often a coping mechanism to deal with things that make us uncomfortable and disabilities make many of us extremely uncomfortable.

NOTE: If there are only one or two people in your group who have obvious disabilities, it is important to address and acknowledge them. Tell the group that there are many people with disabilities and, although they might want to ask questions of one person, that person's experience cannot be generalized to all people with disabilities. Let the person(s) with disabilities decide whether he/she is comfortable sharing experiences or answering questions.

2. Divide participants into groups of three or four. Say the following: "Imagine that you are blind. You rely on a walking stick and a seeing eye dog or another person to help you get around." Ask,

- How do you think people would react to you?
- How would you like people to react to you?

Pause for 2 minutes to let participants discuss these questions in their groups. Then continue: "Now, each of you think about the last time you were interested in someone and wanted to let that person know. You wanted to make some connection with him or her that might lead to a more intimate relationship." Ask,

- How would you go about making that connection with your disability?
- Would it be more difficult with your disability?
- How do you think that person would react to you?
- How would you like that person to react to you?

Allow 3 minutes for small group discussion of these questions.

3. Repeat this exercise four times with each of the following disabilities. Imagine you

- are in a wheelchair, with paralyzed legs, unable to walk.
- have a severe speech impediment that makes it difficult for people to understand you when you talk.
- are mildly but observably retarded.
- have a severe facial disfigurement caused by burns sustained in a fire.

NOTE: You may choose to use different disabilities, depending on your group. The ones listed here were chosen to represent a range of disabilities. Do not use a scenario that would describe a member of your group.

4. Bring all the participants together to discuss the following questions:

- How did it feel to imagine yourself with various disabilities?
- Was it difficult to imagine yourself in these situations?
- Were certain disabilities more difficult to deal with than others when you were thinking about making a connection with someone you like? Which ones? Why would they be more difficult to deal with?
- Does this exercise make you think about how you react to or interact with people with disabilities?
- What factors would make it easier for a person with a disability to express romantic or sexual interest in someone else?

5. Conclude by saying, "This exercise helps us look at one group of people for whom society may make the expression of sexual needs and desires more difficult. We can pay attention to people we interact with who have some form of disability. Do we automatically discount them as sexual beings? Consider how they might see themselves. Think about how we might change how we see and behave toward others."

Variations of Imagining Disabilities Activity

1. If your group is small, keep the whole group together for this activity.

2. Conduct the activity as a series of role plays. Ask for a volunteer to play the role of a person with the disability you describe. Ask for additional actors to play the roles of peers without visible disabilities. Establish simple scenarios that provide familiar opportunities for interaction among a group of teenagers. For example, a youth with a disability is new to the school. He/she enters the cafeteria at lunch time and sits at a table where a group of students who know each other well are talking about an upcoming school dance. Another familiar scenario could involve a party in someone's house. Consider using props, such as a wheelchair. Have the whole group process each role play with the following questions:

Ask the ROLE PLAYERS

- How did it feel to play the role of a person with a disability?
- How did you react to the person with a disability?
- Was it difficult to play these roles? Why or why not?

Ask the OBSERVERS

- How did you feel watching this role play?
- What did you observe about the interactions of all the players?

Ask the WHOLE GROUP

- Does this exercise make you think about how you react to or interact with people with disabilities?
- What factors would make it easier for a person with a disability to express romantic or sexual interest in someone else?

RATIONALE

Our culture tends to assume and teach that heterosexual marriage is the only acceptable option for adult expressions of emotional and sexual intimacy. There are, however, a great many alternatives to heterosexual marriage that may be acceptable and even preferable. In this activity, participants learn about and clarify their values concerning some alternative relationships.

Time Required: 35 minutes

GOALS

To help participants
- develop an awareness of the wide variety of sexual relationships.
- determine which types of relationships would be acceptable to them.
- clarify their values concerning various types of relationships.

OBJECTIVES

By the end of this workshop, participants will be able to
- display a knowledge of a variety of sexual relationships by responding to definitions and completing a worksheet.
- identify their own feelings about a wide variety of sexual relationships.
- participate in a discussion about sexual relationships in which they share their feelings and opinions and listen to those of others.

MATERIALS

☐ Index cards
☐ Handout 11, How I Feel
☐ Leader Resource 16, Sexual Relationship Definitions
☐ Pens or pencils

Optional

☐ Handout 3, Our Whole Lives Program Values, from the parent orientation

PREPARATION

- Review this workshop and decide how to share leadership responsibilities with your coleader.
- Write each term and definition from Leader Resource 16, Sexual Relationship Definitions, on one side of an index card.

- Photocopy Handout 11, How I Feel, for all participants.
- If you wish to use it as a reference during the discussion, enlarge (or copy onto newsprint) and post Handout 3, Our Whole Lives Program Values.
- Post the ground rules from the opening session.

Activity

SEXUAL RELATIONSHIPS   25 minutes

1. Tell participants that this activity is about the ways in which people choose to express their sexuality over time. Make the point that, while we hear mostly about heterosexual marriage and living together, there are many ways for people to experience healthy relationships and express their sexuality. Some of these expressions may be familiar, while others may seem strange; some are chosen and some are not. Remind participants of the group's ground rules for sharing and discussing controversial or sensitive issues.

2. Distribute Handout 11, How I Feel, and pens or pencils to each participant. Explain that each participant will draw an index card that has a sexual relationship written on it. Tell participants that each one will read his/her card aloud and everyone will have a chance to ask the leaders clarifying questions about that definition. Say that after each definition has been read and questions answered, participants will fill in the corresponding parts of the worksheet, expressing how they feel about that type of sexual expression or relationship for themselves and for other people in their lives. Depending on the size of the group, some participants may draw more than one card. Let participants know that their worksheets will be private but that they will be invited to share selected parts of them with the group.

3. With cards face down, have one participant select a card and read it aloud. Answer any questions about the definition listed and then give participants about one minute to fill out their worksheets. Repeat the process until all cards have been read and worksheets have been completed.

SEXUAL RELATIONSHIPS DISCUSSION   10 minutes

1. Use the following questions to help participants share their perspectives:
- Was anything in this activity surprising to you?
- When you look at your completed worksheet, what impression do you get about yourself? Are you a fairly conservative person, a fairly open person, or somewhere in between?
- Does a person have control over the sexual expression or relationship they choose?
- What will you do if one of the relationships you are not comfortable with turns out to be practiced by a person close to you?
- What role do values play in your decisions about sexual expression and relationships?

2. Summarize by saying that it is important to understand that the most commonly practiced relationship is not always the best type for everyone. Individual needs and preferences are important; at different stages in our lives, we may find that different sexual relationships are more or less appropriate for us. Note that if a person is happy and healthy, then he/she should be able to practice and enjoy the sexual expression or relationship that satisfies him/her.

Handout 11

HOW I FEEL

Listen to the term and definition given. In each box below, write a word or phrase that expresses how you feel in each case.

To express *my* sexuality in this way would make me feel

1. Celibacy _____
2. Open marriage _____
3. Heterosexual marriage _____
4. Cohabitation _____
5. Gay/Lesbian "marriage" _____
6. Divorce _____
7. Child-free relationship _____
8. Interracial relationship _____
9. Polygamy/Polyandry _____
10. May-December relationship _____
11. Monogamy _____
12. Singlehood _____
13. Multiple serial relationships _____

If my *best friend* expressed his/her sexuality in this way, I would feel

1. Celibacy _____
2. Open marriage _____
3. Heterosexual marriage _____
4. Cohabitation _____
5. Gay/Lesbian "marriage" _____
6. Divorce _____
7. Child-free relationship _____
8. Interracial relationship _____
9. Polygamy/Polyandry _____
10. May-December relationship _____
11. Monogamy _____
12. Singlehood _____
13. Multiple serial relationships _____

If one or both of *my parents* expressed their sexuality in this way, I would feel

1. Celibacy _____
2. Open marriage _____
3. Heterosexual marriage _____
4. Cohabitation _____
5. Gay/Lesbian "marriage" _____
6. Divorce _____
7. Child-free relationship (Not applicable) _____
8. Interracial relationship _____
9. Polygamy/Polyandry _____
10. May-December relationship _____
11. Monogamy _____
12. Singlehood _____
13. Multiple serial relationships _____

If *my child* expressed her/his sexuality in this way, I would feel

1. Celibacy _____
2. Open marriage _____
3. Heterosexual marriage _____
4. Cohabitation _____
5. Gay/Lesbian "marriage" _____
6. Divorce _____
7. Child-free relationship (Not applicable) _____
8. Interracial relationship _____
9. Polygamy/Polyandry _____
10. May-December relationship _____
11. Monogamy _____
12. Singlehood _____
13. Multiple serial relationships _____

When I hear about *people I don't know* expressing their sexuality in this way, I feel

1. Celibacy _____

2. Open marriage _____

3. Heterosexual marriage _____

4. Cohabitation _____

5. Gay/Lesbian "marriage" _____

6. Divorce _____

7. Child-free relationship _____

8. Interracial relationship _____

9. Polygamy/Polyandry _____

10. May-December relationship _____

11. Monogamy _____

12. Singlehood _____

13. Multiple serial relationships _____

Leader Resource 16

SEXUAL RELATIONSHIP DEFINITIONS

CELIBACY   a person does not participate in any sexual behaviors, either with a partner or with him/herself.

CHILD-FREE RELATIONSHIP   two people in a long-term, committed relationship choose not to have or adopt children.

COHABITATION   intimate partners live together without a legal contract but typically are monogamous and emotionally committed to each other. For male/female couples, this may be a step between courtship and marriage or may never lead to marriage.

DIVORCE   the termination of a marriage through a legal process.

GAY/LESBIAN "MARRIAGE"   two people of the same gender live together with the same commitment and affection that may be found in a heterosexual marriage but without the legal status that is available only to heterosexual couples.

HETEROSEXUAL MARRIAGE   a legal and emotional bond between a man and a woman.

INTERRACIAL RELATIONSHIP   an intimate sexual and emotional relationship between two people of different races. The relationship may also include legal marriage.

MAY-DECEMBER RELATIONSHIP   an intimate sexual and emotional relationship between two people who differ in age by ten years or more. The partners may be an older man and younger woman, older woman and younger man, or a gay or lesbian couple with differing ages.

MONOGAMY   having one intimate partner/spouse and reserving sexual intimacy for that partner.

MULTIPLE SERIAL RELATIONSHIPS   a person moves from one relationship to another throughout her/his life rather than entering into a long-term committed relationship with one person. Each of these relationships may be long- or short-term.

OPEN MARRIAGE   legally married partners agree to have significant, intimate sexual relationships outside the marriage.

POLYGAMY/POLYANDRY   having more than one spouse or being one of a number of wives or husbands to one person.

SINGLEHOOD   not being involved in a significant, committed, long-term relationship with another person.

RATIONALE

Like the previous closure activity, this workshop gives participants the chance to reflect on the significant insights and feelings they have experienced during Sessions 4–6. Such deliberate contemplation enables them to incorporate new knowledge and understanding into their lives.

Time Required: 10 minutes

GOALS

To help participants
- find meaning in what they have learned in Sessions Four, Five, and Six.
- identify how they will use what they have learned in their own lives.

OBJECTIVES

By the end of this workshop, participants will be able to
- describe their beliefs and feelings about the topics in Sessions Four, Five, and Six.
- listen to others' beliefs and feelings about what they have learned and share their own.

MATERIALS

☐ Handout 12, Sentence Completions
☐ Pens or pencils

PREPARATION

- Review this workshop and decide how to share leadership responsibilities with your coleader.
- Make a photocopy of Handout 12, Sentence Completions, for each participant.
- Post the ground rules from the opening session.

Activity

SENTENCE COMPLETIONS   10 minutes

1. Distribute copies of Handout 12, Sentence Completions, and pencils or pens. Ask participants to take five minutes to complete the sentences on the worksheets. Tell them that they will not be asked to hand in the worksheets but they will be invited to share at least one item with the rest of the group.

2. After five minutes, go around the group and ask each person to share at least one completed sentence from his/her worksheet.

3. Thank participants for their hard work in these workshops.

Handout 12

SENTENCE COMPLETIONS

I learned that a person's sexual orientation

I learned that being pregnant is

I learned that being a parent is

I learned that if I ever have children, I will

I learned that how a person expresses his/her sexuality is

I learned that if I became disabled in some way, my sexuality

If I discovered that someone close to me was expressing her/his sexuality in an untraditional relationship, I would

I think that the way I express my sexuality now is

WORKSHOP 21 **Verbal and Nonverbal Communication**

RATIONALE

To have healthy relationships, partners need to understand and be understood by each other. This workshop helps participants think about how they communicate nonverbally (consciously and unconsciously) as well as verbally. It provides opportunities to practice expressing and interpreting difficult nonverbal and verbal messages using facial expressions, touch, and language.

Time Required: 40 minutes

GOALS

To help participants understand

• the role of nonverbal communication in sexual relationships.
• the importance of making nonverbal messages consistent with verbal messages.
• the possibility of misinterpreting nonverbal messages because of individual differences in communication styles.
• the role of facial expressions and physical touch in relating emotions, thoughts, needs, and desires.
• how verbal and nonverbal communication interact.

OBJECTIVES

By the end of this workshop, participants will be able to

• demonstrate an understanding of the importance of nonverbal communication by naming ways in which nonverbal communication plays a role in sexual relationships.
• demonstrate an understanding of the role of both verbal and nonverbal communication in relationships by stating ways in which they interact.
• discuss actions they might take in future relationships to reduce the possibility of sending mixed messages or of being misinterpreted.

MATERIALS

☐ Blue, yellow, and white index cards. (Having cards of different colors is not strictly necessary but will make it easier to keep the cards for different activities straight.)
☐ Leader Resource 17, Communication Cards
☐ Leader Resource 28, Communication Scenarios

Optional

□ a bell or chime to call time

PREPARATION

- Review this workshop and decide how to share leadership responsibilities with your coleader.
- For the Facial Expressions activity, make six blue index cards for each pair of participants. On each blue card, print a statement describing an emotion for participants to express using facial expressions only. Use sentences from Leader Resource 17, Communication Cards, or make up your own. Choose statements that are suited to the maturity level and sophistication of your group; make sure each pair has both difficult and easy emotions to express. You may decide to use the same emotions for every pair, or to vary the cards so that the teams have different statements with which to work.
- For the Touch activity, prepare six yellow index cards for each pair of participants. On each card, print a statement from Leader Resource 17, Communication Cards, or write your own statements expressing a desire for or concern about a relationship. Use the same guidelines for selecting sentences as in the Facial Expressions activity.
- For the Role-Play activity, photocopy the scenarios from Leader Resource 18, Communication Scenarios, cut them apart, and paste them onto white index cards. There should be a complete set of scenario cards for each pair.
- You may wish to bring in a pleasant-sounding bell or chime to call time, as you will be signaling the group at 30-second intervals.
- Post the ground rules from the opening session.

Activities

FACIAL EXPRESSIONS   8 minutes

1. Divide participants into pairs. If you have an uneven number, have one person act as an observer/recorder. Be sure there is at least one male/male pair, one female/female pair, and one male/female pair.

2. Explain that this activity is designed to explore the ways in which we communicate with each other without using words or language. Ask, "Can anyone think of any ways we communicate without using words?" Allow a few people to call out some answers; then explain that participants are going to take turns sending messages to their partners using only facial expressions.

3. Give each dyad six blue cards face down, three to each person. (Be sure each person has both difficult and easy expressions to communicate.) Tell participants they are not to look at the cards until they are instructed to do so.

4. Have participants decide which member of the dyad will go first. Then give the following instructions:

> The person you have chosen to go first is the sender, and the other player is the receiver. After I give the signal to start, the sender should look at his/her first card (without showing it to anyone) and take a few seconds to express the state-

ment on the card using facial expressions only. The receiver should then begin guessing what message the sender is trying to send. When the receiver understands the message correctly, the sender will say "yes" and you will stop and wait until the other pairs are ready. You will have about 30 seconds for each card. After the sender has completed three cards, you will switch roles and the receiver will become the sender.

5. Play the game with each of the six cards. Do not allow a great deal of discussion during the game.

6. When all pairs have finished, ask participants to keep their cards so they can discuss the activity later.

TOUCH   8 minutes

1. Give each dyad a set of six yellow cards, face down, three cards to each player. Tell participants that they may not look at their cards until they are instructed to do so. Give the following instructions:

> Now we are going to do the same kind of activity, but we are going to use *only* our sense of touch. First, both of you should close your eyes, join hands, and without talking, determine which one of you will be the sender first. When you have decided this, the senders should open their eyes, read their cards silently, turn them over, take their partners' hands again, and try to relay the message to the receiver using only touch.
>
> There are three rules: you may not touch in any way that will cause pain; you may only touch hands; and you must maintain touch throughout the exercise. After a few seconds, the receiver may try to guess what the sender is trying to convey. If the receiver is correct, the sender should stop and pat the receiver's hand three times. I will call time after 30 seconds. When the first sender has used three cards, you will switch roles.

2. Continue the game until all six yellow cards have been played. Allow 30 seconds after each card is drawn and make sure that receivers keep their eyes closed and refrain from talking. Also, watch to see that all touching remains appropriate to the activity.

3. Ask participants to keep their cards so that they will be able to discuss the activity later.

COMMUNICATION ROLE PLAY   8 minutes

1. Explain that the next part of this activity involves using both verbal and nonverbal communication. Ask the members of each pair to face each other and determine who will be A and who will be B. Explain that you are going to hand out index cards with situations that participants will have two minutes to act out.

2. Hand out the first set of cards and allow participants about two minutes to act out the scene. Repeat the process for the second and third sets of cards.

DISCUSSION

1. Bring participants together for a discussion of the activity, using the following questions:

  • What was easy about communicating using only facial expressions? Using touch?

  • Which messages and/or feelings were most difficult to express?

  • Was it harder to *send* a nonverbal message or to *interpret* one?

  • What was surprising to you? Did you think you were sending a clear message and then discover that it was not clear to your partner?

  • What are some of the differences in the way you communicate verbally and nonverbally with your parents and with your friends? What about with sexual partners?

  • How did the people in same-gender pairs feel during these activities? [Have the group consider and talk about how homophobia can interfere with clear communication between people of the same gender.]

  • What about the mixed-gender pairs? Are there differences in the ways men and women communicate nonverbally?

  • In what ways does nonverbal communication play a role in sexual relationships?

  • In what ways did you use, or could you have used, nonverbal communication to support your words when you were acting out the situations?

  • How could a person send mixed messages using verbal and nonverbal communication?

  • How might you use what you learned in this activity to enhance your nonverbal communication in the future?

2. Conclude the workshop by saying something like:

> Communication in intimate relationships can take many forms. How we come to meet and become interested in another person is often a direct result of nonverbal communication. How we continue to grow and become more involved with others can be either helped or hurt by our nonverbal communication. The gender of the person with whom we are interacting can have an effect on how we send and interpret messages, but our own needs, motivations, and background can also affect the way we communicate. As we have seen, it is important that both our verbal and nonverbal messages be clear and consistent if we are to be understood and respected.

Leader Resource 17

COMMUNICATION CARDS

For the Facial Expressions activity, choose six of the following statements or write your own:

I feel angry.

I feel sad.

I feel happy.

I am surprised.

I am proud.

I am jealous.

I am suspicious.

I am aroused.

I am scared.

I am excited.

For the Touch activity, choose six of the following sentences or write your own:

I am impatient with you.

I am confused about us.

I'm feeling guilty.

I am not interested in you.

I am sorry that I did that to you.

I'm here for you.

I respect you a great deal.

I am very attracted to you.

I want to get to know you better.

You are making me uncomfortable.

Leader Resource 18

COMMUNICATION SCENARIOS

Scenario One

PARTNER A: You just got a new haircut. The style is very different from your last hair-cut, and you're not sure of it. Although you think it's pretty cool, you ask your friend B's advice about it; you can probably change it if your friend really thinks it's awful. You know B will be honest. Ask B what he/she thinks about your hair.

PARTNER B: Your friend A asks you what you think about his/her new haircut. You think it looks really awful. Because A asked, you tell your friend your true feelings.

Scenario Two

PARTNER A: You and B have gone out on one date. You really like B and would like an-other date with him/her. Ask B for another date.

PARTNER B: You think A is a nice person, but you do not really want to pursue a rela-tionship with him/her. When B asks you out again, find a way to say no.

Scenario Three

PARTNER A: You and B have been dating for a few months, and you have both decided that you do not want to have sexual intercourse or do anything that might result in STDs or pregnancy. You get really excited when you are with B and want to be sexu-ally intimate, but you don't want to take risks. Tell B how you feel.

PARTNER B: You and A have been dating for a few months, and you have both decided that you do not want to have sexual intercourse or do anything that might result in STDs or pregnancy. Now, A wants to be sexually intimate with you, and although you don't object to safe acts, you want A to be clear about what you are both willing to do before things get too hot and heavy.

What Makes a Good Relationship?

RATIONALE

Whether one is already involved in significant relationships or just beginning to seek them out, it is useful for every individual to understand what he/she values and needs most. This workshop gives participants the opportunity to identify and prioritize the important characteristics of a healthy relationship. By listening to the ideas of their peers, participants gain additional insights into what makes a good relationship.

Time Required: 45 minutes

GOALS

To help participants
- think about what they are seeking or might seek in the future in a life partner relationship.
- prioritize these characteristics for themselves.
- learn which characteristics are most important for their peers.

OBJECTIVES

By the end of this workshop, participants will be able to
- share their ideas about what makes a good relationship.
- demonstrate the ability to prioritize relationship characteristics by choosing the single most important characteristic for themselves.
- show an ability to discern reasons for their choice by explaining it to the group.

MATERIALS

☐ At least 30 sheets of 8 1/2" × 11" paper
☐ Newsprint, markers, and masking tape

PREPARATION

- Review this workshop and decide how to share leadership responsibilities with your coleader.
- Post the ground rules from the opening session.

Activity

WHAT MAKES A GOOD RELATIONSHIP? 45 minutes

1. Begin by telling participants that people are attracted to one another and enter into sexual relationships with each other for many different reasons. Explain that this workshop will help everyone think about which of these reasons are most important for them.

2. Ask for volunteers to act as recorders. Use as many volunteers as you wish, as long as there are enough markers for each to have one. Give each recorder a marker and a stack of blank paper. Tell the group that you would like them to name all of the characteristics that they might look for in developing a lasting relationship with someone. As participants offer ideas, have volunteers take turns writing each one in big letters on a sheet of paper.

The group may come up with as many as twenty to thirty characteristics. If participants have difficulty getting started, suggest a few of these:

- attractiveness
- honesty
- faithfulness
- good sex
- same religion
- same age
- same race
- good looks

- trust
- sense of humor
- similar interests
- same political beliefs
- love
- equality
- good communication

3. After about 5 minutes, or when the group has exhausted its ideas, have the recorders hang the sheets on the walls around the room. Invite participants to look at all of the characteristics and decide which one they think is the most important in establishing and maintaining a good long-term relationship. Each person may choose only one characteristic, even though they are likely to think many are important. Ask participants to stand near the sheet with the characteristic most important to them.

4. After everyone has chosen a characteristic, give participants a few minutes to think about why they believe the characteristic is the most important one and, if there are other people standing at the same sheet, to talk with the others about why they have chosen that one.

5. Go around the room and ask participants to explain why they chose the characteristic they did. Point out that people may have chosen the same characteristic for different reasons. For participants who have difficulty articulating the reasons for their choices, the following prompts may be helpful:

- What is so important to you about this characteristic?
- Why is it more important than some of the other characteristics?
- Is there a relationship between the characteristic you chose and some of the other characteristics?

Tell participants that if they hear something that changes their minds, they may move to a new trait and share their reasons for the move.

6. After everyone has had an opportunity to explain her/his choice, bring the group back together to discuss the activity, using some of the questions below.

- Are there themes in the choices that people made?
- How can you tell if a person or a relationship has a particular characteristic that you are looking for?
- Do you have the characteristics you identified as most important?
- Were you surprised by anything you heard?
- Did you change your mind about what is important to you in a relationship?
- Would your choice have been different if we had asked for the most important characteristic in a relationship with a best friend? How would it have been similar?
- What traits or characteristics were really easy to dismiss as less important?
- Which characteristics were almost as important as your first choice?
- Was it hard to choose just one?
- How might your priorities for relationships be different at a later time in your life?

7. Ask participants if they can reach a consensus on the most important traits for a healthy relationship. Give the group a few minutes to list these on newsprint. (You may wish to save this list for use in Workshop 27.) Then ask the group to consider what characteristics might lead to an unhealthy relationship.

8. Conclude by saying something like, "People usually have many reasons for choosing a partner or choosing to stay with a partner. Sometimes, however, it doesn't make sense to start or stay in a relationship if something very important is missing. For example, if sharing the same religion is a priority for a person, then it might be a good idea not to become involved with someone of a different religion. It is useful to think about these issues before starting a relationship, because once you are in a relationship, it is often more difficult to maintain your priorities. Similarly, you may not think that something is important, but you find once you are in a relationship that it is. Can someone give me an example in which this might be the case? It is important to identify what is missing or negative in our relationships so that we can learn and grow and avoid similar problems in the future."

Questions of the Other Gender

RATIONALE

The ability to discuss specific, personal sexual issues is essential for good sexual communication. This workshop gives participants the opportunity to practice asking such questions as well as answering the questions that others pose to them. The more participants practice talking about sex-related topics, the easier it will be for them to have necessary conversations with sexual partners in the future. Because this workshop involves men asking questions of women and vice versa, it gives both genders insight into similarities and differences between and within gender groups.

Time Required: 60 minutes

GOALS

To help participants
- practice communicating about sexual issues.
- become more comfortable asking and answering questions about sex and sexuality.
- gain any information they seek about the sexuality of another gender.

OBJECTIVES

By the end of this workshop, participants will be able to
- identify questions they have about the other gender by writing them down.
- demonstrate increased comfort discussing sex-related issues.

MATERIALS

☐ Newsprint, at least four markers, and masking tape

Optional

☐ Index cards

PREPARATION

- Review this workshop and decide how to share leadership responsibilities with your coleader.
- Choose either the standard approach to conducting this activity or one of the two alternatives.
- Post the ground rules from the opening session.

Activity

QUESTIONS OF THE OTHER GENDER   60 minutes

1. Tell participants that being able to talk about sexual issues, to ask questions and to answer them, is important, even though it can be embarrassing or difficult. Explain that this workshop will provide a chance to practice asking questions and having them answered.

2. Divide participants into two same-gender groups. Give each group at least two markers and two sheets of newsprint. Tell the groups that they will have 15 minutes to write all of the questions they have about the other gender. Explain that the questions can be about any subject but they must be directed to the other group in general, not to any specific person. All questions posed by members of the group should be written down; the group does not need to reach consensus on the questions to be asked. Advise the groups that after they have written their questions, they will trade lists and provide answers to the other group's questions. Ask participants to leave enough space between questions to write answers.

   NOTE: This might be a good time to review the group's ground rules, particularly the following:
   • No direct questions toward a particular person.
   • No killer statements (or questions) or put-downs.
   • Respect different ideas and opinions.
   • Allow one another to speak and be heard.
   • Maintain confidentiality within the small group discussions (authorship of specific questions should not be revealed; the list belongs to the entire group).
   • Everyone has the right to pass.

3. After 15 minutes, have the groups trade lists. Ask them to spend 15 minutes thinking about and writing answers to the questions posed by the other group. Encourage participants to answer as truthfully as possible since they will want to receive answers that are truthful. If there is no consensus on a single answer to a question, groups may provide more than one answer. Suggest that participants write their answers beneath each question in a different colored marker.

4. After 15 minutes, ask each group to post the questions and answers on the wall. Give everyone 5 minutes to read the answers silently. Then have the groups take turns choosing questions about which they would like additional clarification or information. Have each group respond accordingly. Remind participants that no one is required to speak on any particular question or to speak at all. Encourage participants to provide as much accurate information from their own perspectives as they can comfortably. Allow groups to go back and forth asking and answering questions for 20 minutes.

5. Even if all questions have not been answered, take about 5 minutes for discussion, using questions such as:
   • How did it feel doing this activity?
   • Was this activity useful or helpful in any way?
   • Did anyone learn anything new about the other gender?
   • Did anyone learn anything new about his/her own gender?

Alternatives

1. The standard approach to this activity as described above gives participants the opportunity to discuss their answers to the other group's questions within their same-gender group before answering the questions face-to-face. If your participants are ready for more direct interaction, have the groups post their lists of questions and then immediately begin a give-and-take question and answer period. While it can be much more threatening and difficult to respond to questions without preparation, the process can provide a more honest and realistic experience.

2. If your group seems particularly shy or reticent, and you feel that generating questions within a group might be too threatening, have participants write their questions anonymously on index cards. Give each participant at least three or four cards. While providing more participant anonymity, this approach also increases the possibility of inappropriate questions. Therefore, you will want to collect the cards from participants, shuffle them, and then read the questions. Do not edit or censor sincere questions but eliminate truly inappropriate questions or comments, such as those directed at specific participants. Then divide the cards into piles for males and females, divide participants into same-gender groups, and have the groups write their responses either on newsprint or on the cards themselves.

Intimacy, Masturbation, and Lovemaking **8**

WORKSHOP 24 **Defining Intimacy**

RATIONALE

Throughout life, human beings need intimacy to survive. Infants thrive with cuddling, holding, and caressing; children enjoy sitting on a parent's lap, holding hands with friends, sharing dreams and fantasies. Many adolescents meet their need for intimate contact through sexual behavior. It is important, however, for young people to realize that closeness can be found within many different relationships and shared in many different ways. This workshop helps participants expand their definition of interpersonal intimacy beyond genital and sexual intimacy. Participants are encouraged to consider how they can experience the feeling of intimacy through emotional, intellectual, and platonic relationships with people of any gender and by themselves.

Time Required: 25 minutes

GOALS

To help participants to
- understand that intimacy does not have to be expressed genitally or sexually.
- recognize the value of a variety of interpersonal relationships with people of other genders.
- consider the importance of platonic, emotional, and intellectual closeness with another person.
- understand that a person can enjoy intimacy by himself/herself.

OBJECTIVES

By the end of this workshop, participants will be able to
- demonstrate an understanding that intimacy can be experienced in a variety of ways by filling out a worksheet describing intimate behaviors.
- demonstrate an understanding that intimacy can be experienced within a variety of different relationships by writing the names of different people with whom they would like to share various activities.
- show recognition that people can enjoy activities by themselves by identifying such activities.

MATERIALS

☐ Handout 13, With Whom Would You Do It?
☐ Pens or pencils

PREPARATION

- Review this workshop and decide how to share leadership responsibilities with your coleader.
- Photocopy Handout 13, With Whom Would You Do It? for all participants.
- Post the ground rules from the opening session.

Activity

WITH WHOM WOULD YOU DO IT? (Part 1)   25 minutes

1. Introduce this activity by saying that as human beings, we all crave intimacy, or closeness to another person. Point out that intimate relationships are essential to our health and survival, but where we find intimacy depends a lot on how we think about intimacy for ourselves. Quite often people define intimacy very narrowly as explicitly sexual behavior and often only with people in whom we are romantically interested. Tell participants that, in this workshop, they are going to consider pleasurable and intimate activities other than genital ones, and kinds of closeness other than sexual closeness.

2. Give each person a copy of Handout 13, With Whom Would You Do It? Ask participants what comes to mind when they hear the expression "do it." Sexual intercourse is often assumed to be the most intimate act. Say that they are going to consider other forms of intimacy.

3. Ask participants to list on Handout 13 the name of a male and a female with whom they would choose to do each activity. They may use names more than once. Ask them to add any other activities that they think would be pleasurable or intimate and to fill in a male and female name for each of these activities. Stress that the handouts will not be collected; participants should not put their names on them. Explain that these handouts are for their personal use only. Allow participants 10 to 15 minutes to fill in the handout.

4. After participants have filled in the names of males and females, ask them to go over the list again and circle those activities they would enjoy doing alone.

5. When participants have finished, take 10 or 15 minutes to discuss the activity. Use the following questions to stimulate discussion:

- Was it harder to come up with male or female names for most of the activities? [Males usually have more difficulty with males, and females, to a lesser degree, with females.] How do homophobia and heterosexism interfere with our ability to think about intimacy with people of the same gender? [Note that homophobia may be defined as fear or hatred of people who are gay, lesbian, bisexual, or transgender. Homophobia may be manifest in acts of violence, ridicule, discrimination, or exclusion. Heterosexism is the assumption that all people are heterosexual or should be.] How does heterosexism interfere with our willingness to engage in activities with someone of the same gender, even when those activities are not sexual?
- Did you use different criteria for partners for different activities? Why are some people appropriate for some activities but not for others?
- Which of these activities are based on relationships in which there is emotional closeness? Physical closeness? Intellectual closeness? Other kinds of closeness?

- Was there anything similar about the activities you enjoy doing by yourself? Did it surprise you to see a list of activities you would enjoy by yourself?
- Did any of the names you put on your list surprise you?
- Did you learn anything interesting about yourself?

6. Conclude by saying that we need intimacy throughout our lives and express that need in a variety of ways. Note that sexual or genital intimacy may not always be possible or desirable. There are people with whom we might like to share intimacy but not sexual activity. In addition, we all have times in our lives when we are alone, but being alone does not have to mean being lonely. Often being by ourselves can be enjoyable as well as healthy.

Handout 13

WITH WHOM WOULD YOU DO IT?

	Male	*Female*
Spend an evening in front of a fire	_____	_____
Dine at an elegant restaurant	_____	_____
Go on a picnic	_____	_____
Go to a basketball game	_____	_____
Drive across the country	_____	_____
Work on a school project	_____	_____
Sleep in a hammock	_____	_____
Go sailing	_____	_____
Spend a weekend in a mountain cabin	_____	_____
Share personal problems	_____	_____
Change clothes in front of	_____	_____
Dance	_____	_____
Get a backrub from	_____	_____
Go to a concert	_____	_____
Share secrets	_____	_____
Go shopping for clothes for yourself	_____	_____
Go skinny-dipping	_____	_____
Discuss your future	_____	_____

Masturbation Myths and Facts

RATIONALE

Much of the common wisdom about masturbation is both negative and inaccurate. Masturbation is not physically harmful, and it can be a safe and even educational form of sexual expression for people of all ages. This workshop is designed to clarify facts and dispel myths about masturbation and to provide opportunities for participants to explore their own beliefs about and level of comfort with the subject.

Time Required: 30 minutes

GOALS

To help participants
- identify the messages they have received about sex and masturbation from a variety of sources and determine whether those messages were positive or negative.
- explore myths and facts about masturbation.
- discuss their own fears, feelings, and concerns about masturbation.

OBJECTIVES

By the end of this workshop, participants will be able to
- identify the connotation embedded in some of the messages they have received about sex and masturbation.
- distinguish myths from facts about masturbation and know correct factual information to counter each myth.
- demonstrate an understanding of the benefits and/or risks associated with masturbation.

MATERIALS

☐ Four large index cards
☐ Leader Resource 19, Myths and Facts About Sex and Masturbation
☐ One box of graham crackers or Kellogg's Corn Flakes™ wrapped in foil or wrapping paper.

PREPARATION

- Review this workshop and decide how to share leadership responsibilities with your coleader.
- Write MYTH on two of the index cards and FACT on the other two.

- Become familiar with Leader Resource 19, Myths and Facts About Sex and Masturbation. Decide which facts and myths to discuss with your group; you may choose to use only the questions about masturbation or to use questions about the other topics as well.
- Post the ground rules from the opening session.

Activities

MESSAGES ABOUT SEX
10 minutes

1. Explain that this workshop focuses on masturbation. Acknowledge that people often find this subject difficult or embarrassing to discuss and that the group will explore why this topic may cause more discomfort than other topics in this program. Encourage participants to be aware of how comfortable or uncomfortable they feel throughout the workshop.

2. Divide participants into two groups of equal size. Have one group form a circle with all participants facing outward. Have the second group form a circle around the first group facing inward. All participants should align themselves so that they are standing face to face with another participant.

3. Explain that you will give participants an issue to discuss and that each person will have one minute to talk; after one minute, the second partner will talk. After each partner has talked, the inner circle will rotate in a clockwise direction so that everyone has a new partner, and you will provide a new statement for the dyads to discuss.

4. Begin with the following topic:
- What your parents or other adult family members told you about sex when you were a child. After each partner has spoken for the allotted time, have the inner circle rotate and begin again. Repeat this process for each of the following topics:
- What your parents or other adult family members told you about masturbation when you were a child.
- What your peers or siblings told you about sex and masturbation when you were a child.
- The messages you currently receive about sex and masturbation.

5. Help participants process this activity by using the following questions to stimulate discussion:
- How did it feel to discuss sex and masturbation in this way?
- Were the messages you received during childhood generally positive or negative?
- How do you think the messages you received have influenced your current feelings about sex and masturbation?

MYTHS AND FACTS ABOUT SEX AND MASTURBATION
20 minutes

1. Have the two groups from the last activity form two teams.

2. Explain that this is a game about masturbation myths and facts. You will read a statement aloud and each team will have to determine whether the statement is a myth or a fact. When the team has an answer, one member of the team should hold up either the MYTH or FACT card. The team that gets the correct answer first will re-

ceive one point, and that team will have a chance to earn an additional point by giving the correct information if the statement is a myth.

3. Give each team one MYTH card and one FACT card. Using Leader Resource 19, Myths and Facts About Sex and Masturbation, read a statement aloud and determine which team has the correct answer first. If the statement is a myth, ask the team to supply the correct information, and use the information on Leader Resource 20 to supplement the team's information.

4. When all the questions have been asked or there is no more time, determine which team has won and give it the wrapped box as a prize. Explain as members open the package that graham crackers and Kellogg's cereals were invented as calming, mild foods which were to be given to children to inhibit their sexual urges. It was believed that if children masturbated it would cause mental illness or lower intelligence. Ask participants how many of them were given graham crackers as children. Read the following quote about masturbation by J.H. Kellogg. M.D., inventor of corn flakes.

> In solitude he pollutes himself, and with his own hand blights all his prospects for both this world and the next. Even after being solemnly warned, he will often continue this worse than beastly practice, deliberately forfeiting his right to health and happiness for a moment's mad sensuality.
>
> J.H. Kellogg, M.D., *Plain Facts for Old and Young*, 1882.

5. Have the winning team share its prize with the other team. Summarize by discussing how myths and misinformation about masturbation have been passed on throughout history and how we are often influenced by what was believed long ago, even when we realize that the old information is incorrect. Conclude by saying that masturbation is healthy and natural, and only becomes a problem if a person feels guilty about it or does it to the exclusion of all other activities.

Leader Resource 19

MYTHS AND FACTS ABOUT SEX AND MASTURBATION

1. Most women masturbate by inserting something (finger, cucumber, dildo) into their vaginas.

MYTH. Most women masturbate by using their fingers to directly or indirectly stimulate their clitoris and labia.

2. Woman are more likely to have orgasms with clitoral stimulation than with vaginal stimulation alone.

FACT. In fact, most women are not able to experience orgasm with vaginal stimulation alone; they need clitoral stimulation.

3. Sexual fantasies are always about things we secretly want to do.

MYTH. Sexual fantasies are frequently about things we do not really want to do in real life but are curious about or feel turned on by thinking about.

4. If a person masturbates a lot during adolescence, he/she will not enjoy sexual experiences with a partner as much when he/she is older.

MYTH. Masturbating is a good way for young people to express their sexual feelings safely. It can also help people discover what kinds of stimulation they like so that they can share that information with sexual partners and thus have more pleasurable sexual experiences in the future.

5. Boys who masturbate together in groups are *not* showing early signs of being gay.

FACT. Some boys masturbate together in groups during adolescence. This form of sex play has more to do with curiosity and competition than with sexual orientation. Both gay and straight boys participate in this kind of group masturbation.

6. If members of a couple masturbate, something is lacking in their sexual relationship.

MYTH. Masturbating privately and/or as part of a couple's shared sexual expression is common among married or partnered couples and does not at all indicate sexual problems. Sometimes one partner may want sex when the other does not. Also, orgasms experienced during masturbation are often different from those experienced with a partner, and sometimes a person will want to have the masturbation experience rather than the partner experience. Some people find watching their partner masturbate or being watched while masturbating to be very arousing.

7. If a man gets an erection he needs to have an orgasm, or the erection will be very painful.

MYTH AND FACT. For some men, especially younger men, an erection may become painful. The erection will, however, go away with or without orgasm. A man may choose to masturbate to relieve the sexual tension in a pleasurable and relaxing way. It is not harmful for a man to have an erection and not have an orgasm; it is certainly never a reason to have unsafe or coerced sexual intercourse.

8. A lesbian will be attracted to anybody who is female and a gay man will be attracted to anybody who is male.

MYTH. Just as heterosexual females are not attracted to all men, lesbians are not attracted to all women; and just as heterosexual males are not attracted to all women, gay men are not attracted to all men.

9. A man always wants and is ready to have sex.

MYTH. The belief that men are always interested in and ready for sex is a stereotype. Men often think that they should be ready for sex all the time and are worried when they are not. Both men and women experience sexual desire and readiness on and off throughout their lives. It is common for people to be uninterested in sex from time to time and should not be of concern unless the lack of interest in sex becomes a problem for a couple or an individual who may want to experience more sexual desire.

10. Once a man gets turned on to a certain point with a partner, he just cannot stop.

MYTH. There is never a point at which a person cannot stop or ask his/her partner to stop. If a man is having intercourse and he thinks he can stop before he ejaculates, he may find he is not able to pull out in time, and the couple may risk pregnancy or STD transmission. Being turned on, however, even being very aroused, is a condition that can be stopped and is never an excuse for unsafe or coerced sex.

RATIONALE

Teenagers often participate in sexual acts that are very physically intimate without being able to talk about what is happening. This workshop defines many sexual behaviors in a nonthreatening manner and gives participants the opportunity to consider whether or not they would participate in such acts and with whom. Through this activity, young people may improve their ability to make choices rather than just "let things happen" and to think about sexual behaviors within the context of loving, intimate relationships.

Time Required: 35 minutes

GOALS

To help participants
- learn the names and definitions of a wide range of specific sexual behaviors.
- explore their own feelings and values about the sexual behaviors defined in this workshop and determine whether they would participate in those acts and with whom.

OBJECTIVES

By the end of this workshop, participants will be able to
- discuss the definitions of a wide range of sexual behaviors.
- determine for themselves which behaviors they would consider participating in and with whom.

MATERIALS

☐ Index cards
☐ Leader Resource 20, Sexual Behaviors Definitions
☐ Handout 14, Sexual Behaviors Continuum
☐ Pencils or pens

PREPARATION

- Review this workshop and decide how to share leadership responsibilities with your coleader.
- Prepare the sexual behaviors cards as described in Leader Resource 20, Sexual Behaviors Definitions.
- Photocopy Handout 14, Sexual Behaviors Continuum, for all participants.
- Post the ground rules from the opening session.

Activity

WITH WHOM WOULD YOU DO IT? (Part 2)   35 minutes

1. Explain that this activity defines a wide variety of sexual behaviors. Remind participants that there is no assumption that they have or have not engaged in any particular sexual behaviors and that people find some sexual acts appealing and others unappealing. Remind the group not to judge others.

2. Give each participant a copy of Handout 14, Sexual Behaviors Continuum, and a pen or pencil. Explain that when they hear a sexual behavior named, they should write that behavior on their continuum, placing it under or near the type of relationship in which that act would be comfortable to them. Point out that one choice is "no one." Be sure participants understand that they may choose places between the headings as well as under them. Also inform participants that they should not put their names on the handouts and that they will not be asked to share what they write.

3. Shuffle the sexual behaviors cards and spread them face down in no particular order. Have a participant select a card and read the act and, if provided, its definition. Allow participants to ask any questions they have, before writing the act on their continuums. Repeat this process with a new participant and a new card. Go through as many cards as time allows or as otherwise appropriate.

4. Help the group process the activity with the following questions:

- How did it feel to do this activity?
- What was surprising to you?
- Were you able to put the acts in certain places? Were some acts harder than others to place?
- What personal values were important in making decisions about these sexual behaviors?
- Did you consider how safe the act was in terms of STDs? Pregnancy? Emotional risks?
- Do you think you might consider certain acts at different times in your life?

5. Summarize by explaining that sometimes young people become sexually active without thinking about the meaning of the acts in which they are participating. Many people begin their sexual experiences without knowing the variety of sexual behaviors and the many ways in which people can express their sexuality without intercourse.

6. Ask participants to bring in at least one example of a popular song or music video that deals with love, sex, or relationships for the next workshop. They may bring in a CD, cassette, videotape, DVD, or printed lyrics to read to the group. Plan to bring in your own examples and to have audio and video equipment for the samples.

Leader Resource 20

SEXUAL BEHAVIORS DEFINITIONS

Instructions: Write each of the following sexual behaviors on an index card with its definition when supplied and if needed. You may choose to use all the behaviors listed, select specific ones, or add your own to meet your group's needs and time limits.

- *Hold hands*
- *Dry kiss:* mouth to mouth kissing in which both people's mouths remain closed.
- *French kiss:* mouth to mouth kissing in which both people's mouths are open and their tongues touch.
- *Get undressed:* Changing clothes or disrobing so that another person sees you nude or partially nude.
- *Cuddle*
- *Spoon:* Sleeping or lying down with another person like spoons in a drawer [make a diagram on the card].
- *Give a massage:* rubbing and kneading the shoulders, neck, and back of another person.
- *Get a massage:* allowing another person to rub and stroke your shoulders, neck, and back.
- *Skinny-dip:* swimming in the nude.
- *Stimulate someone's nipples:* touching or kissing someone's nipples.
- *Have your nipples stimulated*
- *Take a shower*
- *Lick someone's ears, or have your ears licked*
- *Read erotic books*
- *Watch an erotic movie or video*
- *Fondle someone's genitals:* touching or stimulating another person's genitals.
- *Have someone fondle your genitals*
- *Watch another person masturbate*
- *Masturbate in front of someone*
- *Give fellatio:* sucking, licking, and stimulating a man's penis with your mouth.
- *Give cunnilingus:* sucking, licking, and stimulating a woman's vulva with your mouth.
- *Receive oral sex (fellatio or cunnilingus):* having another person use his or her mouth and tongue to stimulate your genitals.
- *Have vaginal intercourse*
- *Insertive anal intercourse:* putting your penis into another person's anus.
- *Receptive anal intercourse:* having a man put his penis in your anus.

Handout 14

SEXUAL BEHAVIORS CONTINUUM

I would participate in this behavior with

Someone I just met	Someone I am casually dating	Someone with whom I am in a committed relationship	My life partner (spouse)	No one

Images of Love and Sex in Music and Video

RATIONALE

We do not develop our ideas about appropriate and inappropriate sexual behaviors in a vacuum; popular culture plays a major role in conveying information and shaping our values. Music has long been a particularly powerful means of both reflecting and shaping cultural beliefs about love and sexuality. Music videos, which are particularly popular among adolescents and young adults, have added a new layer of storytelling and ideas to musical expression.

This workshop encourages participants to examine the portrayals of love, sex, and relationships in popular music and music videos with a critical eye. Recent studies have suggested that music videos tend to be sexist and misogynist; that they equate violence (often against women) with sex and love; that they are heterosexist; and that they tend to explore negative aspects of relationships more often than positive aspects. This activity asks participants to identify and assess the messages expressed in popular music lyrics and videos and to think about how these messages relate to their own values.

Time Required: 30 minutes

GOALS

To help participants
- think critically about the messages about love and sex in popular music.
- recognize the negative as well as positive impact music and music videos can have on their beliefs and values regarding sex, love, and relationships.
- become more discriminating consumers of popular culture.

OBJECTIVES

By the end of this workshop, participants will be able to
- demonstrate an ability to listen to popular music critically by being able to identify the messages about love, sex, and relationships in particular songs.
- demonstrate an understanding of the potential influence of video by discussing how the addition of video to music can change or accentuate messages.
- show an ability to evaluate such messages as healthy or unhealthy.

MATERIALS

☐ CD/tape player
☐ VCR/DVD player/TV
☐ Examples of popular music and/or music videos about love, sex, and/or relationships

PREPARATION

- Review this workshop and decide how to share leadership responsibilities with your coleader.
- Arrange to have a CD/tape player as well as a television and VCR or DVD player in the meeting room.
- Select some examples of popular songs about love, sex, or relationships in case participants do not bring any to this session. CDs, cassettes, videotapes, and printed lyrics are all appropriate. If necessary, ask a young person you know for suggestions of current groups and their music. Two "classic" examples are Pink Floyd's "The Great Gig in the Sky," from the *Dark Side of the Moon* album, and Meat Loaf's "Paradise by the Dashboard Light" from his CD, *Bat Out of Hell*.
- If you saved the group's list of the characteristics of a good relationship from Workshop 22 as suggested, post it for review.
- Post the ground rules from the opening session.

NOTE: Although intended to be a 30-minute workshop, this activity can easily be expanded to 60 or 90 minutes. For a longer session, have participants break into small groups and have each group work on a few songs. Have the groups answer specific questions about each song. Then have each small group report its findings to the large group. With more examples to study and more group discussion, participants may be able to identify patterns and tendencies within popular music that will give them a deeper understanding of the issues.

Activity

IMAGES IN MUSIC   30 minutes

1. Tell participants that being able to listen critically to lyrics and other messages in music is an important skill for people who spend a lot of time listening to music. Point out that even though most of us develop our beliefs and values from many different sources, music and music video can have a strong impact on how we think and feel about love, sex, and relationships. This is especially true for people who have had fewer real-life experiences to compare to the music and other media images they hear and see.

2. Invite participants to take turns playing the songs or videos or, if they prefer, reading the lyrics they have selected. After each song has been played or read, ask these questions of the group:

- What images come to mind when you are listening to this song?
- What are your gut feelings as you listen?
- What story does this song tell?

3. Take a few minutes to review with participants the consensus they had reached in Workshop 22 about the characteristics of a healthy relationship. Ask participants to keep those characteristics in mind when thinking about the messages that come from the song lyrics and video images. Ask:

- What is the message in this song about relationships? Sex? Love?
- Are love and sex connected?
- Does the song treat men and women equally?

- Does the song promote healthy or unhealthy relationships?
- Do the music and the lyrics send the same message?

If a music video is presented, ask:

- How does the addition of video change or accentuate the messages?
- Do the lyrics and the visuals communicate the same feelings and ideas?

4. After each person has shared a song or a piece of a song—or, when time has run out—help participants process the activity with the following questions:

- Do you see any themes or patterns in the songs we have heard?
- Do you think popular music influences the way we view our own relationships? How?
- If music and videos were someone's main sources of information about sex, love, and relationships, would that person have a healthy or realistic view of these topics? Why or why not?

5. Conclude by telling the group that although each musician, song, and video is different, music and music videos tend to emphasize some ways of thinking and acting, often unhealthy ways, over others. It is important to evaluate the messages we receive from the media so that we can develop our own ideas and values.

Recognizing Unhealthy Relationships

9

WORKSHOP 28 **Power and Responsibility**

RATIONALE

Although dependence is a part of all relationships, it can become unhealthy if one partner assumes too much power over decisions that affect the other's well-being, and/or if one person is expected to take care of many needs for the other. Even though societal roles are changing, women for the most part, are accustomed to giving up individual power in their relationships (both sexual and other), while men are less so. This workshop is designed to give men the experience of giving up control and women the feeling of both power and responsibility.

Time Required: 30 minutes

GOALS

To help participants
- experience, in a safe and nonthreatening way, power differentials between men and women.
- experience (for men) both the frustration and freedom of having another person in control of their well-being.
- experience (for women) both the responsibility and power involved in controlling another person's well-being.

OBJECTIVES

By the end of this workshop, participants will be able to
- demonstrate their understanding of power and powerlessness in relationships by discussing their experience of the power walk activity.
- identify, through discussion, ways in which giving up control in a relationship can be both positive and negative.
- discuss and share their experiences of being in positions of control and positions of submission.
- through discussion, make connections between this activity and the real-life experiences of men and women.

MATERIALS

☐ Pink and blue index cards
☐ Blindfolds (bandanas or scarves) for each pair

Optional

☐ Stickers—a different one for each pair

PREPARATION

- Review this workshop and decide how to share leadership responsibilities with your coleader.
- Select a pink card for each female in the group. Select a blue card for each male. Place one of the matching stickers or a written symbol on a pink card. Place the other sticker or the same written symbol on a blue card.
- Practice a power walk with your coleader.
- Post the ground rules from the opening session.

Activity

POWER WALK   30 minutes

1. Tell the group that this activity will give them a chance to think about how power and responsibility are shared in relationships.

2. Hand out a pink index card to each woman and a blue index card to each man. If you have too many of one gender, you may pair same-gender couples. If you have an uneven number of participants, select one to be the observer. Have participants locate their partners by finding the person with the matching sticker or symbol on his/her card.

3. Give blindfolds to the women in all mixed-gender pairs and to one member of each of the same-gender pairs and have them blindfold their partners. Tell the women that they are now responsible for the safety and well-being of their partners. Each woman should take her partner's arm and lead him/her out of the room. The pair may go as far as the woman chooses within the limits of the building's rules. The male partner may make requests and talk with his guide, but the woman is in charge. Instruct the participants to return within 10 minutes. Observers may follow along but may not intervene in a pair's interaction.

4. After all the pairs have returned, have the blindfolded partners remove their blindfolds. Ask participants to gather in a circle, sitting next to their partners. Use the remaining time, about 15 minutes, to process the activity with the following questions:

- How far away did you go?
- If you were blindfolded, did you make any requests that were refused?
- How did it feel to hand your safety to another person and to be led around?
- How did it feel to lead another person around and to be responsible for that person's safety?
- Is there anything about this experience that surprised you?
- Would you have liked to have switched roles?
- Do observers [if any] have anything to report?
- If you were a same-gender pair, do you think your experience was different from that of the mixed-gender pairs?

Now help participants relate this activity to relationship experiences, using questions like the following:

- Does this activity remind you of any experiences in real life?
- In what ways do people give up control in their relationships?
- Which of the ways we give up control are positive? Which are negative?
- How do you know when you have given up too much control?
- Why do some people give up too much control? Why do some people not give up any control?

5. Conclude by explaining that, although sometimes it is helpful to give up control and let someone else lead in a relationship, it is risky and unhealthy to let someone else always make decisions for you, even if you trust them. Men and women often play power games, and women frequently give up more control than is healthy, while men sometimes expect to take more control than is healthy. Recognizing this issue and talking about it can help keep relationships, both sexual and nonsexual, from becoming unbalanced.

RATIONALE

Men and women usually experience the division of power in relationships very differently. This workshop gives female and male participants the opportunity to "listen in" to each other's conversations about power in relationships. The activity allows the groups to learn how power is experienced by the other gender (as well as by others of their own gender), to gain empathy with the other gender, and to find alternatives to imbalances of power in their own relationships.

As this activity follows Workshop 27, participants should be primed for the discussion.

Time Required: 40 minutes

GOALS

To help participants
• gain an understanding of how another gender views and experiences power and powerlessness.
• increase empathy for others and their experiences with unequal power in relationships.
• gain insight into how unequal power in a relationship is unhealthy and how to share power and responsibility.
•gain a greater understanding, empathy, and compassion for members of another gender and thereby experience better communication.

OBJECTIVES

By the end of this workshop, participants will be able to
• demonstrate a knowledge of how others think and feel about power and powerlessness in relationships by stating at least one way in which members of their own gender agree or disagree about the subject.
• state at least one new or unexpected concept they learned about how another gender feels or thinks about power and powerlessness in relationships.
• identify at least one way in which the views expressed by another gender might have an impact on relationships between genders.
• identify at least one way in which their participation in this activity might help them improve the relationships they have with people of another gender.

MATERIALS

None

PREPARATION

- Review this workshop and decide how to share leadership responsibilities with your coleader.
- Be sure that there are at least three members of each gender present for this activity.
- Decide whether men or women should speak first. If you feel that this exercise will be threatening for female participants, have the men go first. Alternatively, if the women in your group have been more willing than the men to express feelings and opinions in previous sessions, have them begin.
- Arrange participants' chairs so that there is an inner circle and an outer circle, with all chairs facing inward. Keep in mind that in some cultures (for example, among some Native American tribes), it is inappropriate for certain groups to sit in a dominant position above or outside another group. In such a cultural context, adapt the activity accordingly.
- Post the ground rules from the opening session.

NOTE: Although designed as a 40-minute exercise, this workshop can easily be extended to an hour or more. The longer each group has to speak in the inner circle and to provide feedback from the outer circle, the deeper the conversation and the learning will be.

Activity

FISHBOWL   40 minutes

1. Divide participants into same-gender groups. Select one group to go first. Instruct the group you have chosen to sit in a circle and ask the other group to sit in a circle around the first group. Explain that this activity provides an opportunity for each gender to hear and be heard by the other gender.

2. Explain that members of the inner circle will discuss a topic among themselves, while the outer circle observes without interruption or comment. Assure members of the outer circle that they will have time to speak later; instruct them to listen carefully and to note their responses to what they hear. Remind the inner circle of the relevant ground rules: no put-downs; no direct questions of a particular person; use "I" statements; allow others the opportunity to speak and to be heard; everyone has the right to pass.

3. Ask members of the inner circle: "When have you felt pushed around in a relationship?" Encourage members of the inner group to discuss the question among themselves and allow the conversation to continue uninterrupted for as long as it remains productive. If the group becomes overly excited or wanders off the subject completely, guide members back by repeating the question, by asking them to respond to something pertinent that one of them has said, or by posing other questions that will deepen and focus the discussion.

4. When the conversation reaches a natural end or after approximately 5 minutes, ask: "When have you felt powerful in a relationship?" Follow the same format as with the first question. Take a total of 10 minutes for both questions.

5. Then, while the participants remain seated, ask the outer circle to give feedback about what they heard and saw during the discussion. Tell them they may express their feelings about what was said but they should not answer the two questions that were asked. Use the following questions to elicit feedback:

- How did you feel while you were listening to this conversation?
- How did it feel not to be able to respond?
- What was said that made you strongly want to respond?
- What did you hear that was surprising or told you something new?
- Give the outer circle approximately 5 minutes to provide feedback. The inner circle should not interrupt during this time.

6. Have the participants switch places so that the outer circle is sitting in the inner circle and vice versa. Review the rules for both the inner and outer groups; then, repeat steps 3 through 5.

7. After both groups have conversed and given feedback, ask participants to arrange themselves in one large circle so that they are mixed together by gender.

8. Help participants process the activity using the following questions. Encourage them to be as specific as possible in their answers.

- Overall, what did you think of this activity?
- What did you learn about another gender? About your own gender? Did anything surprise you during this activity?
- How might what you have learned influence how men and women negotiate power in relationships with each other?
- Did all the members of the same gender feel the same way about a subject?
- In what ways might you use what you learned in this activity in your future interactions with men and women?

RATIONALE

At some point during their lives, most people will need to break off a significant relationship, either because it is not meeting their emotional, spiritual, physical, or sexual needs, or because it is unhealthy for them in some way. However, ending a relationship can be extremely difficult, even after the decision is made. This workshop gives participants the opportunity to identify and discuss common relationship difficulties and to practice the communication skills necessary to end relationships when necessary.

Time Required: 40 minutes

GOALS

To help participants
- identify and discuss reasons for ending, rather than continuing, a relationship.
- develop and practice the skills necessary to end a relationship.

OBJECTIVES

By the end of this workshop, participants will be able to
- display an understanding of why a relationship should end by creating a list of reasons as a group.
- demonstrate skills for ending a relationship by role playing with a partner.
- demonstrate the ability to know when a relationship is not worth saving by discussing the issue as a group.

MATERIALS

☐ Newsprint, markers, and masking tape
☐ Leader Resource 21, Breaking Up: Role Plays

PREPARATION

- Review this workshop and decide how to share leadership responsibilities with your coleader.
- Decide which of the role plays your group will act out and in which order.
- Post the ground rules from the opening session.

Activity

ROLE PLAYS

40 minutes

1. Explain that many people who know they are not happy in their relationships stay in unhealthy situations because they do not know how to get out. This workshop looks at what kinds of issues can make relationships unhealthy and how people can end relationships when they need to.

2. Invite participants to brainstorm a list of reasons why a person or couple might choose to end a relationship. List the reasons on newsprint.

   After a few minutes ask, "What are some ways that people get out of relationships?" Then ask, "What are some things you can say to break up?"

   Allow participants to share responses for a few minutes.

3. Ask participants to form a circle. Place two chairs, facing each other, in the center of the circle. Ask for two volunteers to begin role-playing a situation that you will read to the group.

4. After you have chosen the two volunteers, instruct the rest of the participants that they may jump into either role to share a different response to the situation at any time during the role play. When a participant wants to enter the role play, she/he should tap a player on the shoulder. That player will then get up and relinquish the role to the new player. If at any time a role player would like to be replaced, he/she may raise his/her hand and another volunteer should take his/her place.

5. Read one of the role-play situations you have selected to the group and allow the volunteers to begin. Have participants continue each role play until it has been exhausted by the group (5 minutes or so). Then select another role play.

6. When the group has finished the role plays, help them process the activity with the following questions:

   - How did it feel to act out trying to end a relationship? What was difficult about it? What was easier than you expected?
   - How did it feel to play the role of the person who wanted to keep the relationship going? How does it feel to be dumped?
   - If someone wanted to break up with you, how would you like them to do so? Which would you prefer: a straightforward approach, euphemisms and evasions, or something else?
   - How do you know when it makes sense to try to work things out in a relationship?
   - How do you know when a relationship is hopeless?

7. Summarize by saying that ending a relationship is not an easy thing to do but it is often the best thing. It is important to be able to identify when a relationship is not good for us and to find ways to end it, even if it means hurting another person's feelings. Sometimes it is necessary and appropriate to allow your own needs to come first and it is better for everyone if a relationship is ended before either partner is led on or made very unhappy.

Leader Resource 21

BREAKING-UP ROLE PLAYS

Role Play 1: Kyle and Jo

Kyle: You and Jo have been together for three months. Your relationship has been very serious and heavy from the very beginning. You had sex with each other right away, and you vowed to be faithful to each other. Although things have happened really fast, it has all felt right to you. You've had more fun with Jo than you've ever had with anyone, and the sex has been fun, too. Jo is fairly experienced and knows a lot of sexual things. You have been very intimate and have trusted Jo a great deal.

Since last weekend, however, you have been hearing rumors that Jo went out with someone else while you were visiting your grandmother. In fact, someone has told you Jo was making out with someone at a party and later they drove off together in Jo's car. You cannot believe it. You feel angry and betrayed and completely vulnerable. You can't trust Jo anymore and feel the need to break things off altogether.

Jo: It's been really great between you and Kyle. You have a lot of fun together, and Kyle is willing to do the sexual experimenting that you like. You promised not to see other people, and until last week, you managed to keep that promise. Last weekend you kind of slipped up, and you're afraid Kyle will find out and freak out. The other person you fooled around with was just a fling, nothing serious. You like Kyle a lot and you really want to keep being together. You hope Kyle will understand that being faithful has never been one of your strong points.

Role Play 2: Jesse and Dale

Jesse: You and Dale have been sweethearts since junior high. You have been through a lot together and have a very solid relationship. You love Dale's family, and they love you. You feel as though you and Dale are destined to be together. The two of you waited three years before starting a sexual relationship, and you have been faithful and very careful and safe. You see yourself growing old with Dale. It all feels very secure and planned, and it makes you feel really good. Knowing that you have Dale gives you the confidence you need to try new things and work hard at school.

Dale: You have always loved Jesse. Even before you became a couple, Jesse was your best friend. What you share together is truly special, but you can't help wondering what it would be like to be with another person. You have never even dated anyone else, and it scares you to think that if you and Jesse make a formal commitment, you will never find out. You love Jesse with all your heart, but it seems scary to make a decision that will affect the rest of your lives when you're both only 17. You feel the need to see other people, just to have that experience and to know for sure that you won't end up hating Jesse for preventing you from learning about yourself. You don't really want to break up, and you realize that Jesse may not be thrilled with your wanting to see other people, but you need to say something.

Role Play 3: Chris and Terry

Chris: You are very much in love with Terry and wish that you could spend every waking (and sleeping) moment together. You wish that you could find jobs together this summer so that you could spend all day together. You've arranged all of your classes so that you and Terry are together in class and for study hall and lunch. You love to kiss Terry in the halls between classes, so that everyone knows you are a couple. After school, it's fun to call Terry on the phone and talk until bedtime. Sometimes, however, Terry seems a little distant. Terry doesn't always want to meet after school or talk on the phone for hours. You have no idea what you've done wrong, but you're sure that you can fix it by just being with Terry and expressing your love and passion in every way possible. As far as you are concerned, the only way to have a relationship is all the way. Cutting back your time with Terry would be devastating.

Terry: In the beginning, it was great to be with Chris. No one had ever been so devoted to you before. Chris would send little notes in class and make a big deal about seeing you in the hall after class. It was really flattering. Now it's beginning to feel like too much. Chris seems to think it's necessary for the two of you to be together all the time. You sometimes want to be alone or go out with your friends. Your grades are slipping because Chris insists on talking on the phone every night and you can't get your homework done. You are feeling really suffocated and need to get out. You really don't want to hurt Chris, but you are being smothered and it's making you crazy.

Role Play 4: Robin and Pat

Robin: You have been going out with Pat for almost six months. Both of you are seniors, and you love each other a lot. You have taken this relationship slowly and have not pushed anything because you really want things to go well this time. From the beginning, Pat has said that sexual intercourse would not be a part of the relationship. At first, you accepted this because you figured if the relationship became serious, sex would become a part of it naturally and Pat would be okay with that. Now, you really want to express your love for Pat in a sexual way; you get so worked up when you are together that you can hardly stand it. It's hard for you to understand how Pat can keep saying "stop." You feel you are both old enough to be having serious sexual relationships and you don't see why Pat isn't ready. You're in love with Pat and will increase the pressure until Pat agrees to have sex.

Pat: From the beginning, you have told Robin that sex would not be part of your relationship. You feel very strongly that sex is not appropriate for people who are young and inexperienced. From what you've seen of your friends, sex makes people do foolish things. You're not a goody-two-shoes, but you are really committed to your stance to stay abstinent, at least for now. You really love Robin, and you really want the relationship to continue, but you are not happy about all the pressure Robin is putting on you to have sex. You just don't see why it is so important. Because you have been so honest and direct about your feelings, when Robin tries to push the sex issue, you feel betrayed and angry. You just don't understand why Robin would think that you would all of a sudden change your views about something so personal and important. If the pressure to have sex keeps up, you're going to have to break up with Robin.

Role Play 5: JP and Corey

Corey: Ever since you and JP have started dating, you have felt on top of the world. JP is very popular and being together has made you part of a very exclusive group at school. For the most part, JP is affectionate and loving with you and seems to take pride in your relationship. Other people call you the "golden couple." Sometimes, however, JP seems to want to tell you what to do a little too much. JP wants to talk about what you wear and how you cut your hair and has been pretty controlling about the things you do together. Last week, when you suggested that the two of you go out alone instead of going to a party, JP slapped you across the face and called you selfish. Afterward, JP was really sorry and swore it would never happen again. But yesterday, when you wanted to talk with some friends, JP grabbed your arm so hard that it left fingernail marks. This is beginning to scare you, and you think maybe you should break things off before you get really hurt.

JP: You love being called the "golden couple" at school. Corey is so attractive and being together has made you both feel wonderful. Sometimes Corey tries to do things that don't really fit the image you have worked to create, and that's a big problem. It has taken years to feel like you mattered at school, and now you want to stay on top; you won't let Corey's lack of experience ruin things for you.

Lately, it's been pretty stressful trying to hold everything together, and Corey keeps making little mistakes about the things you do together and people you associate with. Although you never intended to hurt anyone, you've been a little forceful with Corey and that's bad. You have sworn not to do it again, and you mean it, but sometimes you get so pissed off. You know you need to be more careful; breaking up would not look good at all.

RATIONALE

This workshop asks participants to draw on what they have learned about building healthy relationships and avoiding unhealthy ones. By committing their ideas about good relationships to paper, participants have the opportunity to integrate the information and skills they have learned in Sessions 7–9 with their beliefs, values, and plans for the future.

Time Required: 10 minutes

GOALS

To help participants
- reflect on what they have learned in Sessions Seven, Eight, and Nine.
- identify how they will use what they have learned in their own lives.

OBJECTIVES

By the end of this workshop, participants will be able to
- articulate, by composing a personal ad, their desires and hopes for future relationships.
- share their beliefs and feelings, and listen to those of others, by participating in a discussion of the activity.

MATERIALS

☐ Handout 15, Personal Ad
☐ Pens or pencils

PREPARATION

- Review this workshop and decide how to share leadership responsibilities with your coleader.
- Photocopy Handout 15, Personal Ad, for all participants.
- Post the ground rules from the Opening Session.

Activity

PERSONAL AD 10 minutes

1. Distribute a copy of Handout 15, Personal Ad, and pens or pencils to each participant. Ask participants to take about five minutes to write their own personal ads. Suggest that they include everything that is important to them in a relationship and specify what they would like to avoid. Tell participants that they should not put their names or other identifying marks on their papers because they will hand in their ads and have other members of the group read them aloud.

2. When participants have completed their sheets, collect, shuffle, and redistribute them. Have each participant read one personal ad out loud. Have participants discuss and give feedback on the ads without trying to guess authorship.

3. Thank participants for their hard work in the last three sessions.

Handout 15

PERSONAL AD

Write a newspaper personal ad for the kind of relationship you would like to have now or in the future. Include all aspects of the relationship that are important to you and things that you *do not* want in the relationship.

Before starting your ad, ask yourself the following: What interests, values, and beliefs should the person have? What personal qualities are important? How much sexual intimacy do I want, if any? Would I want something long-term, committed, monogamous, casual? Someone older or younger? What religion, gender, ethnicity?

People who place personal ads usually use abbreviations to save space (and money). Some commonly used abbreviations are:

S = Single	NS = Nonsmoker	So, SWF = Single White Female
M = Married	M = Male	DGM = Divorced Gay Male
D = Divorced	G = Gay	BiMNS = Bisexual Male Nonsmoker
F = Female	L = Lesbian	
W = White	Bi = Bisexual	
B = Black		

Sample Ads

BiBMNS, age 17, seeks fun-loving, caring person, M or F, for companionship. Religion not important, but spirituality is. I love the Mets, Knicks, Giants, and Rangers, also Carmen and Mme. Butterfly. I'm adventurous, enjoy trying new things, looking for a friendship or something more if we share values and outlook. I'd like to snuggle, kiss, and share dreams with someone special. Is that you?

SWF, age 16, seeks SWM for long-term relationship. Interests include: jazz, bike riding, shopping, movies. Must love children, animals, be vegetarian, nonsmoking, gentle, caring, and willing to be intimate without sexual intercourse.

RELATIONSHIP WANTED, must be...

Reproductive Rights

10

WORKSHOP 32 **Abortion**

RATIONALE

The abortion debate is fueled by a tremendous number of complex concerns, including emotional, political, ethical, social, economic, religious, moral, and medical issues. Although young people often view the issue as a simple conflict between "pro-life" and "pro-choice" factions, opinions about and understandings of abortion are generally far more complex. This workshop illustrates some of the complexities and gives participants an opportunity to try on opinions that they may not have previously explored. While not designed to change participants' values, this activity may help participants clarify their beliefs and determine if they wish to change or cherish them.

Time Required: 60–80 minutes

GOALS

To help participants to
- be aware of and understand the many issues involved in the abortion debate.
- explore opinions and issues about abortion with which they may not agree.
- clarify their own values about abortion.

OBJECTIVES

By the end of this workshop, participants will be able to
- demonstrate their understanding of the complexity of the abortion debate by participating in a group role play.
- demonstrate the extent to which they have affirmed or reconsidered their opinions about abortion in discussion of the role play.

MATERIALS

☐ Large index cards
☐ Leader Resource 22, Abortion Debate Role Play
☐ Leader Resource 23, Abortion Mini-Lecture

Optional

☐ Props for the dinner-table role play, such as a large table, plates, glasses, hats, etc.

PREPARATION

- Review this workshop and decide how to share leadership responsibilities with your coleader.
- Photocopy Leader Resource 22, Abortion Debate Role Play. Cut and paste one role onto each large index card. Note that the role play involves nine roles and at least one observer; if your group has fewer than ten participants, eliminate some roles. If you will have more than one observer, make extra cards for them.
- Decide whether or not to give the abortion mini-lecture as part of this workshop. If you do, determine whether it should come before or after the role play and be sure to include information about the abortion laws in your state or province. Take the additional 20 minutes needed for the lecture from Workshop 33 or from the role play.
- Become familiar with the information in Leader Resource 23, Abortion Mini-Lecture, so that you can answer any questions about abortion procedures even if you don't give the lecture.
- Post the ground rules from the Opening Session.

Activities

ABORTION MINI-LECTURE (Optional)   20 minutes

You may choose to include the mini-lecture outlined in Leader Resource 23, Abortion Mini-Lecture, now, after the role play, or not at all. If your group needs information about abortion procedures and you wish to provide it, give the mini-lecture. One way to introduce the lecture is to ask, "What do you want to know about abortion?" You can then address the medical and legal questions that participants have.

ABORTION DEBATE ROLE PLAY   60 minutes

1. Begin by telling participants that the abortion issue is extremely complicated and that people have many different points of view, not just "pro-choice" or "pro-life." Explain that this workshop is going to explore some of the different ways people understand abortion.

2. Explain that the group will do a role play together. Set the stage for participants:

> A young woman who is pregnant is seeking an abortion. She has a large dinner with her friends and family to talk about her decision. Some people support her choice, others do not, and everyone has a rationale for his/her opinion.

Tell participants that each of them will have a role, either as a player or as an observer. If they draw a role with which they do not agree, they should still play the role and not let their personal views interfere.

3. Hand out the index cards, face down, to the participants. You may wish to "plant" the roles to give participants the chance to argue a view counter to their own and to use the talkative and shy participants most effectively.

4. Divide participants into three groups—those playing characters supporting the young woman's decision, those portraying characters that do not support her decision, and observers. Give members of the first two groups about 10 minutes to read their cards, develop their characters, and discuss any questions they have about their roles. Ask participants who are going to be observers to set up the room to look like a family dining room. Tell them that you do not want them to discuss the issue or attempt to listen to the groups as they prepare.

5. Have everyone take their places. Have the players, beginning with Lois, introduce themselves one by one and describe their relationship to Lois and her family. Ask the participant playing Lois to begin the discussion by telling the gathering that she is pregnant and seeking an abortion. Other family members should react to the news in character and express their feelings about the situation. Allow the role play to take no more than 30 minutes. Keep a very careful watch on the time.

6. After 30 minutes, or when the energy is winding down, invite the observers to give feedback on the role play as described on the index cards they received. Use these questions to continue processing the role play:

- What did it feel like to act out your roles? How did it feel to play a role that differed from your true feelings? [Allow each person to respond for 1 minute or less.]
- What did you learn about the abortion issue?
- Which arguments had you not heard before?
- What surprised you about the different opinions?
- Did this exercise challenge or reinforce your own point of view? How?

Allow no more than 20 minutes for the feedback and large group discussion.

7. Conclude by reminding participants that, regardless of their personal opinions on this issue, it is very important to respect others' beliefs and to understand the many facets of the controversy. Encourage participants to remember that people's values and opinions about abortion can change over the course of their lives.

Leader Resource 22

ABORTION DEBATE ROLE PLAY

Supports the Abortion

Lois: You are a seventeen-year-old woman. You are ten weeks pregnant. You were using a diaphragm with spermicide. You had lost weight and had not had your diaphragm refitted and believe this is why it became dislodged during sex. You want an abortion, but you are very conflicted. You were raised in a conservative home, and your parents oppose abortion. You want to go to college and to medical school but feel you won't be able to with a child. You are also concerned because you had a lot of alcohol in the first few weeks of pregnancy before you knew you were pregnant, and you are afraid of fetal alcohol syndrome. You are close to your family and want to be honest and up front with them about the situation. You have decided to tell your family the situation at a family dinner. You have invited some friends to support you.

Mike: You are the seventeen-year-old male partner of Lois, a seventeen-year-old girl who is pregnant by you. You agree with her wish to have an abortion. You don't feel you are ready to get married now although the two of you have discussed getting married after you have both finished college. You are not financially able to care for a baby and would have to quit the football team to get a job. You are hoping to get a football scholarship to pay for college and could not if you had to quit to become a father. You have already indicated that you will not be involved in raising the child if Lois chooses to have the baby.

Nancy: You are Lois's eighteen-year-old friend. You became pregnant when you were fifteen, and had a baby at sixteen. You dropped out of school and are now getting your GED at night while your parents, with whom you live, take care of the baby. You work full-time to support yourself and your child and realize that college is out of the question, at least for now. Although your boyfriend offered to marry you, you decided that would not be a good idea since you were both so young. You feel that you have lost some of the best years of your life because you have no social life and rarely have time to see your friends anymore. You love your child very much, but you worry that she will not have the opportunities she might have had if you had been able to get a degree and a better job. You often don't feel that you are providing her with everything she needs, and you are frequently depressed. If you had it to do over again, you would have an abortion and are urging Lois to have one.

Josh: You are Lois's older brother, age twenty. You feel strongly that Lois should be able to have an abortion if she wishes. You believe that no one has a right to make that decision for her. You feel that it is her body and her life. Knowing how young Lois is and that her boyfriend Mike will not marry her or help her if she keeps the baby, you believe that her life will be altered drastically by having a baby. You understand that Lois tried to prevent the pregnancy by using contraception, but an accident occurred. You think the baby and Lois will really suffer if she is forced to have the baby; she will not be able to go to college, she will become a financial burden on either her parents or the welfare system, and she will lose her childhood.

Does Not Support the Abortion

Mom: Your seventeen-year-old daughter is pregnant and wishes to have an abortion. You are opposed to abortion, but in this situation, religion is not your main concern. You are worried about how an abortion will affect your little girl's health, her emotional well-being, and her ability to have children in the future. Lois is your baby, and you are afraid she'll be consumed by guilt and remorse if she has the abortion. Motherhood is not such a bad option. After all, you've loved being a mom.

Dad: You are strongly opposed to abortion. Your seventeen-year-old daughter is pregnant and is considering having an abortion. You believe that Lois should not have had sex before she was married. You really feel that once a person makes a mistake, they must take responsibility for it and pay the consequences. The only way to make things right now is for Lois to marry her boyfriend and have the baby. You feel that Mike should be forced to marry your daughter.

Aunt Becky: You are Dad's younger sister and Lois's aunt. You believe that abortion is murder. You feel that Lois's unborn child has not done anything wrong and has a right to be protected. There are many childless couples who would love to have a child. You know of organizations that offer financial support for Lois to have the baby and put it up for adoption.

Laura: You are Lois's twenty-five-year-old sister. You became pregnant as a teen, were too afraid to talk to your parents, and decided to have an abortion, which you now regret. Because of the stress over the decision to have an abortion, you and your boyfriend broke up. Although you have gone on to marry and have two children, you often think about the baby you did not have and feel very sad and guilty about it.

Additional Roles

Uncle Hugh: You are Mom's brother, Lois's uncle, and a doctor. You do not have strong opinions for or against abortion, but you want Lois to have the medical knowledge she needs to make the decision. You believe that, medically speaking, abortions are very safe if done under legal conditions by a qualified clinician in the first trimester. You know that having more than two first-trimester abortions or having a second-trimester abortion does increase a woman's risk for miscarriage during future pregnancies.

You also believe that women may have emotional difficulties after having abortions, especially if they feel they were forced to have the abortion, do not receive adequate counseling, or experience extreme conflict over whether or not to have an abortion.

Observers: After the dinner gathering, it will be your job to decide who made convincing arguments and to lead a discussion about the values and opinions expressed. Do all of the supporters of the abortion express the same values and arguments? Do all of those who oppose the abortion express the same values and arguments?

Leader Resource 23

ABORTION MINI-LECTURE

Abortion is defined as the purposeful termination of a pregnancy.

First-Trimester Abortion (up to 13 weeks)

After her pregnancy is confirmed, a woman who chooses to terminate that pregnancy may make an appointment for an abortion with her doctor or at a reproductive health clinic. At the beginning of the most common procedure, known as *vacuum curettage*, the woman is usually offered a tranquilizer to help her relax. The clinician then opens, or dilates, her cervix slightly and inserts a small tube into the cervix through which the contents of the uterus are suctioned out. Once this is done, the tube is removed, and the clinician uses a spoonlike instrument, called a *curette*, to be sure that all fetal and placental tissue has been removed from the uterus. The woman usually experiences pain or discomfort similar to menstrual cramping.

The woman rests at the clinic for an hour or more and then is allowed to go home. Because dilation of the cervix somewhat increases the risk of infection, usually a woman receives antibiotics and is told not to use tampons, douche, have sexual intercourse, or exercise heavily for a few weeks.

Having one first-trimester legal abortion does not affect a woman's ability to have children in the future. Having more than one first-trimester abortion does increase the risk of miscarrying subsequent pregnancies. Illegal abortions, those not done by a skilled clinician under sanitary conditions, are very dangerous and can lead to serious medical complications or even death.

Second-Trimester Abortion (14–26 weeks)

Second-trimester abortions are performed between the fourteenth and the twenty-sixth week of pregnancy. Because the fetus is larger and the placenta is fully formed, the woman's cervix must be dilated to remove the contents of the uterus. Dilation is often done over the course of one or two days by using laminaria. *Laminaria* are small sticks made out of seaweed or plastic that are inserted into the cervix and left overnight. The sticks swell as they absorb moisture from the vagina and cervix. As they swell, they gently dilate the cervix so that the clinician can insert a vacuum tool and a curette. Usually, once the cervix has been dilated, the sides of the uterus are gently scraped and the uterine contents are suctioned away. This procedure is often called a *dilation and curettage*, or *D&C*. After the abortion, the woman rests for an hour or more at the clinic and then is allowed to go home.

In an alternate procedure for second-trimester abortions, a chemical is injected into the amniotic fluid, which aborts the pregnancy.

While second-trimester abortions are considered medically safe, having one does put a woman at a slightly greater risk for miscarriage during future pregnancies. In addition, dilation of the cervix puts the woman at a somewhat greater risk of infection. Second-trimester abortions also carry with them a greater risk of uterine perforation.

First- and second-trimester abortions are safer for a woman, in terms of risk of death, than pregnancy and childbirth.

Third-Trimester Abortion (after 27 weeks)

Third-trimester abortions are not legally available unless the mother's life is in danger or the fetus is severely deformed.

Summary

Having one legal first-trimester abortion does not affect a woman's ability to have babies in the future. Having more than two first-trimester legal abortions, a second-trimester legal abortion, or an illegal abortion does put a woman at greater risk for future miscarriage.

Although every woman is different, most women do not have emotional problems after having a legal first-trimester abortion. If a woman has made the decision of her own free will and has had adequate counseling, she can usually cope with any negative feelings she may experience following the procedure. If, however, she feels forced to have the abortion, does not understand her feelings and beliefs about abortion beforehand, or receives insensitive care from health professionals or family members, she may experience significant emotional stress and require professional counseling to cope with her feelings.

RATIONALE

Recent technological advances have given many couples previously considered unable to bear children the opportunity to become parents. Yet, the new procedures have also raised difficult legal and ethical issues for society. This workshop provides information about some of these issues and gives participants the opportunity to clarify their values regarding parenthood, the beginning and value of life, and medical technology.

Time Required: 35–50 minutes

GOALS

To help participants
• explore the range of reproductive options available to infertile couples.
• get in touch with their own feelings about what defines parenthood.
• think about the ethical and legal issues raised by new technological advances in the area of fertility.

OBJECTIVES

By the end of this workshop, participants will be able to
• demonstrate an understanding of the ethical dilemmas involved in reproductive technology by discussing the critical ethical and legal issues they believe are at the core of individual case studies.
• show the ability to make decisions about difficult issues by identifying the reasons behind their choices.

MATERIALS

☐ Newsprint, markers, and masking tape
☐ Leader Resource 24, Reproductive Technologies Case Studies
☐ Handout 16, Sexual Exploitation and Sexual Harassment

PREPARATION

• Review this workshop and decide how to share leadership responsibilities with your coleader.
• If possible, be familiar with recent news articles about reproductive technology issues. These will help you prepare for participants' questions.
• Read Leader Resource 24, Reproductive Technologies Case Studies.

- Decide which case studies to discuss and how much time (between 35 and 50 minutes) your group will spend on this workshop. Each case study takes between 10 and 15 minutes.
- Prepare two large signs, one marked YES and the other, NO, and hang them on opposite ends of the room. Put a stack of newsprint, a marker, and tape near the signs.
- Photocopy Handout 16, Sexual Exploitation and Sexual Harassment, for all participants.
- Post the ground rules from the Opening Session.

Activity

FORCED CHOICE CASE STUDIES   35–50 minutes

1. Explain to participants that this workshop will explore reproductive rights from a different point of view: How technology can help infertile couples become parents. The new methods have been very helpful to many people, but they raise some serious issues that society has not yet been able to solve. Tell participants that this workshop will help them learn about some of the new alternatives available and some of the concerns that they raise.

2. Tell participants that you are going to explain some of the most commonly used new reproductive alternatives. After each explanation, you will present a case study that poses some ethical or legal questions. After hearing the case study, participants will decide on which side of the issue they would put themselves.

3. Read the description of the first procedure you have chosen and then the case study. Tell participants that every person must make a decision and move either to the YES side or the NO side of the room. Once they are there, they should talk together to find out why each chose that side. Ask each side to list on newsprint the core ethical and/or legal issues involved.

4. After about 7–10 minutes, have each group post their lists on the wall. Ask the groups to take turns reading their lists and explaining why they made their decisions. Inform participants that they are free to change their minds and move to the other side of the room if they are convinced by the other side's arguments.

5. Repeat this procedure for each case study you have chosen. After all have been discussed or time has run out, have the group consider the following questions:
- What was the most difficult part of this exercise?
- Is it possible that there are no "right" answers for some issues?
- Is it okay to make decisions such as these on a case-by-case basis?
- Are there important issues that are involved in all of these cases? What are they?
- Many of these procedures are quite expensive and are not typically covered by health insurance. Is this fair? Should couples be allowed access to these procedures without cost? What about people who cannot afford the many thousands of dollars required for such procedures?
- In general, whose rights take precedence? The fetus's? The biological mother's? The biological father's? The adoptive parents'? Society's?

6. Conclude by saying that our society has been able to create new technology much faster than it has thought through the accompanying moral and legal issues. Equally difficult issues, such as selective abortion and human cloning, are either on the horizon or here now. Each of us needs to think about our fundamental beliefs about the nature of life, birth, and parenthood in order to make some of these difficult choices for ourselves and our world.

7. In preparation for the next session, give each participant a copy of Handout 15, Sexual Exploitation and Sexual Harassment. Ask participants to read "Examples of Sexual Harassing Behaviors Reported in U.S. High Schools" and to spend some time before the next session looking for examples of sexual exploitation and/or sexual harassment in the real world. Ask participants to bring in, for the next meeting, one example of sexual exploitation or sexual harassment they have observed or learned about from school, print (book, magazine, newspaper, Internet, etc.), television, or an interview with someone they know. Explain that they should record their observations on the handout and bring the handouts to the next session.

Be sure to bring in your own examples to share with the class as well.

Leader Resource 24

REPRODUCTIVE TECHNOLOGIES CASE STUDIES

Artificial Insemination by Husband (AIH) and Artificial Insemination by Donor (AID) involve placing semen into a woman's vagina by means other than vaginal intercourse in order to produce a pregnancy. AIH is often used if a man has a low sperm count. Several samples of the man's semen are collected, usually through masturbation, and then pooled to create a semen sample with enough sperm to make fertilization possible. This sample is placed in the woman's vagina at the time she is ovulating. AID is used when a man is completely sterile (no viable sperm). In this situation, a donor (usually anonymous) provides semen to impregnate the woman. Because sperm can be frozen and thawed at a later date without damage, a man who is about to undergo radiation therapy for cancer, which can render him sterile, can first store sperm in a sperm bank for later use. Likewise, a man who is dying can donate sperm for his wife to use after he is gone so that she may have children by him. It is estimated that approximately 250,000 babies are conceived as a result of artificial insemination in the United States each year. AID is also used by women who wish to become single parents or are partnered with other women.

CASE STUDY ONE   Because of the large demand for sperm donors, sperm banks have opened in increasing numbers. There, men can receive payment for donating their sperm anonymously. Some sperm banks have criteria that donors must meet in order to donate. For example, to increase the chance of producing extremely bright babies, one sperm bank only collects sperm from Nobel Prize winners and will only offer the sperm to young women who have high IQs. Other sperm banks provide full descriptions of the donors (height, weight, eye color, attractiveness, religion, IQ, etc.) to prospective mothers so that the woman can choose the characteristics she wants for her child. In your opinion, should there be restrictions on this type of selectivity by sperm banks? YES or NO?

CASE STUDY TWO   In 1995, a couple in the Netherlands gave birth to twins after undergoing artificial insemination by the husband. As the infants grew, it became apparent that they were of two different races since one was white with blond hair and blue eyes and the other was black. Feeling ostracized by their neighbors and friends, the angry couple went to the clinic for answers. It turned out that the syringe used to inseminate the woman with her husband's sperm had not been properly cleaned, so that it had contained sperm from another man from the Caribbean who had come to the clinic with his wife. The man from the Caribbean and his wife had successfully conceived a child of their own and returned home. The sperm of the man from the Caribbean had apparently fertilized one of the woman's eggs while her husband's sperm fertilized the other, resulting in twins with two different ethnicities. Although the couple is suing the clinic, they have decided they want to keep both children. If you were the clinic's administrator, would you feel compelled to tell the man who had accidentally become the biological father of one of the babies that he had a child in the Netherlands? YES or NO?

Embryo Transplant involves removing a fertilized egg that has grown into an embryo from the biological mother's womb and transplanting it into the uterus of another woman who carries the fetus to term. This technique is sometimes used when a woman can conceive but is unable to carry the developing fetus without miscarrying or when a woman does not produce any viable eggs but can carry a fetus to term. If a woman can conceive but cannot carry the fetus to term, another woman, acting as a "surrogate mother," can carry the fetus to term, at which time the baby is given to the biological parents. If a woman does not produce any viable eggs, her male partner's sperm can be used to artificially inseminate another woman (who has donated her egg), and the fertilized egg can then be transferred to the first woman's uterus. In this case, the surrogate mother and the biological father raise the child.

CASE STUDY THREE   A young woman could not carry a fetus to term without miscarrying. Her sixty-year-old mother, well past menopause, offered her uterus to carry the baby until it was born. Thus the mother, at age sixty, became the oldest known person to give birth to a baby. After the birth, the grandmother returned the infant to its biological mother, her daughter. Do you feel this is a justifiable arrangement? YES or NO?

After a discussion of this case, ask if it would make a difference if the daughter asked her mother to carry the baby because she was a model and pregnancy would interfere with her work.

Surrogate Motherhood may be an option when a woman is unable either to conceive or to carry a fetus to term. In this case, a couple may hire a surrogate mother, a woman who donates her egg, is inseminated by the man, and then carries the fetus in her uterus until it is born. In this case, the surrogate mother is genetically related to the baby and gives birth to it.

NOTE: Surrogate mothers are not necessarily paid. Someone, particularly a family member, may volunteer to provide this service.

CASE STUDY FOUR   In 1985, William and Elizabeth Stern signed a contract with Mary Beth Whitehead that stipulated that Whitehead would be artificially inseminated with Stern's sperm, that she would carry the fetus to term, and that she would then surrender the child to the Sterns. In return for her expenses and a compensation of $10,000, Whitehead agreed to renounce all parental rights to the child. When the baby was born, Whitehead changed her mind, refused to give back the baby, and fought for custody. If you were the court, would you require Mary Beth Whitehead to honor the contract and give up the baby to the Sterns? YES or NO?

After discussion, explain that although a lower court originally ruled in favor of the Sterns, the New Jersey State Supreme Court overturned that finding and said that surrogate mother contracts cannot be enforced. The court granted partial custody and visitation rights to Mary Beth Whitehead.

In Vitro Fertilization (IVF) may be used if a woman is unable to conceive because her Fallopian tubes are blocked, preventing a man's sperm from reaching her egg. With IVF, conception takes place outside of the woman's body. The woman takes drugs that either stimulate her ovaries to ovulate (Clomid) or that cause her to ovulate several eggs instead of the usual one (Perganol). The eggs (usually between four and six) are collected in a procedure in which a doctor makes a small incision in the woman's abdomen and, using a long thin telescopic instrument called a laparoscope to find them, extracts the eggs with a long hollow needle. The eggs are then placed in a glass petri dish, drops of sperm are added, and the container is stored in an incubator. (The term "test tube baby" refers to this practice.) In a day or two, when the fertilized eggs have divided into eight-cell embryos, they are placed in the woman's uterus. As many as three embryos may be placed in the uterus to increase the chances of a successful pregnancy, but the practice also increases the chance of a multiple birth. The remaining embryos can be frozen and saved in case the first attempt fails to achieve a pregnancy.

CASE STUDY FIVE   A couple who were unable to have children because the wife's Fallopian tubes were blocked decided to try in vitro fertilization. In the process, ten eggs were harvested and fertilized. Three were implanted into the woman's uterus and the remaining seven were frozen. The first attempt failed to result in a pregnancy. After this attempt, the couple decided to divorce. A year after the divorce was final, the woman decided she wanted to use the remaining frozen embryos to try to become pregnant. She reasoned that because she was thirty-eight years old, her ability to become pregnant was diminishing; if she waited until she found a new partner, she might be too old to conceive. Her ex-husband, who had remarried and was trying to have children with his new wife, did not want her to use the frozen embryos because, he argued, he did not want to father any children by her as they were no longer married. He went to court to block her from using the embryos. In court, he argued that he should have a right not to have children with someone against his will. His former wife argued that the frozen embryos had already been conceived. She claimed that he had made the choice when he first agreed to inseminate her, and now it was just a matter of bringing these potential lives to fruition. If you were the judge in this case, would you allow the woman to use the embryos she created with her former husband? YES or NO?

CASE STUDY SIX   A couple chose to try to have children through in vitro fertilization. Several embryos were implanted, and eight were frozen for further tries. The first attempt failed, and sometime later, both the man and woman were killed in an airplane crash.

• What should be done with the remaining embryos?

• Should the clinic throw them out?

• Should the clinic be allowed to use these embryos for another couple looking to have a child?

• Does the sexual orientation of the couple seeking to have a child matter in this decision?

FYI: Other Reproductive Technology Options

Gamete Intra-Fallopian Tube Transfer (GIFT)

This procedure is similar to IVF as the ova and sperm are mixed outside the body. With GIFT, however, the ova and sperm are placed into the woman's Fallopian tube *before* fertilization takes place. Because fertilization occurs naturally in the Fallopian tube rather than in a petri dish, this procedure has a much higher implantation rate than IVF.

Zygote Intra-Fallopian Transfer (ZIFT)

As in IVF and GIFT, the sperm and ova are collected, and as in IVF, they are allowed to fertilize outside of the body in a petri dish. However, the resulting fertilized zygote is placed in the woman's Fallopian tube and allowed to travel to the uterus to implant naturally.

Handout 16

SEXUAL EXPLOITATION AND SEXUAL HARASSMENT

Sexual exploitation is the use of sex or sex-related activities to take advantage of another person or group of people for one's own benefit or financial gain, without regard for how these actions affect the other person or group's well-being. **Sexual harassment** is "unwanted attention of a sexual nature from someone in school or the workplace; also includes the use of status and/or power to coerce or attempt to coerce a person into having sex, and unwelcome sexual jokes, glances, or comments." (Janell Carroll and Paul Root Wolpe, *Sexuality and Gender in Society*, Reading, Mass.: Addison-Wesley, 1996.) A broader, more concise definition is "sexual pressure imposed on someone who is not in a position to refuse it." (Catherine MacKinnon, *Feminism Unmodified*, Cambridge, Mass.: Harvard University Press, 1987.)

Between now and the next session, look for examples of either sexual exploitation or sexual harassment in the places listed. Use this handout to write down what you have observed or heard.

School

Print (books, magazines, newspapers, Internet, etc.)

Television

Personal interview with someone who has experienced sexual exploitation or harassment. (Please do not name the person.)

EXAMPLES OF SEXUAL HARASSING BEHAVIORS REPORTED IN U.S. HIGH SCHOOLS

- touching (arm, breast, buttock, etc.)
- verbal comments (about parts of the body, what type of sex the victim would be "good at," clothing, looks, etc.)
- name-calling (from "honey" to "bitch" and worse)
- spreading sexual rumors
- leers and stares
- cartoons, pictures, and pornography
- using the computer to leave sexual messages or graffiti or to play sexually offensive computer games
- gestures with the hands and body
- pressure for sexual activity
- cornering, blocking, standing too close, following
- conversations that are too personal
- "rating" an individual (for example, on a scale from 1 to 10)
- obscene T-shirts, hats, pins
- showing R-rated movies during class
- "snuggies" (pulling underwear up at the waist so it goes between the buttocks)
- sexual assault and attempted sexual assault
- rape
- massaging the neck; massaging the shoulders
- touching oneself sexually in front of others
- graffiti
- making kissing sounds or smacking sounds; licking the lips suggestively
- howling, catcalls, whistles
- repeatedly asking someone out when he or she isn't interested
- "spiking" (pulling down someone's pants)
- facial expressions (winking, kissing, etc.)
- "slam books" (list of students' names with derogatory sexual comments written about them by other students)
- "making out" in the hallway.

—From *Sexual Harassment and Teens: A Program for Positive Change* by Susan Strauss and Pamela Espeland (Minneapolis: Free Spirit Publications, 1992).

Power and Control

11

Sexual Exploitation, Sexual Harassment, and Erotica

RATIONALE

This workshop encourages participants to open their eyes to the prevalence of sexual exploitation and sexual harassment in everyday life and in the mainstream media. By asking participants to search for examples, this exercise helps participants gain a better understanding of exploitation and harassment and how they differ. Participants will also examine examples of nonexploitive erotica and begin to understand how sexual, nonexploitive material and/or behaviors differ from those that exploit individuals or groups.

Time Required: 45 minutes

GOALS

To help participants

- distinguish between sexually exploitive and nonexploitive representations and behaviors.
- explore the extent to which sexual harassment and sexual exploitation are part of their lives.

OBJECTIVES

By the end of this workshop, participants will be able to

- demonstrate that they can recognize sexual harassment and sexual exploitation by collecting examples of each.
- show that they can distinguish between sexual harassment and sexual exploitation by identifying the correct term to apply in specific cases.
- show that they understand the difference between exploitive representations and behaviors, such as those found in pornography, and nonexploitive sexual behaviors and representations by looking at examples of erotica and noting the differences between erotica and the exploitive examples they discussed.

MATERIALS

- ☐ Newsprint, markers, and masking tape
- ☐ Age-appropriate examples of nonexploitive erotica from art or literature
- ☐ Handout 16, Sexual Exploitation and Sexual Harassment (from Workshop 33)

PREPARATION

- Review this workshop and decide how to share leadership responsibilities with your coleader.
- Before this session begins, give participants copies of Handout 16, Sexual Exploitation and Sexual Harassment, and have them record examples of sexual exploitation and harassment if they have not already done so in preparation for this workshop.
- Bring in examples of sexual exploitation and sexual harassment that can be used to help guide the discussion, to supplement participants' choices, or to point out particular instances that participants may have missed.
- Write the definitions of sexual exploitation and sexual harassment from Handout 16 on newsprint and post them on the wall.
- Review the definitions of pornography and erotica given in this workshop. Bring in age-appropriate examples of erotica for the group to discuss.
- Post the ground rules from the Opening Session.

Activity

DISCUSSION OF SEXUAL HARASSMENT
AND EXPLOITATION   45 minutes

1. Explain that this workshop will explore how power and control can be misused through sexual harassment and exploitation. Ask participants to pass in the handouts they completed during the week.

2. Read aloud each example from participants' handouts, supplementing as necessary from your own materials. As you read each example, ask participants to decide whether it is a case of sexual harassment, sexual exploitation, both, or neither. Ask them to give reasons for their choices using the definitions posted on the wall as guidance.

3. When all examples have been read and discussed, ask:
- Was it difficult or easy to find examples for this assignment?
- Which source (school, print, television, or personal interview) was the most difficult from which to find examples? Which was the easiest?
- How are sexual exploitation and sexual harassment related? What do they have in common?
- Is sexual harassment one type of sexual exploitation?
- How common is sexual exploitation in our culture? Sexual harassment?

4. Ask the group to list the characteristics their examples had in common. Ask, "What defines sexual harassment or sexual exploitation?" As participants call out answers, write them on newsprint. Be sure that the concept of a power differential is included on the list you write. When the list is complete, write EXPLOITIVE at the top.

5. Explain that pornography is generally considered exploitive because it depicts individuals who are being forced to do something sexual or who are doing something sexually degrading. Tell the group that not all sexually explicit materials are exploitive or degrading; not all of them are pornography.

6. Show or read aloud the examples of erotica you have brought in. As you show or read each example, ask participants if it meets the criteria for "exploitive" they brainstormed earlier. Ask, "What characteristics do the erotica have in common with the exploitive examples? What characteristics set them apart?"

7. Ask participants to define erotica. Then, present the definitions below and ask participants if they find them acceptable.

> EROTICA: Sexually arousing material that is not degrading to women, men, or children (Janet Sibley Hyde, *Understanding Human Sexuality*, Whitehall, Ohio: McGraw, 1990).

> EROTICA: Sexually oriented media that are considered by a viewer or society as within the acceptable bounds of decency (Janell Carroll and Paul Root Wolpe, *Sexuality and Gender in Society*, Reading, Mass.: Addison-Wesley, 1996).

8. Conclude with a discussion of the following questions:
- Should there be legal restrictions on sexually explicit materials?
- Should the First Amendment of the Constitution, which grants freedom of speech, be interpreted to protect any sexual material or behavior, no matter how exploitive?
- Who should decide what is erotica and what is pornography?
- What criteria should be used to determine whether or not something is acceptable for public consumption?
- Which is more important, protecting those who are hurt or degraded by exploitive pornography by banning it or protecting the right of individuals to write, publish, and read what they wish as long as they are not harming anyone?

WORKSHOP 35 **Date Rape**

RATIONALE

Acquaintance, or date, rape is a serious concern for young people. Poor communication and sex role stereotyping can put adolescents in exploitative and violent sexual situations. This workshop helps participants to avoid such situations by identifying strategies that reduce the risk of misinterpreting another person or of being misinterpreted.

Time Required: 40 minutes

GOALS

To help participants
- analyze why date rape might occur in a given situation.
- identify how date rape might be prevented.

OBJECTIVES

By the end of this workshop, participants will be able to
- demonstrate their understanding of factors that increase the risk of date rape by discussing, as a group, why date rape may have taken place in a fictional story.
- develop, through group discussion, strategies that men and women can employ to prevent date rape.

MATERIALS

☐ Newsprint, markers, and masking tape
☐ Handout 17, Diane's Story, and Handout 18, Mark's Story

PREPARATION

- Review this workshop and decide how to share leadership responsibilities with your coleader.
- Make copies of Handout 17, Diane's Story, and Handout 18, Mark's Story, for all participants.
- Post the ground rules from the Opening Session.

Activity

AVOIDING DATE RAPE   40 minutes

1. Tell participants that this workshop deals with date rape, also called acquaintance rape. Explain that date rape is a sexual assault that occurs between people who are in a dating situation, even though it may be the first date. Unlike stranger rape, date rape involves people who have some kind of relationship; they may even have had a sexual relationship in the past. Date rape can occur between people of all ages, but it is very common among people between the ages of sixteen and twenty-five.

2. Acknowledge that rape can be hard to talk about and tell participants that they may pass on participating in the discussion if they wish to do so. (Keep in mind that a member of your group may have firsthand experience of rape or abuse.) Explain that understanding why date rape occurs and working on ways to prevent it are sometimes the best ways to deal with the feelings of fear, anger, and helplessness that talking about rape can bring up.

3. Divide participants into two groups. Explain that each group will read and discuss a story about a dating situation. Have each group select three volunteers to take turns reading the group's story out loud, one paragraph per person. After the stories have been read, have each group discuss the questions that follow the story.

4. Ask the groups to sit away from each other so that the conversations do not disturb them. Give Handout 17, Diane's Story, to the members of one group and Handout 18, Mark's Story, to the other. Tell participants that they will have about 10 minutes to read the stories and discuss their responses.

5. When time is up, bring two large groups together and have a participant read Handout 17 to the whole group. Then have someone read Handout 18 to the whole group. Use the questions that accompany the stories to lead a group discussion. Invite participants to compare how they felt about the characters before and after they heard the other side of the story. Use the following questions to discuss the activity:

- When a person is very aroused and wants to continue sexual activity but isn't sure what a partner wants, what should she/he do?
- When a person is unsure what he/she wants to do as a sexual encounter continues, what should she/he do?
- What do you think Mark would say if Diane accused him of rape?
- What will happen if Diane does not say anything?
- What could Mark and Diane have done differently?
- Some colleges have a code of dating etiquette that requires couples to ask permission before engaging in any sexual activities. For example, one partner may ask, "May I kiss you?" or "May I touch your breasts?" Is this type of code useful?

6. Ask the group for ideas about what can be done to prevent date rape. Have the group brainstorm a list and record their responses on newsprint. Then make two additional lists: one of things that men can do to prevent date rape and another of things that women can do to prevent date rape.

Handout 17

DIANE'S STORY

Diane and Mark were going on their second date, and Diane could not believe her luck! She'd only been at college for a month, and already she was dating a great guy. Mark was a junior, captain of the soccer team, in a great fraternity, and really cute. Her friend Joan told her that she thought Mark was an honor student, too, but he was too modest to tell anyone. On their first date, they had gone to a party at his fraternity and Diane had met a lot of his friends. Most of them seemed really nice but a little rowdy. At the end of the date, he had driven her back to her dorm and been a perfect gentleman. She had thought he was really cute and she had felt so attracted to him that she would have loved to have kissed him, but she was glad to see that he was a really nice guy and not too pushy. Diane really wanted to make a great impression on him for the second date. She dressed carefully and spent more time than usual on her hair and makeup.

On their second date, Mark took her to a very fancy and expensive restaurant; all of her friends had been impressed when she had told them where they were going. "He must really like me a lot," she thought. Mark ordered a bottle of wine with dinner, and it was so good that they finished the whole thing, something Diane almost never did. Mark was funny and easy to talk to, and he seemed really interested in her. She felt as though she would just melt into his brown eyes. After dinner, she didn't want the date to end. She was happy when he asked her back to his frat house. They walked there from the restaurant, holding hands and stopping every once in a while to kiss gently. When they got back, they sat on the couch in the main room and watched some television with his fraternity brothers, and Mark had a few beers. After a while, the guys were getting loud and Mark asked her if she would prefer going up to his room. She said sure.

When they got to his room, he asked her if she'd like to hear some music. She said yes, and he put on something low and jazzy. Then, he asked her to dance. As they moved together, they kissed and he rubbed her back. She felt beautiful and sexy and very aroused. She felt that she could keep kissing him and dancing forever. She held herself close to him and moved her body against his. She was really getting into it, and then she realized that she could let things go too far if she didn't get a hold of herself. She gently pulled back from Mark and asked him if he could drive her home in a few minutes. He said yes, but then he said he felt pretty drunk and didn't think it would be such a good idea for him to get behind the wheel. Diane didn't feel sober enough to drive either. Mark suggested that she stay over and sleep in his bed. He said he would sleep on the floor. He sounded so responsible and caring that she agreed. They started dancing again and kissing. It felt so good, and she was really attracted to him. She didn't stop him when he moved her over to the bed, and they sat down next to each other. They made out for a while, and then he took off his shirt. Diane decided there was no harm in that; she wanted to feel his skin against hers, so she took her shirt off too, and they held each other and touched each other for a long time. When Mark put his hand inside her pants, Diane tried to squirm away. She was very turned on, but everything was happening so fast. She kept on kissing him, whispering "no" between kisses. He climbed on top of her and they lay together, moving against each other. Mark kept trying to push her pants down, and she kept trying to squirm away. Before she knew what was happening, Mark was yanking her pants down and pushing her legs apart. All of a sudden she felt him pushing his penis inside her. She was trying to scream "no," but his mouth was over her mouth and he was so strong.

Discussion Questions

- Would you define this situation as rape?
- Why or why not?
- What could Diane have done to prevent this situation from occurring?
- What could Mark have done differently?
- What should a person do when she/he wants to be sexual but doesn't want to have intercourse?
- Do you think Mark planned to have sex with Diane from the beginning of the date?

Handout 18

MARK'S STORY

Mark really liked this new girl, Diane. Although she was pretty young, she seemed smart and together, and she was just beautiful. His fraternity brothers had been really impressed when he had shown up at the party with her last week. He was proud of himself, too, because he hadn't even tried to kiss her at the end of their first date, even though he was dying to! He didn't want her to think he was just after sex. For their second date he wanted to let her know how much he liked her, so he made reservations at the best restaurant in town. She sounded pretty thrilled when he told her about it. When he picked her up, she looked fantastic, even more beautiful than before. It was exciting to be out with someone so pretty. He ordered wine with dinner, and before he knew it they had finished the whole thing! They talked about everything, and she was really smart and funny. He really enjoyed being with her. As they walked back to his frat house after dinner, they held hands and stopped every once in a while to kiss gently. Although he would have loved to have taken her up to his room and made love to her, he had no idea if she would be into it and he didn't want to offend her by just blurting it out, so he decided to wait and see if she gave him any signals. They sat and watched television with his buddies for a while and Mark had a few beers. Then the guys started getting kind of loud, and he asked Diane if she'd like to go up to his room with him. She said sure.

When they got to his room, he asked her if she'd like to hear some music and she said yes, so he put on something low and jazzy. Then he asked her to dance. They moved together on the floor and kissed. Her body felt so great as she pressed herself against him, and she smelled so good that Mark was really getting turned on. His head felt kind of fuzzy from the wine and beer and the music, and he just wanted to keep touching her and feeling her. Then she gently pushed back from him and asked him to drive her home in a few minutes. First he said sure, but as he tried to clear his head, he realized that he was pretty drunk, and he said that he was too drunk and it wouldn't be safe to get behind the wheel. He offered to let her have his bed and he would sleep on the floor. Although she seemed to hesitate, she agreed and they went back to dancing.

Mark was really turned on, but he was getting tired of standing, so he maneuvered Diane over to the bed and they sat down. They touched and made out for a while. Mark was really getting aroused, and he felt that she was, too. Then he took of his shirt. He wanted to see what she would do, and he was just dying to touch her bare skin. She took off her shirt, too, and they touched for a long time. It seemed that she was as into him as he was into her. When he tried to put his hands inside her pants, she squirmed away, but she didn't seem mad, so he kept kissing her. He laid her back on the bed and climbed on top of her, and they moved against each other. Mark felt as though he would just explode. He wanted her so badly. She seemed to want him; she was moving against him and kissing him back, and she had taken off her shirt! Mark thought that she really wanted him but she probably didn't want him to think she was too easy. He just wanted her so much and she was moving under him and if he pulled hard he could get her pants down and then he could get inside her. She was squirming under him . . . and he could hear her say no, but he wanted her and she really wanted him . . . and he really wanted to do it . . . and he pushed her and he was inside her.

Discussion Questions

- Would you define this situation as rape?
- Why or why not?
- What could Mark have done to prevent this situation from occurring?
- What could Diane have done differently?
- What should a person do when they want to be sexual but don't want to have intercourse?
- Do you think Diane planned to have sex with Mark from the beginning of the date?

RATIONALE

Even though it is very important, young people often do not understand the concept of consent and are frequently unsure in sexual situations of how to determine if they have given consent or if it has been given to them. In addition, adolescents often have not decided in advance what they want from an encounter when they are faced with a sexual situation and/or how far they would like the encounter to go. To prepare them to make healthful decisions in their own lives, this workshop helps participants explore the concept of consent and analyze some morally ambiguous sexual situations.

Time Required: 35 minutes

GOALS

To help participants
- define and explore the concept of consent.
- identify how they would respond in a variety of morally ambiguous sexual situations.

OBJECTIVES

By the end of this activity, participants will be able to
- demonstrate their understanding of the concept of consent by voting whether or not a given situation implies consent and discussing their opinions with others.
- state, during a large group discussion, how they feel about a given sexual situation and determine how they might respond if they found themselves in a similar situation.

MATERIALS

☐ Red, green, and white index cards
☐ Leader Resource 25, Consenting Situations
☐ Leader Resource 26, "What If?" Cards

PREPARATION

- Review this workshop and decide how to share leadership responsibilities with your coleader.
- Prepare voting cards for all participants by gluing or stapling one red and one green card together.
- Photocopy Leader Resource 26, "What If?" Cards. Cut and paste each situation on a white index card.
- Post the ground rules from the opening session.

Activities

WHAT IS CONSENT?   15 minutes

1. Explain that while we are all familiar with the phrase "consenting adults," not everyone knows exactly what consent is or how to know if they have it. Sexual consent means "agreeing to participate in a particular sexual behavior." Sometimes, not being sure of whether or not a person has consented to a behavior leads to confusion, which can lead to sexual assault or rape. Explain that this workshop will explore how to think about and determine what constitutes someone's consent.

2. Give a voting card to each participant. Say to the group, "I will read a statement, and then you will vote on whether or not the statement implies consent to have sexual intercourse. If you think the statement implies consent, hold up the green side of the card; if you do not think the statement implies consent, hold up the red side of the card. If you think the situation is too ambiguous to judge, wave the card back and forth. Remember that the couples involved may be of the same gender or different genders." (Allow the gender of the people in the situations to remain ambiguous.)

3. Read the statements on Leader Resource 25, Consenting Situations, in order. After each statement, allow participants to vote; then ask if they have any thoughts or comments to share. If participants seem confused or indecisive, ask what would have to happen in the scenario to make it clearer. When there are no further comments or questions, go on to the next situation. Spend about 5 minutes on the voting process.

4. After all of the situations have been voted on and discussed, take about 10 minutes to discuss the following questions:

- Was it difficult to determine whether or not consent had been given?
- Do you think a person should state out loud in every situation what sexual acts they will or will not participate in or verbally ask permission to initiate a sexual act?
- Is body language enough to constitute consent?
- What gender issues exist around the issue of consent? Do men and women view this issue the same way? Are there distinct gender differences?

WHAT IF?   20 minutes

1. Explain that this activity explores the issues of implied consent by asking participants to determine if having sexual intercourse seems comfortable and/or appropriate in various situations.

2. Shuffle the cards you prepared from Leader Resource 26, "What If?" and fan them out face down. Have a volunteer pick a card and read it to the group; then lead a group discussion about each card. Continue the activity by having different volunteers select and read as many cards as can be discussed in 10 minutes.

3. Use the remaining 10 minutes to help participants process the activity with the following questions:

- Were some situations easier to decide about than others? What did they have in common?
- When thinking about these situations, does the gender of the participants make any difference to your decision? Do the men and women in this room seem to look at these issues differently? If so, what kinds of differences did you notice?

- Is anything that happens sexually between two consenting adults acceptable?
- What are some strategies we can use in our own lives to assure that we are respected and treated well by our future sexual partner(s) and that we respect and treat our future partners well?

Leader Resource 25

CONSENTING SITUATIONS

Ask: Is someone consenting to have sexual intercourse with you if he/she

- gets into your car with you?

- goes out on a date with you?

- lets you buy dinner?

- goes on a picnic to a secluded place with you?

- gets drunk with you?

- goes up to your bedroom with you when your parents are not home or goes to your dorm room with you when your roommate is not there?

- makes out with you clothed?

- makes out with you naked?

- has oral sex with you?

- does not say anything when you start to have sexual intercourse?

- says no but keeps responding physically in a sexual way?

- says yes but his/her body seems to be saying no?

- says yes, yes, yes?

Leader Resource 26

"WHAT IF?" CARDS

What if your partner is very drunk, incoherent, and pretty passive? Do you have sexual intercourse with her/him?

What if your very drunk partner passes out just as you are about to have intercourse? Do you continue?

What if your partner is a virgin and says he/she wants to have sex to "get it over with"? Do you want to have sexual intercourse?

What if you meet someone at a party for the first time. You spend the entire evening together. You go back to your room to make out but decide at some point that you're not really in the mood for sexual intercourse. You are both naked and about ready to have sexual intercourse. What would you do?

What if your boyfriend/girlfriend has admitted that he/she had once forced someone to have sexual intercourse against that person's will? Do you want to have sexual intercourse with him/her?

What if your partner tells you that he/she really is not ready to have sexual intercourse with you but would be willing to do it to keep from losing you? Do you have sexual intercourse with this person?

What if you start to have intercourse and your partner does not refuse, but you think he/she would rather not have sexual intercourse? Do you proceed? How, if at all, would your response differ with someone you just met as opposed to someone you had been with for a long time?

What if you know that your partner does not want to have sexual intercourse with you, but you know that you could talk him/her into it? Do you? What about someone you just met?

What if you have been with your boyfriend/girlfriend for over a year. You have had intercourse once, and now your partner tells you he/she thinks the two of you made a mistake and would like to take things more slowly. Do you try to convince him/her to have sexual intercourse anyway?

What if you could get something you really want—a job, an opportunity, an experience, an object—by having sexual intercourse with a person who has power over you? Would you do it?

What if you know that someone over whom you have power wants to have sexual intercourse with you to get something that he/she wants or needs? Do you have sexual intercourse with him/her?

WORKSHOP 37 **Gay Pride Parade**

RATIONALE

Previous sessions have been concerned largely with personal sexual behavior, values, and decision-making, but sexuality also has political implications. This workshop considers one way in which sexuality and politics are connected: legal discrimination against gay, lesbian, and bisexual people. By making gay rights posters and imagining taking part in a gay pride parade, participants have the opportunity to understand one of the ways in which sexuality and politics are connected, to examine their own levels of homophobia and heterosexism safely, and to consider how society may be transformed.

Time Required: 1 hour

GOALS

To help participants
- identify important issues related to gay rights.
- demonstrate their views about gay rights through artistic expression.
- develop an awareness of their own levels of homophobia and heterosexism.

OBJECTIVES

By the end of this workshop, participants will be able to
- identify gay rights issues during a brainstorming activity.
- represent their own beliefs about gay rights by creating a poster.
- describe, following a guided imagery exercise, what participating in a public gay rights demonstration would be like for them.

MATERIALS

☐ Poster board and poster paints
☐ Newsprint, markers, and masking tape
☐ Writing paper
☐ Pens or pencils

PREPARATION

- •Review this workshop and decide how to share leadership responsibilities with your coleader.
- • Practice reading Leader Resource 27, Gay Pride Parade, aloud.
- • Post the ground rules from the opening session.

Activities

GAY RIGHTS POSTERS   45 minutes

1. Tell participants that often when people think about sexual orientation, they think about with whom and how people have sex. But sexual behavior is just one part of who we are as individuals, and sexual behavior is just one part of any relationship. Because our culture sees homosexuality and bisexuality as outside the norm and sometimes as wrong or perverted, people who are bisexual, gay, and lesbian, whether they are in committed relationships or not, face many challenges trying to enjoy the rights that heterosexual people take for granted.

2. Ask participants to brainstorm all the issues they think of when they think about gay rights. Write their responses on newsprint. Be sure the list includes gay parenting, gay adoption, gay marriage, sharing property, visiting partners in hospitals, medical insurance for partners, public affection, sharing housing, estate planning, and employment.

3. After the list is complete, ask participants to imagine that they have been asked to create banners or placards to be carried in a gay rights parade. Invite each participant to choose an issue that expresses something they believe about gay rights. Tell them their posters may use a slogan, a visual image, or both.

4. When they have completed their posters, have participants post their creations on the wall and explain them if they wish.

Alternative

Have participants create posters in small groups.

GUIDED IMAGERY   15 minutes

1. Invite participants to get into comfortable positions for a guided imagery. Tell them that this exercise will allow them to get a feel for a situation in a safe, nonthreatening, and personal way that they might not otherwise have an opportunity to explore. Dim the lights.

2. Read Leader Resource 27, Gay Pride Parade, slowly and clearly.

3. Immediately after bringing participants back from the guided imagery, ask them to remain silent as you hand out pens or pencils and writing paper. Then invite participants to record their thoughts and feelings during the imagery. Explain that they will not be asked to hand in what they have written.

4. After 5 minutes, ask for volunteers to share some of what they have written. Have as many as feel comfortable do so.

5. Help participants process the activity for 10 minutes with the following questions:

- During what portion of the imagery did you have the most powerful response?
- Overall, what seem to be some common responses to the imagery experiences?
- Are there gender differences in how people responded?
- Given that all of us are raised in a homophobic environment and have been taught a great deal of misinformation about homosexuality, all of us are at least a little homophobic. Even gay people can internalize the homophobia of our culture. To what degree do you think you have become aware of your own homophobia?

6. Point out that because we live in a culture that is for the most part ignorant about sexuality, most of us must spend time relearning what we have learned from our culture and the media. Often, when we discover that we have been insensitive to or unaware of others' feelings, we feel uncomfortable. It is useful, however, to know what we truly think and believe because only when we understand our feelings and values can we choose to change or to hold on to them.

7. Conclude by inviting participants to bring to Workshop 38 recordings of songs that say something about gender equality or inequality.

Leader Resource 27

GAY PRIDE PARADE

Read the following guided imagery slowly, calmly, and clearly.

Close your eyes and take several deep breaths. As you inhale, feel yourself filling with warmth and serenity. As you exhale, try to let out any stress or tension you may feel. Relax your feet and legs . . . your pelvis and lower back . . . your chest and neck . . . your jaw and forehead. Allow your arms and hands to rest comfortably. Let your mind be blank for a moment.

Imagine a brilliantly sunny day in your neighborhood. The air is fresh, and the sky is bright blue. It's a perfect day for a parade. A local human rights organization is having its annual parade. You hear bands playing, and you see people marching along carrying banners with all kinds of slogans and images.

Imagine that you are marching along in the parade carrying the poster you made today. Many of the people marching near you are wearing T-shirts and carrying banners representing the Gay Pride Alliance, a local gay rights group. As you turn a corner you see a group of your friends standing outside a local store watching the parade. You are not sure if they see you or not.

What are you thinking about at this moment? How are you feeling?

Now you are home from the parade, waiting for dinner to be ready. Your family is sitting together watching the local news, and there you are on the screen holding your poster. The video freezes on the picture of you as the announcer reports on the parade.

What do you think would happen in your house? How would your family members respond to your participation in the parade? How do you think you would feel?

Assume that most of the people you know have seen the news report—your friends, teachers, coworkers, other relatives, coaches, etc.

What responses will these people have? How do you feel about being seen by them?

Take a few more seconds to identify how you are feeling, what issues are being raised for you. I am going to ask you to bring some of those feelings back to this room with you.

Slowly begin turning up the lights. Ask participants to remain silent.

RATIONALE

Most people are familiar with the issue of gender equality, but many have not clearly defined their attitudes toward and beliefs about this topic. Using a song from the 1970s as a trigger, leaders encourage participants to look at the movement for gender equality from a historical perspective and to reach some conclusions about what issues have changed and what emphases have shifted since the song was recorded. Participants then have an opportunity to use their creativity to devise their own songs expressing their views of gender equality. This exercise helps participants to begin to focus on their own values and beliefs about this topic.

Time Required: 50 minutes

GOALS

To help participants
- examine their own views about gender equality.
- express their ideas about gender equality in a creative manner.
- explore the ways in which issues of gender equality have changed since the women's movement of the 1970s and the ways in which the issues have remained the same.

OBJECTIVES

By the end of this workshop, participants will be able to
- show their comprehension of the major issues involved in the fight for gender equality by identifying those issues through large group discussion.
- express their own values around the issue of gender equality.

MATERIALS

- ☐ Recording of the song, "I Am Woman" by Helen Reddy
- ☐ One or more recordings of contemporary songs that address the theme of gender equality in society or within a relationship
- ☐ Copies of Handout 19, I Am Woman, for each participant
- ☐ Tape player/CD player
- ☐ Paper
- ☐ Pencils

PREPARATION

- Review this workshop and decide how to share leadership responsibilities with your coleader.
- Bring in at least one recording of a contemporary song that addresses gender equity issues that is about a male experience. Two possibilities are "When I Was a Young Man" by Dar Williams and "Just the Two of Us" by Will Smith. Bring in at least one recording of a contemporary song that raises gender equity issues. Possibilities include: "If You Were the Woman and I Was the Man" by the Cowboy Junkies on their album, *Black-Eyed Man*; "He Thinks He'll Keep Her" recorded by Mary Chapin-Carpenter on her album, *Come On, Come On*; and "Just a Girl" recorded by No Doubt on their album, *Tragic Kingdom*.
- Post the ground rules from the opening session.

Activities

"I AM WOMAN"   10 minutes

1. Tell the group that this activity addresses the issue of gender equality. The fight for gender equality is not a new one. Women have long fought for equal rights and opportunities. Even with the efforts of the women's suffrage movement, it wasn't until 1920 that women in the United States gained the right to vote. The 1960s and 1970s saw a reemergence of the feminist movement and the return of the issue of gender equality to the forefront of America's social and political agenda. Ask if anyone is familiar with the song called "I Am Woman," which pop singer Helen Reddy recorded in 1972.

2. Give participants copies of Handout 19, "I Am Woman." Ask them to read the lyrics while they listen to the song, to think about what the major message seems to be, and to decide whether or not they think the message is applicable to today's efforts at gender equality.

3. Play the song, then ask:

- What are the main messages of this song?
- Are any of these messages relevant to today's issues surrounding gender equality?

4. Invite participants to take turns playing the songs that they have brought in. If no one has brought songs, play some you have brought. After each song ask:

- What are the main messages of this song?
- What is its message about what it means to be male or female? About gender roles?
- What does it suggest about gender justice or injustice?
- Do you agree with the messages in the song?
- Do these messages remind you of an experience you have had at school, at home, or in any other setting?

If no one brought in a song from a male perspective, play the one you brought in and follow the preceding process.

CREATING GENDER EQUALITY SONGS   40 minutes

1. Tell participants that they are going to have the chance to express their own views on the most important issues related to gender equality. Explain that they are going to write lyrics to their own songs about gender equality. They may work alone or in groups of two or three. Encourage them to formulate the message that they would like people to hear. Say they have 20 minutes to write their lyrics and put them to any well-known pop, rap, rock, even childhood tune. When everyone is finished writing, they will take turns singing their songs for the group. Suggest that one way to write the songs might be first to make a list of the major messages they want to include and then turn them into the lyrics of a song.

2. When everyone has finished, ask for volunteers to go first. If participants have worked in groups, encourage everyone in the group to sing, although if members want to have one person present, they may.

3. When all songs have been sung, ask the group:
- Why is gender equality important?
- Who benefits from gender equality?
- Was it difficult to think of the ideas you wanted to express?
- Were any themes repeated in different songs?
- Twenty-five years from now, what will be the main issues on the topic of gender equality?

4. Conclude by suggesting that gender equality is important for both genders. The more freedoms women have to make choices for their lives, the more freedom men have as well. Say something like, "There was a time when men had no choice but to work to support their families. Today, because women are increasingly pursuing careers, many men have the option of staying home and caring for their children while their spouses support the family. Ultimately, we all benefit when people are treated equally under the law and have the same opportunities to pursue in their lives. Therefore, it is important to watch for examples of inequality in our daily lives and to fight against them."

Handout 19

I AM WOMAN

by Helen Reddy and Gary Burton, 1972

I am woman, hear me roar
In numbers too big to ignore
And I know too much to go back, to pretend
'Cause I've heard it all before
And I've been down there on the floor
No one's ever gonna keep me down again

Yes, I am wise, but it's wisdom born of pain
Yes, I've paid the price, but look how much I've gained
If I have to, I can do anything
I am strong, I am invincible—I am woman . . .

You can bend but never break me
'Cause it only serves to make me
More determined to achieve my final goal
And I come back even stronger
Not a novice any longer
'Cause you've deepened the conviction in my soul

Yes, I am wise, but it's wisdom born of pain
Yes, I've paid the price, but look how much I've gained
If I have to, I can do anything
I am strong, I am invincible—I am woman . . .

I am woman watch me grow
See me standin' toe-to-toe
As I spread my loving arms across the land
But I'm still an embryo, with a long, long way to go
Until I make my brother understand

Yes, I am wise, but it's wisdom born of pain
Yes, I've paid the price, but look how much I've gained
If I have to, I can do anything
I am strong, I am invincible—I am woman . . .

RATIONALE

This closure activity brings together some of the underlying themes of this program: equality, freedom for all people to pursue sexually healthy lives, diversity, responsibility, empowerment, and proactive caring for one another. The workshop allows participants to reflect on their thoughts and feelings, learn from them, and use them in the future.

Time Required: 10 minutes

GOALS

To help participants
- find meaning in what they have learned in Sessions Ten, Eleven, and Twelve.
- identify how they will use what they have learned in their own lives.
- think about what actions they can take to make a positive difference in the world.

OBJECTIVES

By the end of this workshop, participants will be able to
- demonstrate an understanding of how their own actions can make a difference by specifying one action they would take to make the world a better place.

MATERIALS

☐ Index cards
☐ Pens or pencils

PREPARATION

- Review this workshop and decide how to share leadership responsibilities with your coleader.
- Post the ground rules from the opening session.

Activity

CHANGING THE WORLD   10 minutes

1. Give an index card and a pen or pencil to each person. Ask participants to take a few minutes to think about what they would do, if they could do anything, to make the world better for oppressed groups or individuals. Tell them they should not write their names on the cards but each of them should write one suggestion. Explain that you will collect the cards, mix them up, and have the group read the suggestions out loud.

2. After participants have had a few minutes to think and to write down their ideas, collect the cards. Mix them up and redistribute them. Have participants read them aloud, one at a time. Discuss any common themes and unique ideas that were shared.

3. Thank participants for their hard work in this workshop.

4. In preparation for the closing session, ask each participant to bring to the next session one small object to share with the group. Explain that they should select something that reminds them of the group or something significant about the group or their experience in it. Items such as rocks, feathers, shells, and marbles are all acceptable. Ask participants not to discuss what they are bringing with other members of the group. If you wish, have the group also plan a party and delegate responsibility for refreshments, etc.

Closing Session

RATIONALE

As this program comes to an end, participants need not only to absorb all of the information and skills they have learned but also to find closure on the relationships they have made within the group. While members of the group may meet again in the future, the group itself will disband and cannot be duplicated. For some participants, this ending may not be significant, but for others, it will represent a considerable loss. The activities in this session are designed to help participants bid farewell to the group and its members.

Time Required: 1 hour

GOALS

To help participants
- say goodbye to the group and its members.
- identify significant learning moments from the program.

OBJECTIVES

By the end of this session, participants will be able to
- explain how each member of the group has played a role in their learning and experience of the program by writing a note to him/her.
- express, through discussion, their feelings about the ending of the group.

MATERIALS

☐ Large box with a lid
☐ Writing paper
☐ Pens or pencils
☐ Low table or small mat
☐ Small memento(s) (for yourself or the whole group) to share
☐ Special refreshments as desired

PREPARATION

- Review this workshop and decide how to share leadership responsibilities with your coleader.
- If participants are bringing in their own small objects (see Workshop 39), then bring only one for yourself and perhaps a few extra. If participants have not been

told to bring objects or if they forget to do so, bring enough feathers, stones, beads, etc. for the whole group. Privately place your item(s) in the box.

- Gather any refreshments you have agreed to bring.
- Set up the meeting area so participants can sit in a circle around a low table or small mat.
- Plan to participate in all of the closure activities as a member of the group.
- Post the ground rules from the opening session.

Activities

SHARING MEMENTOS   20 minutes

1. As participants arrive, ask them to put the small items they have brought (if any) into the box so that no one can see whose item is whose. When all the items have been put into the box, take them out and place them on the center table or mat.

2. Have the group sit in a circle. Invite one participant to go to the table, choose an item that is not her/his own to take home and return to his/her seat. Ask the individual to explain why he/she chose that item and in what way it is meaningful. Or, ask the participant to name what she/he will remember about the group when looking at the item in the future.

3. Ask the person who brought in the item to explain its significance to him/her.

4. Have participants take turns selecting items until each person has a small item to take home as a memento.

AFFIRMATIONS   15 minutes

1. Give each person a sheet of paper and a pen or pencil. Have participants write their name at the bottom of the paper and then pass it to their left.

2. Ask each person to write a note to the person whose name is at the bottom of the paper. Tell participants that the notes should describe, in a positive way, how the person's participation in the group has affected their own experience of the program. After about 1 minute, have participants sign their names to their notes and fold the paper over so that no one can read what is written at the top.

3. Have participants pass the notes to the left again and repeat the procedure. Continue this process until the paper returns to the person whose name is on the bottom. By this time, the paper should include comments from every member of the group, including the leaders.

4. Ask participants to put their notes away for the moment. Explain that they should read the notes privately later.

SIGNIFICANT LEARNING   15 minutes

Go around the circle and have participants take turns naming what they thought was one of the most significant learning experiences for them in the program. Ask them to describe the ways in which their participation in the program will have an impact on their future.

SHARED FAREWELLS

10 minutes

Ask participants to say goodbye to the group by sharing something about the group that they will miss and saying goodbye to it. For example, one might say, "I say good-bye to the way Jane laughed when she was nervous," or "I bid farewell to the way the leader was always calling time outs during our discussions."

PARTY

Enjoy the refreshments and/or other party activities you have planned.

Handout 20

LEADER EVALUATION FORM

Dear Leaders,

Undoubtedly, leading this program had its ups and downs. We would like to suggest that you sit down together in a comfortable setting and reflect on the overall experience. The questions below ask you to generalize to some extent about different dimensions of the program. Where appropriate, circle the number that best represents your response and then explain under "comments." We hope discussing this form will be helpful to you. We know that filling it out and sending it to us will be very helpful to us in improving the program. You can send completed forms to:

UUA Curriculum Director
25 Beacon Street
Boston, MA 02108

1. Overall, how age-appropriate was this program for your group?

1	2	3	4	5
Completely appropriate				Not at all appropriate

Comments: _____

_____

_____

2. Overall, how engaged/interested was your group in the program and its activities?

1	2	3	4	5
Completely engaged				Not at all engaged

Comments: _____

_____

_____

3. How prepared were you to lead this program?

1	2	3	4	5
Completely prepared				Not at all prepared

Comments: _____

_____

_____

4. How supportive were parents of their children's participation in this program?

1	2	3	4	5
Completely supportive				Not at all supportive

Comments: _____

_____

_____

5. If you could add a session to this program, what topic(s) would you add? Why?

_____

_____

_____

6. If you could drop a topic from this program, what topic(s) would you drop? Why?

_____

_____

_____

7. Overall, what do you think there should have been more of in this program?

_____

_____

_____

_____

8. Overall, what do you think there should have been less of in this program?

_____

_____

_____

_____

9. What do you think is the most important learning(s) your participants will take with them from this experience?

_____
_____
_____
_____

10. How would you describe what this experience was like for you?

_____
_____
_____
_____

11. Any other comments or suggestions (you may use the back of this sheet, also)?

_____
_____
_____
_____

Your Name _____

Your Congregation _____

Your Day Phone Number or E-mail _____

Handout 21

PARTICIPANT FEEDBACK FORM

1. What is your overall rating of the program? (Please circle one.)

   Excellent   Good   Average   Fair   Poor

2. What did you like *best* about the workshops you participated in?

   _____

   _____

   _____

3. What did you like *least* about the workshops you participated in?

   _____

   _____

   _____

4. Do you think your workshops were: (Please check one)

   _____ too long   _____ about right   _____ too short

   How long would you like the workshops to be? _____

5. Do you think the number of workshops was: (Please check one)

   _____ too many   _____ about right   _____ too few

6. Are there any workshop topics that you think should be dropped ? If yes, which one(s)?

   _____

   _____

7. Is there any topic that you would like to add to the program? If yes, what was missing for you?

   _____

   _____

8. What is the most valuable learning or experience you will take from this program?

   _____

   _____

   _____

9. Please rate your facilitators' skills in leading the program: (Circle one)

   Excellent   Good   Average   Fair   Poor

10. What suggestions do you have to improve the program?

_____

_____

_____

_____

_____

_____

_____

This form may be used to give your facilitators feedback to help them improve the program the next time it is offered.

This form can also be sent to the developers of the program to help them improve future editions. Copies may be sent to:

UUA Curriculum Director
24 Farnsworth Street
Boston, MA 02210-1409

Resources

SEXUALITY EDUCATION AND INFORMATION

Primary Organizations

Contact these organizations for a variety of up-to-date resources such as newsletters, Web sites, books, reviews, videos, periodicals, etc.

Advocates for Youth
2000 M Street NW
Suite 750
Washington, D.C. 20036
202/419-3420
http://www.advocatesforyouth.org

Produces resources for sexuality educators, including fact sheets, curricula, programs, and advocacy materials. Programs include: HIV Education and Prevention, Teen Pregnancy Prevention, Peer Education, Media Education, Parent/Child Communication, Support for Lesbian, Gay, Bisexual, and Transgender Youth, and a Support Center for School-Based and School-Linked Health Care.

Guttmacher Institute
125 Maiden Lane, 7th floor
New York, NY 10038
800/355-0244
wwwguttmacher.org

Provides current, accurate data on sexual activity, contraception, abortion, and child-bearing in the United States and worldwide.

Centers for Disease Control and Prevention (CDC)
National Prevention Information Network (NPIN)
PO Box 6003
Rockville, MD 20849-6003
800/232-4636
http://www.cdcnpin.org

A national reference, referral, and distribution service for information on HIV/AIDS and STDs run by the United States Centers for Disease Control.

Family Health Productions, Inc.
PO Box 1639
Gloucester, MA 01930
978/282-9970
http://www.abouthealth.TV/index.htm

A nonprofit production company (formerly Media Works) *that produces and distributes television programs, videos, DVDs, companion guides, and books about public health and sexuality education advocacy. Resources include:* Raising Healthy Kids: Families Talk About Sexual Health, In Our Own Words: Teens and AIDS, What Works: Sexuality Education *and* Words Can Work: When Talking with Kids About Sexual Health.

The Gay, Lesbian, and Straight Education Network (GLSEN)
80 Brad Street, 2nd floor
New York, NY 10004
212/727-0135
http://www.glsen.org

Brings together teachers, parents, students, and concerned citizens on the U.S. national and local level to work together to end homophobia in our schools. Focuses on in-school programming, advocacy, and community organizing.

Health Canada
A.L. 0900C2
Ottawa, Ontario
Canada K1A 0K9
613/957-2991
http://www.hc-sc.gc.ca

Health Canada is the federal department responsible for helping the people of Canada maintain and improve their health. The Health Canada home page provides extensive information on many aspects of health, including sexuality education, HIV/AIDS, and STDs. The department's Health Promotion Home Page (http://www.hc-sc.gc.ca/hppb/hpo/index.html) includes information about HIV/AIDS and Comprehensive School Health.

Answer
Center for Applied Psychology
Rutgers University
41 Gordon Road, Suite C
Piscataway, NJ 08854-8045
848/445-7929
e-mail: answered@rci.rutgers.edu
http://answer.rutgers.edu

A coalition of public, private, and nonprofit agencies joined in support of family life education, including comprehensive instruction about human sexuality, in school and community settings. Resources include two newsletters: Family Life Matters *and* Sex, Etc.

Parents, Families and Friends of Lesbians and Gays (PFLAG)
National Office
1828 L Street, NW
Suite 660
Washington, D.C. 20036
202/467-8180
http://www.pflag.org

Supports local chapters throughout the United States, Canada, and world. Publishes resources for families and allies of gay, lesbian, bisexual, and transgender people as well as resources for those who are coming out.

Planned Parenthood Federation of America
434 West 33rd Street
New York, NY 10001
212/541-7800
http://www.plannedparenthood.org

The Planned Parenthood Federation of America provides comprehensive reproductive and complementary health-care services, advocates public policies that guarantee these rights and ensure access to such services, and provides educational programs that enhance understanding of individual and societal implications of human sexuality. Planned Parenthood has affiliate organizations and clinics throughout the United States that offer resources to sexuality educators.

Sex Information and Education Council of Canada (SIECCAN)
850 Coxwell Avenue
Toronto, Ontario
Canada M4C5R1
416/466-5304
www.sieccan.org

Publishes The Canadian Journal of Human Sexuality, *a peer-reviewed, academic journal, and the* SIECCAN Newsletter, *which contains articles and resource reviews for sexuality educators. Their resource, "Common Questions About Sexual Health Education" is designed to assist Canadian sexuality education advocates.*
    NOTE: SIECCAN *is not affiliated with SIECUS.*

Sexuality Information and Education Council of the United States (SIECUS)
1012 14th Street NW, Suite 1108
Washington, DC 20005
202/265-2405
http://www.siecus.org

Develops, collects, and disseminates information, promotes comprehensive sexuality education, and advocates for the right of individuals to make responsible sexual choices. Provides program consultation and assistance to communities. Publications include Guidelines for Comprehensive Sexuality Education, Community Action Kit, *the bimonthly* SIECUS Report, *and the* SIECUS Advocates Report.
    NOTE: SIECUS *is not affiliated with SIECCAN.*

TOPICS IN SEXUALITY EDUCATION

Web Sites

The Complete HIV/AIDS Resource
http://www.thebody.com

A clearinghouse for AIDS/HIV information and resources on the Internet, founded by former civil rights lawyer Jamie Marks. The most frequently visited AIDS-related Web site according to the Medical Library Association.

Coalition for Positive Sexuality
http://www.positive.org

Provides factual, comprehensive sexuality education information. It operates under the premise that youth have the right to complete and honest sex education. This site can help youth demand information from their school, health-care providers, and parents.

Go Ask Alice
http://www.goaskalice.columbia.edu

Provides factual, in-depth, straightforward, and nonjudgmental information to assist readers' decision making about their physical, sexual, emotional, and spiritual health. Go Ask Alice! is supported by a team of Columbia University health educators and health-care providers, along with information and research specialists from health-related organizations worldwide. "Alice" answers questions about relationships; sexuality; sexual health; emotional health; fitness; nutrition; alcohol, nicotine, and other drugs; and general health.

Scarleteen
www.scarleteen.com

Offers inclusive, comprehensive, supportive sexuality and relationship information for teens and emerging adults. Offers archived answers, messageboards, SMS service, and a live chat service.

Sex, Etc.
www.sexetc.org

A Web site by teens for teens sponsored by the Network for Family Life Education (see Primary Organizations). Includes articles, resources, and an anonymous question and answer forum.

Info for Teens
plannedparenthood.org/info-for-teens/

Sexuality and relationship information by teens for teens. Sponsored by Planned Parenthood Federation of America (see Sexuality Education and Information, Primary Organizations).

Videos

In Our Own Words: Teens and AIDS. 20 minutes.

   Available from Family Health Productions, Inc., PO Box 1639, Gloucester, MA 01930, 978/282-9970, e-mail: info@abouthealth.com, www.abouthealth.com.

It's Elementary: Talking About Gay Issues in School and *It's Still Elementary.* Groundspark. 1 hour, 17 minutes and 48 minutes, respectively.

   Addresses the myths that children do not know about gays and lesbians and that schools are not capable of dealing well with these issues. To order: New Day Films, 190 Route 17M, PO Box 1084, Harriman, NY 10926; 1-888/367-9154 (toll-free); e-mail: orders@newday.com.

Books

Bass, Ellen, and Kate Kaufman. *Free Your Mind (The Book for Gay, Lesbian, and Bisexual Youth and Their Allies).* San Francisco: Harper Perennial, 1996.

Brimner, Larry Dane. *Being Different (Lambda Youths Speak Out).* Danbury, CT: Franklin Watts, 1995.

Feinberg, Leslie. *Transliberation: Beyond Pink or Blue.* Boston: Beacon Press, 1998. (A resource for leaders)

Griffin, Carolyn Welch; Marian J. Wirth; Arthur G. Wirth; and Brian McNaught. *Beyond Acceptance: Parents of Lesbians and Gays Talk About Their Experiences.* New York: St. Martin's Press, 1997.

Haffner, Debra. *From Diapers to Dating: A Parent's Guide to Raising Sexually Healthy Children.* Second Edition. New York: Newmarket Press, 2004.

Hutchins, Loraine, and Lani Kaahumanu. *Bi Any Other Name: Bisexual People Speak Out.* 25th Anniversary Edition. New York: Alyson Books, 2015.

Planned Parenthood. *All About Sex: A Family Resource of Sex and Sexuality.* ed. Ronald Filiberti Moglia and John Knowles. New York: Three Rivers Press, 1997.

Sonnie, Amy. *Revolutionary Voices: A Muticultural Queer Youth Anthology.* New York: Alyson Books, 2000.

COMMUNICATING ABOUT SEXUALITY

Filling the Gaps: Hard to Teach Topics in Sexuality Education. SIECUS. 1998.

   Contains excellent lessons to supplement a sexuality education program like Our Whole Lives. Includes exercises addressing abstinence, diversity, sexual identity and orientation, safer sex, and a valuable list of resources. (See SIECUS listing under Sexuality Education and Information, Primary Organizations.)

Raising Healthy Kids: Families Talk About Sexual Health. For Parents of Preadolescent and Adolescent Children. Family Life Productions, Inc. 1997.

A 30-minute DVD/video with accompanying discussion guide. Includes interviews with young people, parents, and experts. Features discussions about values, listening, avoiding absolutes, mixed messages, and relationships. Available from Family Life Productions, Inc. (See Family Life Productions *listing under* Sexuality Education and Information: Primary Organizations.)

Talk About Sex: A Booklet for Young People on How to Talk about Sexuality and HIV/AIDS. New York: SIECUS, 1992.

INTERNET SAFETY

Both www.safekids.com and www.safeteens.com promote ways for young people to remain safe online. Both sites are based on a free brochure written by Larry Magid for the National Center for Missing and Exploited Children.

SEXUAL HEALTH

A number of organizations provide sexual health resources, including books, videos, charts, and pamphlets. You may want to obtain catalogs from the following sources:

American Social Health Association
PO Box 13827
Research Triangle Park, NC 27709-3827
919/361-8400
www.ashastd.org

Educational materials on sexual health and sexually transmitted disease.

ETR Associates
100 Enterprise Way, Suite G300
Scotts Valley, CA 95066
800/620-8884
www.etr.org

Source for pamphlets, books, flip charts, curricula, and videos with an emphasis on sexuality and health education.

The Gay, Lesbian, and Straight Education Network (GLSEN)
"Just the Facts About Sexual Orientation and Youth: A Primer for Principals, Educators and School Personnel"
see contact information on page 250.

This pamphlet was recently distributed to public schools to help make schools safe places for students of all sexual orientations.

Health Edco: The Anatomical Human
PO Box 21207
Waco, TX 76702-9719
254/776-6461
www.healthedco.com

Catalog of professional quality anatomical charts and models.

SEXUALITY AND DISABILITY

(Sex)abled: Disability Uncensored.
Hoffman, Amanda L..
https://vimeo.com/6842318

A video about college student activists around issues of sexuality and disability..

Kaufman, Miriam. *Easy for You to Say: Q & As for Teens Living With Chronic Illness or Disability.* 3rd. Ed. Revised and updated. Richmond Hill, ON: Firefly Books, 2012.

Mairs, Nancy. *Waist High in the World: Life Among the Non-Disabled.* Boston: Beacon Press, 1997.

SEXUAL VIOLENCE

Faith Trust Institute
2414 SW Andover St., Suite D208
Seattle, WA 98106
206/634-1903
www.faithtrustinstitute.org

Print and video resources.

Safer, Andrew, *Healthy Relationships: A Violence Prevention Curriculum*, 2nd Ed. 1994. Men For Change, Box 33005, Quinpool Postal Outlet, Halifax, NS B3L 4T6, Canada. 902/457-4351, www.m4c.ns.ca

Dedicated to ensuring that women, men, and children can live in a world that is free from the culture of violence which is responsible for the deaths of . . . women, this twelve-session curriculum for adolescents addresses topics such as exploring Emotions, Conflict Resolution, Gender Stereotypes and the Media, Assertiveness, Self-esteem, Communication Skills, Relationships, and much more.

MISCELLANEOUS

Chimes

We have had many requests for a source for chimes to gently return a group to focus. One source of Tibetan chimes (or Tingsha) is Dharmacrafts. Contact them at 800/794-9862, www.dharmacrafts.com for a catalog.

Games

Adolescents enjoy games both to express energy and to build the youth group. There are many game books appropriate for youth. Here are some suggestions:

DeepFun: Games and Activities
www.uua.org/re/youth/adults-ministry/deepfun
Games cherished by Unitarian Universalist yourth through the years. Downloadable.

Yaconelli, Mike, and Scott Koenigsaeker. *Get 'Em Talking: 104 Great Discussion Starters for Youth Groups.* Youth Specialties, 1990.